PATHWAYS OF LEARNING

Teaching Students and Parents about Multiple Intelligences

DAVID LAZEAR

Foreword by Arthur L. Costa

Zephyr
Press ®

REACHING THEIR HIGHEST POTENTIAL

Tucson, Arizona

Pathways of Learning
Teaching Students and Parents about Multiple Intelligences

Grades: All ages

©2000 by David Lazear
Printed in the United States of America

ISBN 1-56976-118-3

Editor: Bonnie Lewis
Design and production: Daniel Miedaner
Cover art and design: Daniel Miedaner
Book illustrator: John Reedy

Published by
Zephyr Press
P.O. Box 66006
Tucson, Arizona 85728-6006
800-232-2187
http://zephyrpress.com
http://giftsforteachers.com
http://newways2learn.com

Library of Congress Cataloging-in-Publication Data

Lazear, David G.
    Pathways of learning : teaching students and parents about multiple intelligences / by David Lazear ; foreword by Arthur L. Costa.
        p.cm.
    Includes bibliographical references.
    ISBN 1-56976-118-3 (alk. paper)
    1.   Learning. 2. Multiple intelligences. 3. Cognitive styles. 4. Teaching. 5. Activity programs in education. I. Title.

LB1060 .L386 2000
    370.15'23—dc21   00-033396

PATHWAYS
OF LEARNING

It is of the utmost importance that we recognize and nurture all of the varied human intelligences, and all of the combinations of intelligences. . . . If we can mobilize the spectrum of human abilities, not only will people feel better about themselves and more competent; it is even possible that they will also feel more engaged and better able to join the rest of the world community in working for the broader good. Perhaps if we can mobilize the full range of human intelligences and ally them to an ethical sense, we can help to increase the likelihood of our survival on this planet, and perhaps even contribute to our thriving.

—Howard Gardner

Contents

Foreword

Diversity is the basis of biological survival. Each of us has a particular genetic structure; unique facial features; a distinguishing thumbprint; a distinctive signature; a background of knowledge, experience, and culture; and a preferred way of gathering, processing, and expressing information and knowledge. We even have our singular frequencies in which we vibrate. George Leonard (1986) observes that all living things are oscillators: "The simplest single-celled organism oscillates to a number of different frequencies, at the atomic, molecular, sub-cellular, and cellular levels; microscopic movies of these organisms are striking for the ceaseless, rhythmic pulsation that is revealed. In an organism as complex as a human being, the frequencies of oscillation and the interactions between those frequencies are multitudinous."

Life would be simpler if everybody was similar, but the truth is that all people, deep within their genetic and bodily drives, yearn and strive to exert their individualism. Embedded in many educational practices, however, are policies and procedures that lead individuals toward uniformity: grading on a curve, I.Q. tests, curriculum guides, textbook adoptions, standardized achievement tests, criteria for judging excellence, grade-level demarcation, Carnegie Units, and so forth.

Perhaps Winston Churchill (1987) best illustrates the point:

> I had scarcely passed my 12th birthday when I entered the inhospitable regions of examinations, through which for the next eight years, I was destined to journey. These examinations were a great trial to me. The subjects, which were dearest to the examiners were almost invariably those I fancied least. I would have liked to have been examined in history, poetry, and writing essays. The examiners, on the other hand were partial to Latin and mathematics. And their will prevailed. Moreover, the questions which they asked on both of these subjects were almost invariably those to which I was unable to suggest the satisfactory answer. I should have liked to be asked to say what I know. They always tried to ask what I did not know. When I would willingly have displayed my knowledge, they sought to expose my ignorance. This sort of treatment had only one result, I did not do well in examinations.

I have a close friend whose daughter is dyslexic. The daughter has always had difficulty in school and is invariably enrolled in special education classes. Last year, California State University, Sacramento, awarded her a music scholarship. She plays cello in their symphony orchestra. The "perfect 10" Olympic gold medal diver Greg Louganis was never as adept at learning in school as he is at diving. British Prime Minister John Major was a high-school dropout. Winston Churchill was thought to be retarded because he frequently played with toy soldiers when he was young. Eleanor Roosevelt, Albert Einstein, and numerous other notables were deemed "retarded," "slow," "handicapped," or "disturbed" learners.

As educators, we've known only too well the class clown who keeps us in stitches with puns and anecdotes but flunks math tests. We've marveled at those social magnets to whom other students cling but who are not good in spelling. We've seen students who cannot express themselves in writing but who, when provided with crayons, paints, or clay, can communicate their ideas with great clarity.

Because public education favors a narrow range of verbal and visual intelligence, we miss those more elusive qualities of humanness. The industrial era influenced our picture of education, schooling, and intelligence. When we counted the number of items produced as a measure of work done, workers' efficiency and ability were reduced to numbers. As the Irish social commentator George W. Russell stated, "When steam first began to pump and wheels go round at so many revolutions per minute, what are called business habits were intended to make the life of man run in harmony with the steam engine, and his movement rival the train in punctuality." Educators, influenced by the time-management experts, also viewed student learning capacities numerically. Lord Kelvin is quoted as saying, "If you cannot measure it, if you cannot reduce it to numbers, your knowledge is of a meager and unsatisfactory kind." Thus evolved our image of intelligence as a static numerical score—132, 70, 100—for which we were forever cursed or blessed. Our view of human greatness was counted, summed, and reduced to digits.

In the midst of the postindustrial era, however, we are increasingly cognizant of human potential as our greatest natural resource. Valuing a range of diverse skills and capacities makes a business, a community, a society, and a nation strong. We are realizing that collaboratively drawing on the resources of diversity gives a product, an idea, or a plan greater potential and power. And Howard Gardner's theory of multiple intelligences has not only expanded our list of unique qualities, but also revolutionized our concept of human capacity.

On a recent flight from Chicago to Honolulu, I sat next to a pilot who flies 747s for United Airlines. While he would have much preferred to have been on the flight deck, I was able to engage him in some intriguing conversation. I inquired as to the nature of pilots' training and the rigor required to advance to the status of captain. "Does anyone ever get washed out?" I inquired. "Oh, yes," was his reply. "Just recently, I served on an examination team for a flight engineer who was requesting advancement to second officer. He didn't make it. Part of the examination that United puts us through," he explained, "is a simulation of an in-flight crisis situation. This person did not call upon the resources of the other members of his flight deck team to assist in solving the problem. He thought he could solve the problem all by himself. He was washed out!" This anecdote is indicative of a situation unique to our modern life of complex problem solving. No one person can have all the answers to all the problems. Knowing how to network, how to draw on diverse resources, and how to value others' expertise, views, perceptions, and knowledge is essential to survival. We might view these skills as a new form of interlocking intelligences: collaboratively melding the perceptions, modalities, skills, capacities, and expertise into a unified whole that is better and more efficient than any one of its parts.

Furthermore, people whom we deem most effective seem at home in many areas of functioning. They move flexibly from one style to another as the situation demands it. They have an uncanny ability to read clues from the situation or the environment to determine what is needed. They bring forward from their vast repertoire those skills and capacities needed to function most effectively in any setting.

Music educator Joseph O'Conner and organizational consultant and trainer John Seymour (1990) report that "no system is better in an absolute sense than another; it depends what you want to do. Athletes need a well-developed kinesthetic awareness, and it is difficult to be a successful architect without a facility for making clear, constructed mental pictures. One skill shared by outstanding performers in any field is to be able to move easily through all the representational systems and use the most appropriate one for the task at hand."

It is to the development of more effectively functioning human beings that David Lazear has dedicated his work. His Eight Ways handbooks serve educators and parents in helping students to become aware of and to manage the multiplicity of their own and others' unique forms of intelligence; in knowing how and when to employ and evaluate the usefulness of each intelligence; and in respecting other people's preferences for and levels of intellectual development. Lazear's work also illuminates a vision of an educational community in which each member's range of multiple intelligence capacities is maximally developed.

To adopt this new vision, educators will need to be prepared to "get off the digm"—to experience a paradigm shift. Some of our traditional ways of viewing education, learning, teaching, achievement, and talent will be found to be obsolescent and will demand to be replaced with more modern and relevant policies, practices, and philosophies. As our paradigm shifts, for example, we will need to let go of our obsession with acquiring content and knowledge as an end in itself and make room for viewing content as a vehicle for developing various forms of intelligence; we will dismiss uniformity in deference to valuing diversity; we will give up external evaluation of students in favor of students' self-examination; we will devalue competition and enhance interdependence; we will redefine smart to mean having a repertoire of intelligences and knowing when to use each.

Jean Houston's (1987) comment "Never has the vision of what human beings can be been more remarkable" becomes even more profound as we more clearly envision, more stridently demand, and more eagerly install those educational and societal conditions in which humanness is enhanced. The fullest development of the intellects today will allow our students and all the world's citizens to continue developing future visions of ever more remarkable human beings.

This book provides a pathway to that future.

Arthur L. Costa, Ed. D.
Professor Emeritus
California State University
Sacramento, California

Preface

This revised edition of *Pathways of Learning* represents some of my most recent thinking on how to make teaching students *about* multiple intelligences an ongoing part of the curriculum. Over the years, as I have been working to create ever more ways that multiple intelligences can be incorporated into the task of educating today's young people, I have witnessed often the difference it makes when students understand the intelligences, both in themselves and in each other.

I am a strong advocate for explicitly teaching students about multiple intelligences. It is part of the metacognitive task of teaching them about the teaching/learning process itself. Students should know everything we as teachers know about teaching and learning. They should know about every trick we have in our proverbial instructional bags. They should know and understand all the many strategies we employ to get across the various concepts we have to teach. The more they know and understand about the teaching/learning process itself, the more active and responsible learners they will become.

The same can be said for multiple intelligences. The more students know and understand multiple intelligences as an instructional vehicle and process, the more excited and involved they will become in their own educational process. But the benefits go beyond this. When students learn about their own multiple ways of knowing, their self-esteem is often greatly enhanced. Likewise, their respect for each other and their ability to honor, and even celebrate, the intellectual diversity that exists among the human family is greatly amplified.

The revisions in the year 2000 edition of *Pathways* are an attempt to demonstrate the possibility of creating a parallel multiple intelligence-based curriculum, which can interface with the regular academic curriculum. The focus of this multiple intelligence curriculum is teaching students about the various intelligences, *not* as an add-on, but in and through the regular academic curriculum. As we *consciously* and *explicitly* use the intelligences as a regular, ongoing, and normal part of the teaching/learning process, students gain a more in-depth understanding of themselves and learn how to use the full spectrum of their intellectual capacities to achieve success in school and beyond.

It is my hope that this revision will help you tap the full potentials of your students, as you journey with them in the task of preparing them to become creative, effective, and productive citizens of our world.

This is my third book in a series of eight dealing with implementing multiple intelligences. The first, *Eight Ways of Knowing*, is about teaching *for* multiple intelligences. It focuses on integrating the various intelligence capacities and skills into existing school curricula. The message of this first book is that, if we want our children to be as intelligent as they can be on as many levels as possible, then we must teach the specific skills for using each intelligence in developmentally appropriate ways. This approach takes students on a journey of exploration that moves from the attainment of the basic skills of each intelligence through students' more complex development for acquiring knowledge and processing information. The approach leads them through the higher-order use of the intelligences to solve problems and meet daily challenges, culminating in a variety of vocational and avocational pursuits.

My second book, *Eight Ways of Teaching* (revised), is about teaching *with* multiple intelligences. Its focus is the revitalization of classroom instruction using the eight ways of knowing. The book presents eight full-blown lessons (one for each intelligence) to use in traditional academic areas such as history, math, science and health, language arts, social studies, and the practical and the fine arts. It presents a dynamic, four-stage model for designing lessons—stage one awakens various intelligences in students; stage two gives them an opportunity to practice particular intelligence skills; and stage three utilizes those skills in a content-based lesson. The final stage of the model provides ideas for appropriate assessment and helps students transfer their learning of a given lesson beyond the classroom.

The other books deal with creating multiple-intelligence rubrics for assessment, integrating multiple intelligence into the curriculum, and a series of self-help tapes and workbooks for expanding and enhancing the eight intelligences in our personal lives.

Pathways of Learning is concerned with reinventing the learning process from a multiple intelligence perspective. This book describes ways to expand intelligent behavior, whether in school or in other everyday situations outside of the classroom. It endeavors to give teachers the means for relating multiple intelligence theory and practice to students and parents. *Pathways* now includes references to the naturalist intelligence. The book is devoted to teaching about multiple intelligences and thus presents the metacognitive dimension of this work.

I dedicate this book to the hundreds of teachers, principals, and administrators who are actively working to incorporate teaching for, with, and about multiple intelligences into the typical school and classroom situation. These educators are truly the pioneers of an important new trend that is moving across the United States and Canada, changing the paradigm of education. I have had the privilege of getting to know and working with many of these people in and through various professional development workshops. I believe the ways in which they are applying this new paradigm of human intelligence are on the cutting edge of the next phase of multiple intelligence research.

As always, I must again thank Howard Gardner, the father of the theory of multiple intelligences as we know it today, for his continued support, feedback, advice, and encouragement in completing all of my books on the multiple intelligences. Likewise, the encouragement I receive from my partner, Jim Reedy, is key to keeping me moving forward, continually looking for new and unexplored ways to apply multiple intelligence.

To all of you who have made my life so rich and so full in the years I have been working on my books and professional development activities and workshops, thank you. None of this would have been possible without your prodding, feedback, and support.

David G. Lazear
Maui, Hawai'i
April 2000

Introduction

HELPING STUDENTS TAP THEIR FULL LEARNING POTENTIAL IN SCHOOL

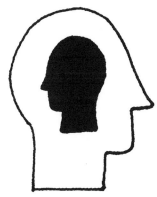

In a school that is a home for the mind there is an inherent faith that all people can continue to improve their intellectual capacities throughout life; that learning to think is as valid a goal for the "at risk," the handicapped, the disadvantaged, and the foreign-speaking as it is for the "gifted and talented"; and that all of us have the potential for even greater creativity and intellectual power.

—ART COSTA, *THE SCHOOL AS A HOME FOR THE MIND*

As far as we know, human beings are the only creatures that possess the ability to be self-reflective; that is, we have the ability to step back from ourselves and watch ourselves, almost like outside observers. This capacity carries with it both the joy of freedom and the burden of responsibility. We are not victims. Once we become aware of something in our lives, our self-consciousness gives us the power to change it, if we so desire. This self-reflective dimension is at the heart of helping students understand their own multiple intelligences, how to improve those intelligences, and how to use them consciously to enhance the students' own and others' lives.

The cognitive research of the last ten to fifteen years overwhelmingly supports the necessity and possibility of teaching students how to increase their skills of knowing, understanding, perceiving, and learning. In his article "Thinking Skills: Neither an Add-On nor a Quick-Fix," Art Costa (1991) makes the following observation:

> For many years we thought that thinking skills programs were intended to challenge the intellectually gifted. Indeed, some thought that any child whose I.Q. fell below a certain static score was forever doomed to remedial or compensatory drill and practice.

Gaining wide acceptance, four fundamental and refreshing concepts underlie modern cognitive curriculum and instructional practices. They are: *The Theory of Cognitive Modifiability* (Feuerstein 1980), the *Theory of Multiple Intelligences* (Gardner 1983), the faith that *Intelligence Can Be Taught* (Whimbley 1975), and Sternberg's thesis that traditional I.Q. scores have very little to do with success in dealing with the problems encountered in daily life (Hammer 1985; McKean 1985).

These theoretical concepts equip us with the realization that all human beings are both retarded in certain problem-solving skills, while simultaneously being gifted in others (Link, as quoted in Makler 1980). The concepts provide us the faith that all human beings can continue to develop their intelligent behavior throughout a lifetime.

Pathways of Learning is about helping all of our students continue to develop their intelligent behavior and their intellectual capacities throughout their lifetimes. I like to call this kind of teaching and learning "meta-intelligence," adapting the idea of metacognition to working with the eight ways of knowing. Stop for a moment and answer the following questions:

- Do you talk to yourself? What do you talk to yourself about?
- Do you answer yourself? Are you often your own best therapist?
- Why do you go through this process? What benefits do you get from it?

Don't worry—talking to yourself is probably not early senility setting in. It's metacognitive behavior! In his article "Mediating the Metacognitive" Art Costa (1984) calls the process of metacognition *inner talking*: "Occurring in the neocortex and therefore thought by some neurologists to be uniquely human, metacognition is our ability to know what we know and what we don't know. It is our ability to plan a strategy for producing what information is needed, to be conscious of our own steps and strategies during the act of problem solving, and to reflect on and evaluate the productiveness of our own thinking." The process of teaching about multiple intelligences, meta-intelligence, is simply intelligence investigating and thinking about itself.

Current research on metacognition documents four distinct levels of information processing, with each level becoming more metacognitively sophisticated than the previous one. I have structured this book around these levels and have adapted them to the task of helping students and parents become more aware of the eight ways of knowing, learn how to use them effectively to be more successful in school, and acquire a full repertoire of intelligence tools and skills for dealing with the task of daily living beyond the classroom. The exercises, or intelligence learning activities, presented in this book are an attempt to catalyze more intelligences in the classroom and to help students transfer the use of the full spectrum of their intellectual potentials to everyday life.[1]

LEVEL 1: TACIT INTELLIGENCE

"I use my eight intelligences everyday, I just never thought about it."

The tacit level of teaching and learning about multiple intelligences involves helping students become aware of capacities and potentials that we generally take for granted. We do many "intelligent" things each day without realizing how really clever we are. Think about what is involved in crossing the street without getting hit by an automobile, listening to music to relax at the end of a day, making a grocery list, parallel parking, drawing diagrams or maps to help someone get from one place to another, using body language to communicate feelings and ideas, telling and understanding jokes, and balancing a checkbook. The tacit level for teaching and learning about the eight ways of knowing involves activities to help students become aware of the capacities and potentials that are the students' legacy as part of the human species and to help them recognize these capacities as intelligent behavior.

LEVEL 2: AWARE INTELLIGENCE

"Now that I have labels for the various ways of knowing, I can practice them and make them stronger."

The aware level of teaching and learning about multiple intelligences involves learning about the neurobiology of the intelligences and how we can improve their functioning. Once we can name the intelligent behaviors we use during the day, it is possible for us to work on strengthening and expanding our "intelligence functioning." In many ways, the intelligences are like any skill we possess—the more we practice them, the better we become at using them.

The aware level involves two tasks: (1) learning how each of the intelligences operates in the brain/mind/body system, and (2) evaluating one's own relative strengths and weaknesses in the various intelligence

---

1. The following description of the levels is adapted with permission from the PDK Fastback series.

areas. Once we have done these tasks, we can become conscious participants in our own intellectual development. If some students discover that they are not very good at using the active imagination (a visual/spatial intelligence capacity), for example, they should also be told about or shown exercises and activities they can use to improve or strengthen this capacity within themselves.

LEVEL 3: STRATEGIC INTELLIGENCE

"Not only do I know about the eight intelligences, but I know when and how to use each one most effectively."

The strategic level of teaching and learning about the eight ways of knowing encompasses the two previous levels of meta-intelligence but adds the conscious decision to employ the eight intelligences regularly to enhance learning, expand creativity, and improve problem-solving abilities. Students suddenly realize that they have many tools in their "kitbags" to help them know, understand, perceive, and learn. For example, if one student is assisting another with schoolwork, the helper may be able to "translate" a lesson into a preferred or stronger intelligence modality for the other student. Or a student might consciously use a variety of ways to solve a problem, including drawing, talking with others, acting it out, thinking about it, or trying to visualize a solution. In other words, the strategic use of the intelligences is using them with intention.

LEVEL 4: REFLECTIVE INTELLIGENCE

"I am learning how to use all eight ways of knowing to help me in my daily life."

The reflective level of teaching and learning about the intelligences involves activities that help students integrate the eight ways of knowing into daily life. Students can use the eight intelligences to approach any problem, challenge, project, or goal. What is more, when we "cook on more burners" as we go about the task of daily living, we can access greater levels of creativity and inventiveness within ourselves than if we use only one approach. Likewise, the eight intelligences not only make various learning tasks more fun; they also broaden and deepen our knowledge base, for we know and understand something in at least eight ways, not just one.

Each level of this model represents an increasingly complex understanding of and facility in using the different ways of knowing. Each level also assumes and contains the previous level within an ever-widening spiral of understanding of and skill in using various intelligence capacities.

TEACHERS TEACHING FOR MORE INTELLIGENCE: THE CASE FOR A PARALLEL CURRICULUM

One of the major assumptions of this book is that we, as educators, need to do whatever it takes to teach students *about* their own multiple intelligences. Current cognitive research has clearly shown that the more conscious students can become about every dimension of the learning process, the better they can and will become as active learners, who recognize themselves as responsible for their own learning. Part of this task is to systematically lead them through the development of what I have called the "meta-intelligence levels." The biggest task of the individual teacher using this book is to create the developmentally appropriate adaptations of the various exercises, activities, and extensions presented.

At first glance, it may seem that teaching students about multiple intelligences involves a big add-on to the existing curriculum. However, I do not believe that this is really the case.

- First, teaching about multiple intelligences is helping students become metacognitive about their own learning process. It makes them aware that they do indeed possess at least eight ways of knowing what they know; eight ways of acquiring knowledge, processing information, learning, and understanding.
- Second, they become aware that not all of their eight intelligences are equally developed; some may be in a state of latency. However, they learn that any underdeveloped or weaker intelligence can be strengthened, empowered, amplified, and enhanced.
- Third, through various self-discovery experiences, such as those suggested in the twenty *Exploration and Discovery Exercises* in this book, students can acquire a sizeable battery of strategies, tools, techniques, and methods to more fully tap into and activate the full spectrum of their intelligence potentials.
- Finally, the more aware students are of their own learning and the bio-neurological and cognitive processes involved in a multiple intelligences approach to learning, the more active, responsible learners they will become.

What I am advocating is a parallel curriculum, in which teachers are continually helping students become more aware of their own cognitive processes while they are studying the daily required material (hopefully using all eight intelligences). While this is not more "stuff" to teach, it is an additional layer of self-consciousness and self-reflectiveness infused into the instructional process and into the process of students' learning.

What Are the Benefits of a Meta-Intelligence Parallel Curriculum?

1. Students become invested in their own education, almost as partners with their teachers. Often they will become advocates for themselves and their own learning needs. Teaching *about* multiple intelligences produces students who are active, eager learners. Is there an educator who could ask for anything more?
2. Understanding of multiple intelligences is a great self-esteem booster. Many of students' negative self-images may come from parent, teacher, and peer put-downs, often when students have attempted to utilize one of the so-called "non-traditional intelligences" to express themselves. Self-awareness and knowledge about multiple intelligences can reverse this very quickly.
3. An understanding of multiple intelligences tends to boost students' esteem for each other. Their perspectives of fellow classmates change. No longer is it necessary (or cool) to put down other students because they are different. Multiple intelligences, in fact, promotes respect for individual differences—celebrating our diversity!

Initially, a bit more time is required to introduce students to the fact that they have eight ways of knowing, not just one. They will not learn this by osmosis. It will require some explicit teaching plus exploration on their part to really understand the intelligences within themselves. But once they gain this understanding and begin to learn how to use their multiple intelligences, it becomes easier to integrate teaching *about* the intelligences into your daily classroom lessons where, hopefully, teaching *with* the intelligences is already part of your normal instructional practice (see *Eight Ways of Teaching*).

Nearly one hundred percent of teachers who have implemented some type of meta-intelligence parallel curriculum agree that the time they have spent teaching *about* multiple intelligences bears many fruits both in students' academic performance and their future life beyond the classroom.

Logical-Mathematical Intelligence

The knowing that occurs through the process of seeking and discovering patterns and through problem solving. It uses such tools as calculation, thinking skills, numbers, scientific reasoning, logic, abstract symbols, and pattern recognition.

Verbal-Linguistic Intelligence

The knowing that occurs through the written, spoken, and read aspects of language as a formal system. It uses such tools as essays, debates, public speech, poetry, formal and informal conversation, creative writing, and linguistic-based humor (riddles, puns, jokes).

Visual-Spatial Intelligence

The knowing that occurs through seeing both externally (with the physical eyes) and internally (with the mind's eye). It uses such tools as drawing, painting, sculpture, collage, montage, visualization, imagination, pretending, and creating mental images.

Intrapersonal Intelligence

The knowing that occurs through introspection, metacognition (thinking about thinking), self-reflection, and "cosmic questioning" (What is the meaning of life?). It uses such tools as affective processing, journals, thinking logs, teaching for transfer, higher-order thinking, and self-esteem practices.

*8 Ways of Knowing**

Musical-Rhythmic Intelligence

The knowing that occurs through hearing, sound, vibrational patterns, rhythm, and tonal patterns, including the full range of potential sounds produced with the vocal chords. It utilizes such tools as singing, musical instruments, environmental sounds, tonal associations, and the endless rhythmic possibilities of life.

Interpersonal Intelligence

The knowing that occurs through person-to-person relating, communication, teamwork, and collaboration. It employs such tools as cooperative learning, empathy, social skills, team competitions, and group projects that foster positive interdependence.

Naturalist Intelligence

The knowing that occurs through encounters with the natural world that involve appreciation for and understanding of the various flora and fauna, recognition of species membership, and the ability to relate to living organisms. It uses such tools as hands-on labs, field trips, sensory stimulation, and attempts to classify and comprehend natural patterns.

Bodily-Kinesthetic Intelligence

The knowing that occurs through physical movement and performance (learning by doing). It employs such tools as dance, drama, physical games, mime, role-play, body language, physical exercise, and inventing.

*Adapted from *Eight Ways of Knowing: Teaching for Multiple Intelligences* by David Lazear (Palatine, Ill.: Skylight, 1998).
Pathways of Learning © 2000 Zephyr Press, Tucson, Arizona • 800-232-2187 • http://zephyrpress.com

A Model for Teaching about Multiple Intelligences:
Dynamics of the Parallel Curriculum

Explorations of the Eight Intelligences

PRACTICE
PRACTICE
PRACTICE
PRACTICE
PRACTICE
PRACTICE
PRACTICE

Intelligence Experiments Beyond the Classroom

There are three general stages to working with this parallel multiple intelligence curriculum. This is discussed in much greater detail on the parallel curriculum pages, following each of the basic *Intelligence Explorations and Discovery Exercises*. The diagram on page 8 and the following explain what is involved in using this curriculum in a systematic way.

1. **Multiple explorations of the eight intelligences.** In the chapters which follow, you will find *Intelligence Exploration and Discovery Exercises* for each meta-intelligence level; namely, the tacit, aware, strategic, and reflective levels. I will refer to these as the "base exercises." The content of the base exercises is the eight intelligences themselves. Research from the cognitive sciences suggests that when teaching students a new skill, it is best to do so in a relatively content-free situation or one in which they are dealing with familiar content. This is to give students the opportunity to focus on the skills and/or capacities you are trying to teach, rather than be worried about something they must know for an upcoming test. Each base exercise involves three dynamics you should keep in mind as you create other intelligence exploration exercises.

   - *Awakening, stimulating, and triggering the intelligences.* Begin with an easy, fun, hands-on activity that quickly catapults students into using their own multiple intelligences; one that captures their attention and interest from the beginning. Remember, the best way to learn about multiple intelligences is by doing it, so don't spend too much time talking about the intelligences. Involve students in doing the exercise as quickly as possible to discover the intelligences for themselves (see *Eight Ways of Knowing* for more exercises and activities for awakening the intelligences).
   - *Amplifying, developing, and enhancing.* This is very much akin to taking your intelligences to the gym and giving them a good workout. When teaching students about the intelligences using the base exercises, you may need to demonstrate the use of an intelligence, a specific skill, or capacity to get them started. Then give students an immediate opportunity to try it out for themselves in as content-free environment as possible. For example, demonstrate how to do graphic representation (a visual/spatial intelligence capacity) by visually representing something that is important to you. Then give them an opportunity to practice the same skill or capacity to express something that is important to them.
   - *Self-evaluation and reflection.* The self-reflective part of working with the intelligences may well be the most important part. At the end of each base exercise is a period for reflection. Never

cut this part to save on time. This is where you are asking students to "harvest" their learning. It is during these reflective times that you are most able to accomplish the teaching *about* multiple intelligences goals for each of the meta-intelligence levels—the tacit, aware, strategic, and reflective. Carefully design this part of the exercise to take students as far as possible into the learning and discoveries of the respective meta-intelligence levels.

2. **Practice, practice, practice, and more practice** (using multiple intelligences in academic content areas). Once students have an understanding (and personal experience) of the various intelligences, you are ready to help them learn how to apply the eight intelligences to the learning of various curriculum-based material. Contemporary cognitive sciences research suggests that it takes three to four times of practice using a particular skill/capacity, in different learning situations, dealing with different aspects of one subject area or totally different subjects, to catalyze the transfer process (Fogarty and Bellanca, 1986). For example, teach them the skill of expressing their ideas through role play, then ask them to apply it to learning math concepts, to understanding a period of history, to performing a scientific experiment, or to understanding characters in literature. There are several key aspects to bear in mind when you are creating these academic applications of the base exercises:

   - *Bridging the base exercises.* The importance of this is to help students create a link between the content-free use of the base exercise and its use with academic content. Many of the dynamics are the same, but now they must utilize the eight intelligences in various ways to help them learn and understand academic content. Learning *about* multiple intelligences is still key. This process is now intensified, however, and they must use their base knowledge about multiple intelligences to help them with the mastery of the academic curriculum.
   - *Academic and multiple intelligences objectives explanation.* Students need to know and understand both the content and the intelligence objectives of the lesson. Clarification of these objectives will maximize their successful processing of the academic material via the eight intelligences. The more they know about and understand the teaching and learning strategies you will be using, and *why* you are using them, the better learners they will become. You may even find them helping you teach the lesson.
   - *Reflection and processing.* Students may successfully complete various multiple intelligence-based learning tasks, around which you have structured a given lesson. Yet this does not

mean they have also mastered the knowledge you wanted them to gain *about* their multiple intelligences. Always make sure there is time for stepping back and reflecting on the learning process that was involved in the lesson. What was it like using multiple intelligences to learn the content? How did multiple intelligences help the learning? What did you learn about yourself and your own intelligences in this lesson? We often don't really know what we know until we step back and explicitly state what we know.

3. **Intelligence experiments beyond the classroom.** After students have learned how to use the eight intelligences in the academic/curriculum content, it is time to encourage them to apply the intelligences outside the school environment. Work with them to help them find ways they can use their multiple intelligences in dealing with various family, individual, and peer relationship situations; such as planning the family summer vacation, deciding electives for the next school term, or solving conflicts and disagreements with friends. In some ways, this stage is the ultimate transfer in teaching *about* multiple intelligences; namely, do students understand the intelligences deeply enough to make them a regular part of their lives? Many of the dynamics mentioned in the previous two sections apply here as well. However, there are several additional considerations:

- *Brainstorming potential connections.* When we try to move learning beyond the confines of the classroom, most students need help in bridging what they have been doing and learning in the classroom environment to their real-life environment. When you ask students to work with the meta-intelligence exercises in their lives beyond the classroom, remember there is a certain amount of risk involved. You will probably need to help them get started with application ideas that minimize the risk but have the potential to maximize their further learning about multiple intelligences.
- *Time to experiment.* Once students have committed themselves to various intelligence experiments beyond the classroom (either ideas in this book or others you create with students), give them lots of support, encouragement, and time to implement their plans. Remember, in order for them to be successful in implementing this part of the parallel curriculum, they may have to do some teaching to others about multiple intelligences. Students will likely need your assistance in short courses they could give to others, especially those people who might be involved in their various intelligence experiments.

• *Time to report (and reflect)*. While students are implementing their intelligence experiments, you may need to provide opportunities for them to share how things are going, and to make mid-course corrections to their initial plans. The reporting and reflecting will show how these intelligence experiments beyond the classroom are working on the reflective level—the tacit-reflective, aware-reflective, strategic-reflective, or reflective-reflective level. These reports are asking students to harvest their learning from the intelligence experiments and to make them part of their regular repertoire for living.

HOW TO USE THIS BOOK

This book is intended as an advanced-level aid for teachers who are working with multiple intelligences in their classroom, both teaching students the skills of the different intelligences as well as integrating multiple ways of knowing and learning into their daily teaching of various content and subjects. The book assumes that you have been able to catalyze students' interest in the eight ways of knowing. The exercises, tools, and techniques presented in these pages are most effective when students are genuinely interested in learning more about themselves intellectually. If that interest is not there already, or if it is weak, the tacit tools will likely be most useful as catalysts of the desire to learn more.

I believe that most exercises and strategies I am suggesting can be easily integrated into daily lessons with careful planning on your part. However, any time you can give where the lesson content is the intelligences will increase students' awareness of the eight ways of knowing, and strengthen their abilities to skillfully use the intelligences in mastering assigned classroom material. The more aware students become about various learning processes in general, and their own unique learning in particular, the better learners they will be, not only in school, but in their lives beyond the classroom as well.

Now let's explore what you'll find in each chapter.

Base Exploration Exercises

Chapters 2 through 5 offer twenty specific meta-intelligence exploration and discovery exercises you can use to help students learn about their intelligences. These are organized by the four meta-intelligence levels—the *tacit*, *aware*, *strategic*, and *reflective* levels. Each intelligence-based exploration exercise focuses on helping students learn about various aspects of their own intelligences.

Some of these exploration exercises may extend over several days and, in at least one case, over several weeks. This is not to suggest an inordinate amount of time must be spent on these exercises. However, you should give a few minutes each day for reflection on the intelligence explorations and discoveries that students are making when you are using those meta-intelligence exercises, which take more time. This is important from two standpoints: (1) students may be experiencing difficulty with certain aspects of a given exercise where you and other students can assist them; and (2) the very act of sharing what is happening to them may serve to heighten and intensify their work with an exercise. Remember, the most important part of each lesson is the reflection at the end, so make sure to allow adequate time.

Each base exploration exercise contains a set of blackline masters for elementary, middle, and secondary level schools. Use them to help you introduce the activity to your students.

The exercise procedures will need to be adapted so they are developmentally appropriate to the grade level you teach. Remember Jerome Bruner's important insight about the "spiral curriculum"—anything can be taught to any age level, if you as the teacher take the time to step inside the students' world view and speak the language that they can understand (Bruner 1956). I have given you spiraled blacklines to help you to create the necessary spiraled exercise procedures.

The Parallel Curriculum Interface

There is a parallel curriculum interface section following each of the base exploration exercises. This section provides curriculum-interface extension exercises in three distinct areas:

1. **Curricular exploration and discovery.** This section presents further extension exercise ideas that are based on the initial exploration exercise. These suggestions are intended to trigger your thinking about other ways to use the base exercise. Using these suggestions and/or others you create can help students learn about how the intelligences function, give an awareness of their own personal strengths and weaknesses, provide ideas for what they can do to improve and/or strengthen all ways of knowing, and show them ways they can help others utilize the full spectrum of their intellectual capabilities.

2. **Academic exploration and discovery.** This section offers several beginning ideas for adapting and applying the base exploration exercise to various academic content areas. In some cases, the suggestions are content specific. In others, they are more generic and could, in principle, be adapted to a variety of distinct subject areas. Again, my goal is to get you started so you can come up with your own applications of the base exercise to your content.

3. **Beyond school exploration and discovery.** The final section is concerned with students' adaptations and use of the base exercise in real life situations outside the classroom. This is the ultimate test of their learning about and understanding of multiple intelligences. The real goal of these sections is to encourage students to make multiple intelligences a regular part of their everyday lives, both in school and beyond.

I suggest that you begin with the base exploration exercise examples and experiment with using some of the additional application extension exercises. The goal of all these exercises is to increase students' comfort level in exploring multiple intelligences, as well as learning how to use the specific exercises.

Use all of the academic extensions provided, and create as many of your own as you can. This is the practice, practice, practice, and more practice stage discussed earlier. The more we use the various intelligences in the teaching and learning process, the better students will genuinely understand the academic content.

Have students experiment with one of the suggested extension ideas. If time permits, have them come up with others on their own. Allow them time to report and reflect on what they are learning and discovering about multiple intelligences as they experiment with them beyond the classroom.

Using the parallel curriculum interface section in this way will at least get you started on the very exciting and revelatory journey of teaching your students about multiple intelligences.

Personal Reflection Logs

At the end of each parallel curriculum section I have included a personal reflection log. These logs are for you as the adult learner. I believe that these logs are the most important part of this book. They provide you with an opportunity to move your own teaching for, with, and about multiple intelligences through the four meta-intelligence levels.

Special Chapter for Parents

I have included a new chapter for parents because I believe they play a critical part of teaching students about their multiple intelligences. Parents must understand what you are doing and why, especially given that this way of teaching and learning "goes against the grain" of how most education is being done in the Western world today. This chapter, entitled "Nurturing Multiple Intelligences at Home," can be the basis for special parent in-services or training sessions on how to develop, enhance, and expand their children's multiple intelligences in and through their family life together. Some of the material on these pages could be used to help you inform parents about multiple intelligences during parent-teacher conferences. The information also could be included in a newsletter to parents. Or, simply present parents with this information to help them understand what you are doing in the classroom and to assure them that it has a solid foundation in educational research.

For Colleagues and Administrators Too

The parents' chapter offers a helpful overview of the theory and practice of multiple intelligences, and may be useful for administrators and colleagues as well. The chapter provides easy-to-understand background information on the eight intelligences. If parents want more, I suggest a copy of *Eight Ways of Knowing*. This gives a thorough introduction and comprehensive explanation of each intelligence.

In addition, invite others to observe your lessons that apply multiple intelligences in the teaching and learning process. Allow them to interview students on what they think about a multiple intelligence approach to teaching and learning. Then ask them to look at test scores and other appropriate multiple intelligence academic assessment methods (which you are hopefully using in your classroom). My guess is that you will be able to show many students succeeding in school who never have before. They will see highly motivated, active learning taking place.

Kitbag of Methods, Tools, and Techniques
for Teaching about Multiple Intelligences

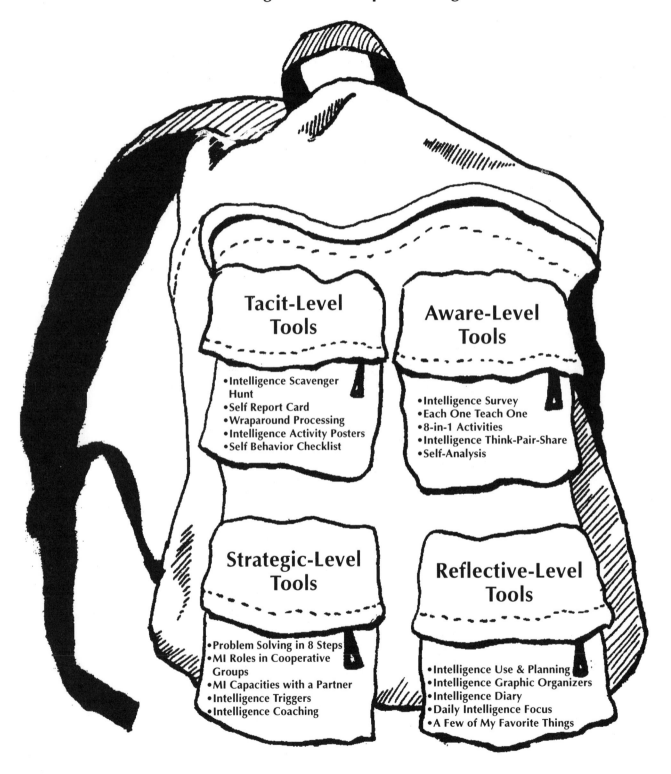

Tacit-Level Tools

- Intelligence Scavenger Hunt
- Self Report Card
- Wraparound Processing
- Intelligence Activity Posters
- Self Behavior Checklist

Aware-Level Tools

- Intelligence Survey
- Each One Teach One
- 8-in-1 Activities
- Intelligence Think-Pair-Share
- Self-Analysis

Strategic-Level Tools

- Problem Solving in 8 Steps
- MI Roles in Cooperative Groups
- MI Capacities with a Partner
- Intelligence Triggers
- Intelligence Coaching

Reflective-Level Tools

- Intelligence Use & Planning
- Intelligence Graphic Organizers
- Intelligence Diary
- Daily Intelligence Focus
- A Few of My Favorite Things

Pathways of Learning © 2000 Zephyr Press, Tucson, Arizona • 800-232-2187 • http://zephyrpress.com

1
Nurturing Multiple Intelligences at Home

A Special Chapter for Parents

The question is *not* "How smart is my child?"
It's rather, "*How* is my child smart?"

THE THEORY OF MULTIPLE INTELLIGENCES: AN OVERVIEW

Some of the latest brain research has discovered that we have many ways of being intelligent, not just one. However, the standardized testing we do in our schools does not address this full range of our intellectual abilities and skills. Dr. Howard Gardner, co-director of Harvard University's cognitive research effort called "Project Zero," looked at human intelligence from a much wider angle than we usually do in traditional, standard intelligence testing.

Dr. Gardner coined the phrase "multiple intelligences" to talk about this reality. In an article, "The Development and Education of Intelligences," published in *Essays on the Intellect*, he proposed a new working definition of intelligence to help us move beyond the biases of the more traditional view of intelligence: "An intelligence entails the ability to solve problems or fashion products that are of consequence in a particular cultural setting."

In other words, in common, everyday life we call someone intelligent if: (1) they can solve the problems they face in their lives, (2) they can creatively meet life's many challenges, and (3) they are able to produce things that are of value to our society. In addition to Gardner's initial definition, I have also suggested that intelligence is the way we know what we know, understand, learn, process information, and acquire knowledge.

This research has identified at least eight intelligences that each of us possesses; eight ways we are smart; eight ways we know what we know. There are probably many others! The overview chart of the eight intelligences Howard Gardner identified is on page 7. You will find a description of each intelligence and some exercises that you can use to explore the eight intelligences in yourself and with your children. You might even find it interesting to try some of these exercises on your friends, or turn them into different kinds of party games!

Pathways of Learning © 2000 Zephyr Press, Tucson, Arizona • 800-232-2187 • http://zephyrpress.com

Verbal/Linguistic Intelligence
(sometimes called "word smart" or "book smart")

We use our verbal/linguistic intelligence when we speak to each other in formal speech or informal conversation. We use it when we put our thoughts down on paper, create poetry, or simply write a letter to a friend. Verbal/linguistic intelligence is involved in story-telling and creating, in all forms of humor involving such things as plays on words, the unexpected ending in a joke, and various funny twists of the language. It is involved in any use of metaphors, similes, and analogies, and, of course, in learning proper grammar and syntax in speaking and writing.

Exercises to Stimulate the Verbal/Linguistic Intelligence

- Learn the meaning of one interesting, new word each day and practice using it in normal conversation with others.
- Get a book of word games and puzzles (for example, crosswords, jumbles, and so on) or play language-oriented table games (such as Scrabble™, Spill and Spell™, and so on).
- Watch a TV drama or detective story, then write your own sequel or tell what you think should happen in the next episode.
- Talk with someone about his/her ideas or opinions. Ask questions, have a discussion, or engage in friendly debate.
- Make a presentation on a topic that interests and excites you (for example, a hobby, a political view, a book you've read, or someone you know).

Logical/Mathematical Intelligence
(sometimes called "number smart" or "thinking smart")

You can see logical/mathematical intelligence in operation most clearly when you are involved in a situation that requires problem solving or meeting a new challenge. It is often associated with what we call scientific thinking. We use our logical/mathematical intelligence when we recognize abstract patterns such as counting by twos, or knowing if we've received the right change at the supermarket. We use it to find connections or see relationships between seemingly separate and distinct pieces of information. Logical/mathematical intelligence is responsible for the various patterns of thinking we use in our daily lives such as list-making, creating priorities, and planning something for the future.

Exercises to Stimulate the Logical/Mathematical Intelligence

- Practice analytical thinking by classifying a group of 12 randomly gathered objects. See if you can create a rationale for organizing them (for example, shape, colors, size, use, and so on).
- Do a project that requires following step-by-step directions; for example building something (not prefab) or cooking from scratch.
- Create a four-point outline telling about a movie you have seen with each of the points having four subpoints, and each subpoint having four more subpoints.
- Create a convincing, rational argument for something that is totally absurd; for example, the benefits of roller skates with oval-shaped wheels.
- Create a sequence of numbers that has a hidden pattern. See if someone else can discover the pattern.

Visual/Spatial Intelligence
(sometimes called "art smart," "seeing smart," or "picture smart")

Visual/spatial intelligence can be seen in its purest form in the active imagination of children involved in such things as daydreaming, pretending to make themselves invisible, or imagining themselves to be on a great journey to magical times and places. We employ this intelligence when we draw pictures to express our thoughts and feelings, or when we decorate a room to create a certain mood. We use it when we use a map get where we want to go. Visual/spatial intelligence helps us win at chess, enables us to turn a blueprint on paper into a real object (for example, a bookshelf or a dress), and allows us to visualize things we want in our lives (for example, new curtains or wallpaper, making a successful speech, planning a trip, projecting a career change, or receiving an award).

Exercises to Stimulate the Visual/Spatial Intelligence

- Look at the clouds with a group of friends and see if you can find such things as animals, people, objects, faces, and so on, hidden in the formations.
- Practice exercises for using the active imagination; for example, imagine yourself living in a different period of history or pretend you are having a conversation with your hero/heroine, a character from literature, or a historical figure.

- Try to express an idea, opinion, or feeling with clay, paints, colored markers, or pens. Use images, shapes, patterns, designs, textures, and colors.
- Plan a scavenger hunt with friends. Make complex and interesting maps for each other to follow that will lead to the "treasure."
- Create a picture montage on a theme or idea that interests you. Cut out pictures from magazines and arrange them to convey what you want to say.

Bodily/Kinesthetic Intelligence
(sometimes called "body smart"
or "movement smart")

Bodily/kinesthetic intelligence could be seen in operation if I gave you a typewriter with no markings on the keys, and asked you to type a letter. If at some time you learned how to type, your fingers would "know" the keyboard and would likely be able to produce the letter with little or no effort. The body knows many things that are not necessarily known by the conscious mind; for example, how to ride a bike, park a car, catch an object thrown to it, or maintain its balance while walking. Bodily/kinesthetic intelligence also involves the ability to use the body to express emotions and thoughts (such as dance or body language), to play a game or sport, to invent a new product, and to convey ideas (such as charades, mime, and drama).

Exercises to Stimulate the Bodily/Kinesthetic Intelligence

- After a presentation, have everyone in a group express their reactions to the presentation through a physical gesture, action, movement, posture, or other body language.
- Pay attention to your body as you do an everyday physical task, such as shoveling snow, washing dishes, or fixing your car. See if you can become aware of your actions, what your body knows how to do, and how it functions.
- Perform different physical activities, such as walking, dancing, or jogging. Try to match your mood. Also try some activities to change your mood.
- Practice using your non-dominant hand to perform any taken-for-granted task (for example, brushing your teeth, eating, buttoning a shirt, and so on). See if you can train your hand to function more effectively.

Musical/Rhythmic (also Auditory/ Vibrational) Intelligence
(sometimes called "music smart" or "sound smart")

We use our musical/rhythmic intelligence when we play music to calm ourselves when we are stressed out or to stimulate ourselves when we're bored and feeling down. Many of us use music and rhythm to attain a steady rhythm when jogging, cleaning the house, or learning to type. Musical/rhythmic intelligence is involved when we hear a jingle on the radio and find ourselves humming it over and over throughout the day. It is active when we use tones and rhythmic patterns (instrumental, environmental, and humans) to communicate how we are feeling and what we believe, for example the sounds of intense joy, fear, excitement, and loss; or to express the depth of our religious devotion or the intensity of national loyalty.

Exercises to Stimulate the Musical/Rhythmic Intelligence

- Make a list of different types of music you own or have access to. Listen to several minutes of each type and note how each affects you; for example, feelings, images evoked, memories sparked, and so on.
- Think of something you want to remember, or something you want to teach someone. Choose a well-known tune and create a simple song using the information to be remembered or taught.
- Experiment expressing your feelings (for example, fear, contentment, anger, exhaustion, exhilaration, and so on) through vocal sounds alone (no words). Try producing different volumes, pitches, tones, and noises to communicate your meaning.
- Listen to the natural rhythmic patterns of your environment; for example, coffee brewing, traffic, wind blowing, rain beating on the window, and so on. See what you can learn from these rhythms and beats.
- Read a story and practice "illustrating" it with various sound effects, music, rhythmic beats, tones, and so on—much like an old-time radio show.

Interpersonal Intelligence
(sometimes called "people smart")

We experience our interpersonal intelligence most directly whenever we are part of a team effort, whether it be a sports game, a church committee, or a community task force. This intelligence utilizes our ability to engage in verbal and nonverbal communication, and our capacity to notice distinctions among ourselves, for example, contrasts in moods, temperament, motivations, and intentions. Interpersonal intelligence allows us to develop a genuine sense of empathy and caring for each other. Through this person-to-person way of knowing, we maintain our individual identity, but also become more than ourselves as we identify with and become part of others. We can stand in another's shoes and understand his or her feelings, fears, anticipations, and beliefs.

Exercises to Stimulate Interpersonal Intelligence

- Get a partner to try to reproduce a complex shape or design you have drawn. These are the rules: (1) verbal instructions only; (2) partner may not look at the drawing; (3) partner may ask you any question; and (4) you can't look at what the person is drawing.
- Explore different ways to express encouragement and support for other people (for example, facial expressions, body posture, gestures, sounds, words, and phrases). Practice giving encouragement and support to others around you each day.
- Practice listening deeply and fully to another person. Force yourself to stay focused on what is being said. Avoid the tendency to interpret what the person is saying and to express your views. Ask relevant questions, make appropriate comments, or paraphrase to check for your own understanding.
- Volunteer to be part of a team effort and watch for positive and negative team behavior (positive behaviors are things that help the team work together and be successful).
- Try disciplined people watching—guessing what others are thinking, feeling, their background, profession, and so on, based on nonverbal clues (for example, dress, gestures, voice tone, colors, and so on). When possible (and appropriate) check your accuracy with the person.

Intrapersonal Intelligence
(sometimes called "self smart")

Intrapersonal intelligence is the introspective intelligence. It allows us to be self-reflective; that is, to step back from and watch ourselves, like an outside observer. Intrapersonal intelligence involves knowledge about and awareness of the internal aspects of the self, such as knowledge of feelings, thinking processes, self-reflection, and a sense of/or intuition about spiritual realities. Both self-identity and the ability to transcend the self are part of the functioning of intrapersonal intelligence. When we experience a sense of unity, have an intuition about our connection with the larger order of things, experience higher states of consciousness, feel the lure of the future, and dream of unrealized potentials in our lives, it is the result of our intrapersonal way of knowing.

Exercises to Stimulate the Intrapersonal Intelligence

- Make a mood graph showing the high points and low points (as well as points in between) of your day. Note the external events that contributed to the different moods.
- Evaluate your thinking strategies and patterns in different situations; for example, a problem arises in a well thought-through plan, an emergency or crisis occurs, or you have to make a decision when there are a number of viable and attractive options.
- In the midst of a routine activity, practice acute mindfulness; that is, an intense awareness of everything going on: thoughts, feelings, physical movements, and inner states of being.
- Keep a daily journal or reflective log where you record your thoughts, feelings, ideas, insights, and important events from your day. Try a variety of recording media such as writing, drawing, singing, acting out, painting, or sculpting your reflections.
- Pretend you are an outside observer watching your thoughts, feelings, and moods. Notice different patterns that seem to kick into gear in certain situations; for example, the "anger pattern," "playfulness pattern," or "anxiety pattern."

Naturalist Intelligence
(sometimes called "nature smart")

The naturalist intelligence deals with all that we know in and through the natural world (as opposed to the world created by humans). This intelligence is highly sensitive to and stimulated by all aspects of nature, including plants, animals, the weather, and physical features of Earth. It includes such skills as recognizing various categories and varieties of animals, insects, plants, flowers, and so on. It involves the ability to grow things and to care for and train animals. And it involves a sensitivity to and love for Earth, as well as a desire to care for and protect its natural resources.

Exercises to Stimulate the Naturalist Intelligence

- Go to a favorite place out in nature and walk slowly around, paying conscious attention to its impact on your five senses. What do you hear, smell, taste, see, and feel?
- Create a mini-greenhouse in your home or yard. See what plants, flowers, herbs, and so on, you can grow.
- Gather a set of CDs or tapes that have environmental or natural sounds. Spend time listening to them, immersing yourself in the sounds of nature. What do they evoke in you?
- Find an object in nature and study it carefully, looking for patterns in your own life that are reflected in this object.
- Spend time with a favorite animal (pet, creature in a zoo, and so on) and really allow yourself to get to know it. Imagine what it is thinking, feeling, and so on.

NURTURING THE FULL POTENTIAL

There are literally hundreds of relatively simple things we as parents can do at home to help our children be all that they can be intellectually. We can work with our children to develop and use all eight intelligences on a regular basis as part of normal life together as a family. There are at least three areas where you can, as a parent, nurture, even evoke, the full spectrum of your child's or children's intelligences.

Look in the sections that follow for hundreds of practical ideas for nurturing your child's many intelligences at home.

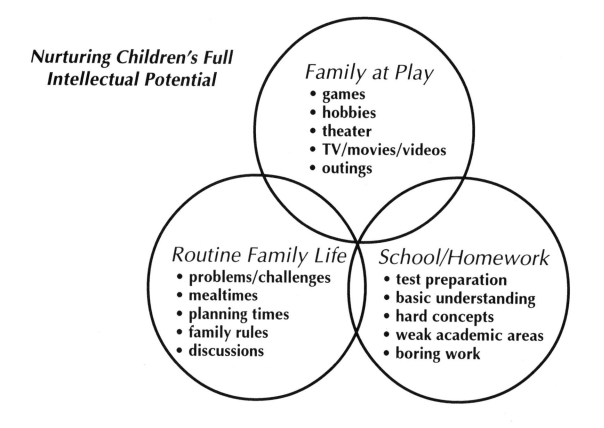

Nurturing Children's Full Intellectual Potential

Family at Play
- **games**
- **hobbies**
- **theater**
- **TV/movies/videos**
- **outings**

Routine Family Life
- **problems/challenges**
- **mealtimes**
- **planning times**
- **family rules**
- **discussions**

School/Homework
- **test preparation**
- **basic understanding**
- **hard concepts**
- **weak academic areas**
- **boring work**

The Family at Play

Think about times when you are doing things together as a family—such as family outings, going to a movie, playing various kinds of games, pursuing favorite activities, and so on. These are excellent occasions to work on the intelligences with your family.

- What kinds of games do you have and play in your home? There are many games available in stores that require the use of different intelligences in the playing of the game itself. Make up new games that use the intelligences.

- After seeing a movie, TV show, or play what do you talk about? This is a great time to have a multiple intelligence discussion about the event; talk about such things as the soundtrack, scenery, costumes, action and/or movements of the characters, natural setting, use of color, and so on.
- Where do you go for vacations and/or family field trips? What you do and see is as important as the locale. Think about all the possibilities related to the intelligences: physical activities you can do; museums or shows where you can experience the art, music, dance, drama, or stories unique to where you are visiting; parks or hikes where you can immerse yourselves in the natural environment, and so on.
- What afterschool or weekend activities do you encourage? Hobbies or family projects provide great opportunities to use and develop different skills from the various intelligences. This allows people to try something new or to work on developing a skill.

Routine Family Life

There are many aspects of ongoing family life that can become tiresome and boring; they happen over and over and over again, day in and day out, every week, month, and year. However, approaching these times using multiple intelligences can often bring new life and excitement into these occasions.

- What is your family problem-solving process and how does it work for you? For many families these are dreaded moments. What could happen if you approached family discussions or problem-solving times on more levels? Try talking about and drawing pictures of issues or problems. Then silently meditate on them, make up funny songs about them, and act out the problem and several solutions.
- How does your family approach making and enforcing family expected behaviors? Sometimes, behavior problems arise in families because the children do not really understand the reasons for certain expected behaviors, or they have had no input into such things. Approaching this area of family life using all of the intelligences can help everyone to internalize these behaviors.
- What usually goes on during mealtimes in your house in addition to eating? Designing the mealtime drama with the eight intelligences in mind can be a wonderful time for reflection on the intelligences.

Think about the visual/spatial appeal of the food and its presentation. Think about the various kinds of background music you could use to enhance different kinds of meals (especially meals from a culture other than your own). How could you relate different foods to the different intelligences?

- When planning a family activity, budget, home improvement, and so on, what planning process do you use? Many of my comments and suggestions on discussing family problem solving also apply here. Do the planning using as many of the intelligences as you can. In addition to talking about what will be done, use visuals, body movements (for example, gestures, facial expressions, and so on), time to reflect on personal feelings, values, and so on.

Schoolwork/Homework

Working with my own daughters on their schoolwork was one of the most enlightening times in my own practical understanding of the theory of multiple intelligences. Neither of them were traditional learners, so I had to find a variety of ways to help them with homework. At that time, I did not have the label "multiple intelligences" to put on some of the things we tried, but as I look back I now recognize that I was using many multiple intelligences strategies to help them succeed.

- "I hate this! It's so boring!" Does your child/children ever say this? This is a wonderful time to pull out all stops of the eight intelligences and find a way to make homework more interesting and fun. This approach will also pay off, as they will likely better remember and understand what they studied.
- How do you help your child/children review for a test? Approaching the review of the required material on as many of the intelligence levels as possible will help them remember the material when taking the test, even if the basic form of the test is written. For example, ask them to show you information by drawing it, making up a rhyme about it, or acting it out. You could turn the review into a TV game show.
- Are there certain subject areas with which your child/children struggle a great deal? When we encounter material that is very hard to understand, we often mistakenly take a "work harder, longer, with more effort" attitude. What we should probably be doing is working on it differently. Here is where using the eight intelligences comes in. If a child is having trouble understanding something in one way, multiple intelligences gives us many ways to translate it into another way of knowing.
- Do you ever feel that your child's/children's basic understanding of some concept is lacking? This is a great time to return to the most

basic parts and approach them using the eight intelligences. This can often cause the "aha!" experience to happen. Future learning can then build on this foundation.

For busy parents, homework is probably the most difficult area of nurturing the intelligences in our children. Also, since most of us have not been in the formal school classroom as learners for some time, dealing with curricular material in multiple intelligences ways can be a bit of a stretch.

However, in working with my daughters, I found that they could often, with my encouragement and support, come up with creative ideas to help themselves with their own learning—ideas which went way beyond the mostly paper-and-pencil tasks that over 95 percent of their homework required of them. In doing these multiple intelligence-based learning activities with the assigned homework, they successfully completed the work, and I found them more motivated as learners. Their understanding of the material greatly increased.

Parents can be of great help to their own children and their teachers. We can help our children transfer their classroom learning beyond the school situation by reinforcing learning about their intelligences. This means that we must ask them to be as intelligent as possible in multiple ways in school, as well as to use their full intelligence capacities in the family situation. This will help teachers by expanding their influence on students beyond the time that a child is in school, thus, making every situation a learning situation. This truly is the key for instilling a passion for lifelong learning in our children.

Please refer to the suggestions at the end of each of the intelligence activities sections at the end of this chapter for specific ideas or ways to try to help children with their schoolwork.

STAGES OF LEARNING, NURTURING, AND DEVELOPING MULTIPLE INTELLIGENCES

The human capacity for learning is awesome. Whenever we learn anything we generally move through four distinct stages before the learning really becomes a part of our lives. Allow me to explain these four stages using learning about multiple intelligences as the example.

Stage 1: Tacit Understanding

"I use the eight intelligences every day, I've just never called them that."
Here your concern is learning to recognize multiple intelligences in the many taken-for-granted things we do every day—those things we do without thinking about them that are in fact using multiple intelligences.

Stage 2: Aware Understanding

> *"Now that I have a label for the different ways of knowing,*
> *I can practice them and make them stronger."*

This stage involves two tasks: (1) learning the basic functioning of each intelligence, including skills and capacities, and (2) evaluating one's own intelligence profile—identifying intelligences which are more developed and those which are still emerging.

Stage 3: Strategic Understanding

> *"I know about the eight intelligences, and I know when and how to use each one."*

This level involves the realization that we have many, many tools in our "intelligence kit bags"—tools which we can use on a regular basis to enhance learning, expand creativity, and help us improve our problem-solving abilities.

Stage 4: Reflective Understanding

> *"I am learning how to use all eight ways of knowing to help me in my daily life."*

At this level we learn how to integrate the eight ways of knowing into our normal repertoire. In other words, as we go about the task of daily living we are automatically accessing greater levels of creativity and inventiveness than if we were using only one approach.

On the following pages, I have provided fuller explanations of these four stages as well as numerous practical activities you can do for each intelligence in these four stages. These stages or levels can help your child/children understand the intelligences, and also provide many ways to nurture the fuller development of each intelligence in the family as a whole.

STAGE 1: TACIT UNDERSTANDING

The main goal of this stage is to help children become aware that they do have different ways of knowing and learning. Some children may have unique ways of approaching a problem that needs to be solved or unorthodox means of dealing with challenges. Sometimes these methods or strategies make a child seem different from other children. They may not understand why one student may need to draw pictures to express what he/she is trying to say, for example, while another needs to act something out in order to really understand. It is important that children learn that we are not all the same, and that an approach to solving a problem that works perfectly well for one child may do nothing at all for another. This is not because the other child is stupid or weird. It's

Pathways of Learning © 2000 Zephyr Press, Tucson, Arizona • 800-232-2187 • http://zephyrpress.com

because we all have many different ways of knowing, understanding, learning, perceiving, and communicating with each other.

The suggested activities for the different intelligences are examples of things you can do to help your child/ children become aware of and to appreciate these differences. The activities are designed to help children become aware of many highly intelligent things they do every day, most of them without thinking, and definitely without labeling them as "intelligent" behavior. Once children can label some of these things as "intelligent," they often gain an entirely new image of themselves and others.

This is extremely important, especially for children who may not be doing well in school. We are often too quick to attach the label "learning disability" to difficulties some students have in working with the verbal/linguistic and logical/mathematical intelligences. These make up most of how school is conducted today. Many times, these difficulties have nothing to do with so-called "learning disabilities" but rather with "learning differences"—ways of knowing, learning, and understanding that our schools have not tapped. Helping children become aware of these differences makes a huge difference in their own self-esteem and can make a difference in how they feel about each other as well.

The eight ways of knowing are inherent in the brain. Therefore, there are things you can do to trigger each of the different intelligences in yourself and your children. This is a matter of awakening the full intelligence potential we already possess. Following are some suggestions you may find helpful to use at home with your own children. These suggested activities and exercises are intended to promote the *tacit* level of understanding the intelligences.

I use the eight intelligences every day; I've just never called them that!

Activities to Support the Tacit Use of the Intelligences

Verbal/Linguistic

★ Play word games which involve understanding the order and meaning of words: Scrabble™; word searches, jumbles, and crossword puzzles in the newspaper; Wheel of Fortune™; hangman.

★ Have them explain or teach something to you they have learned.

★ Tell each other jokes and teach them about puns.

★ Play memory/recall games: trivia games, vocabulary flash cards.

★ Read and tell stories to each other.

★ Get a book of limericks and read them to each other, then make up some of your own.

Visual/Spatial

★ Play games that require the use of visual skills: Pictionary™.

★ Play "I'm thinking of something and its color or shape is . . ."

★ Practice doing something in your imagination before actually doing it, such as a piano recital or sports' game.

★ Make up a story in which your family is the hero and draw pictures to go with it.

★ Ask your child to draw images or symbols to express feelings (including the colors of how he or she is feeling).

★ Play blindfold games: lead each other around blindfolded and guess where you are, or "Pin the Tail on the Donkey."

Logical/Mathematical

★ Play guessing games that involve logical thinking: Clue™, Jeopardy™.

★ Play games that require seeing patterns: Rummy Cube™, Yahtzee™.

★ Play games that involve the development of a strategy to win: Monopoly™, Battleship™, checkers, tic tac toe.

★ Brainstorm a list of possible solutions to a family problem; then prioritize the list.

★ Guess the pattern of a sequence of numbers, a grouping of objects, a set of words, a list of people or places, and so on.

Bodily/Kinesthetic

★ Play games that require physical movement and the use of the body: Twister™, charades.

★ Learn sign language together as a family.

★ Learn and teach each other different kinds of dances.

★ Make up a dance or drama about your family's history.

★ Create a family exercise routine that you do together.

★ Role-play a problem you are facing as a family, trying out a variety of solutions.

★ Make a list of the body language family members use to express themselves and their feelings.

Activities to Support the Tacit Use of the Intelligences

(continued)

Musical/Rhythmic

★ Make a list of the different music family members like at different times of the day.

★ Create a song about your family using a popular tune.

★ Play music recognition games: Name That Tune™.

★ Discuss the use of music in TV shows; for example, to create tension in dramas or action shows.

★ Learn songs and sing them together as a family, for example, popular songs, Christmas carols, Broadway tunes, church songs.

★ Put certain family rules to music and rehearse them by singing the song.

★ List the sounds each member of the family makes to express him/herself at different times and in different situations.

Interpersonal

★ Play various communication games: "telephone" or gossip.

★ Create a family project with each member having a part to complete.

★ Role-play what to do when there is disagreement in the family.

★ Give each other supportive/clarifying feedback on some personal achievement or goal.

★ Teach and practice giving positive encouragement to each member of the family.

★ After watching a TV show or movie, see if you can guess what each member of the family thought about it.

Intrapersonal

★ Play games that require focus and concentration of the mind: Concentration™, card games like Go Fish or Hearts.

★ Have children tell you how they approached a homework assignment .

★ Have each family member keep a journal or diary of his or her thoughts and feeling each day. Designate time each week for sharing.

★ Have each family member create a personal emblem or symbol then explain it to the rest of the family.

★ Practice watching yourself doing routine things; for example, washing dishes, cleaning, homework, and so on.

Naturalist

★ Go on nature walks in favorite natural settings and pay attention to nature's effect on each of your senses.

★ Plant something together and track its development or progress day by day.

★ Play "I'm thinking of an animal" guessing games where the clues are the animals' characteristics.

★ Raise a new pet and/or train a current pet to perform something such as a trick, a helpful task, obedience, and so on.

★ Create and participate in various kinds of nature scavenger hunts with your child, such as finding things from plants, animals, the physical world, and the weather.

STAGE 2: AWARE UNDERSTANDING

Now that I have a label for the different ways of knowing, I can practice them and make them stronger.

The goal of the aware stage of learning about the eight intelligences is to help children discover how the different intelligences work. Children need to know what is involved in using their eight intelligences, what various capacities and/or skills they possess, how to access or trigger them, and what some of the possibilities are for using the different ways of knowing every day.

While everyone has at least eight ways of knowing, not all of them are as developed as others in each person. In fact, most children feel somewhat skillful in one or two of the areas, and much less comfortable and unskilled in others. This is not a reason for discouragement. Since the intelligences are part of our neurology (brain) and physiology (body) as human creatures, a less-developed intelligence can be strengthened through practice. In fact, the intelligences are very much like any skill we have—the more we practice it, generally, the better we become, whether it is our golf swing, parking a car, cooking, or building something.

Each of the intelligences can be activated, or triggered, through activities that stimulate the senses of sight, sound, taste, touch, smell, speech, and communication with others, as well as the "inner senses" such as intuition, metacognition (thinking about one's own thinking), and spiritual insight. At the aware level, we are concerned about learning specific techniques and methods for working with an intelligence to enhance and strengthen its knowing and learning powers.

The aware level of the intelligences also involves learning how to interpret and understand the different kinds of information we receive. We must learn the unique language of each intelligence; that is, how each expresses itself and how we can speak the language of a particular intelligence we want to use. For example, the language of musical/rhythmic intelligence is tones and rhythmic patterns—not words, sentences, writing, and speech. Therefore, if we are to effectively use the musical/ rhythmic way of knowing, we must learn to recognize and reproduce musical tones and rhythm patterns, and to interpret the meaning of different sounds.

You'll find that you can improve your intellectual skills if you consciously exercise them. Practicing the eight ways of knowing is the key to strengthening and improving them. Following is a list of home practice exercises to use to help your children enhance and strengthen the full range of their intelligence capabilities. Try a few of these and see what happens to you and your children. Remember, "Practice makes perfect."

It's exercise only if you push the pedals!

Activities to Support the Aware Use of the Intelligences

Verbal/Linguistic

★ Practice writing about one very ordinary, mundane event each day as if it is the central turning point of history. Use lots of juicy, descriptive words, metaphors, and similes.

★ At dinner, randomly choose a topic to discuss with each person speaking as if he or she were an expert on the topic.

★ Randomly pick a new word from the dictionary each day, learn its meaning, and consciously try to use it in conversations with others throughout the day.

★ Debate the pros and cons of something from the evening news, making sure each person expresses their opinions.

★ Try joint storytelling where you begin telling a tale, stopping at various points, and asking each person to continue the story as it is passed on.

Logical/Mathematical

★ Videotape a TV drama or action show, then watch it, stopping the action at critical turning points. Ask people to predict what will happen next. Continue the tape and check the accuracy of the predictions.

★ Make up a family code and leave notes written in the code for each other.

★ Choose a problem situation from the news, a sitcom, or a soap opera. Brainstorm solutions you can think of to solve the problem, then agree on the "best" solution.

★ Have each family member create a four-point outline on one of their hobbies with each point having four related subpoints, and each subpoint having four sub-subpoints.

★ Create a numbers at the dinner table exercise: the number of fork prongs, the number of fingers not counting thumbs, or the average number of helpings of food people took.

Visual/Spatial

★ Imagine seeing a place the family has visited or lived. Each person describes what they are seeing and helps the others see aspects that may have been neglected.

★ Experiment using various visual media (such as paints, clay, colored markers, or collage) to express what your day was like.

★ Practice leading each other on various fantasy trips in the mind to exotic places and times. Try to actively imagine everything that is suggested in the journey.

★ Practice getting around by reading a map. Go to a place that is not well-known and get lost intentionally. Use a map to get back to a familiar spot.

Bodily/Kinesthetic

★ Role-play/mime an idea, opinion, situation, or feeling using only body movement and physical gestures to communicate.

★ Go for a walk and practice walking in different ways to match certain moods/feelings: the thinking-things-over walk, the angry walk, the walk-of-joy/excitement, the walk-of-sadness/depression, the determined walk, and so on.

★ Several times during the day practice physical mindfulness. Choose some routine activity and perform it in slow motion, carefully observing the body in action.

★ Think of a challenge the family is facing. Is it like trying to blast through a brick wall, being caught in a spider web, or what? Physically act out breaking through the wall, untangling yourself from the web, or whatever matches your image of the problem.

Activities to Support the Aware Use of the Intelligences

(continued)

Musical/Rhythmic

★ Sit alone in several different situations and list every sound you hear. See if you can picture what is making the sound and what is going on.

★ Practice making certain sounds to express emotions: contentment, fear, anger, sadness, excitement, disappointment, and so on. Experiment with using these sounds to punctuate your conversation with others.

★ Decide the major stages of your family's history, then choose a piece of music to go with each stage. Listen to each piece.

★ Experiment with different kinds of music and beats to enhance performance during the day; for example, music to lower stress, promote creativity, make you happy, or help focus on a task.

★ Illustrate a story using sound, rhythm, music, beats, and other tonal patterns or noises.

Interpersonal

★ Try to fully and completely listen to another person. Practice cutting off mind chatter that is continually evaluating and judging what is being said before he or she says it.

★ Practice disciplined people watching to see how much you can learn and how attuned you can become to other people, their feelings, expressions, body language, tone of speech, and so on.

★ In talking with another person, practice extending their response by asking relevant questions which help you understand where they are coming from. Get to know them and their thinking as much as you can.

★ Experiment with different ways to help a group improve its interpersonal skills: create a group motto, emblem, and cheer; list accomplishments on the wall; plan a celebration; or discuss what's going well in the group and what needs improvement.

Intrapersonal

★ Practice watching yourself performing different tasks. Imagine yourself as an outside observer of you, especially in situations that tend to throw you off balance.

★ Pretend that you have your own personal coach or counselor inside your head, one who knows all about you and your needs. Practice going inside to talk with this person about how to reach your full human potential.

★ After any task you accomplish during the day, practice taking a few minutes to step back and evaluate your performance: "What did I do well?" and "Where do I need to improve?"

★ Experiment with keeping a mood chart or graph to track your feelings during the day or week. Note high points, low points, and middle-of-the-road points. Note what kinds of external things were happening at each point.

Naturalist

★ Create a plan to enhance the decor and/or atmosphere of your home with things from the natural world that different family members would enjoy.

★ Get involved in various kinds of animal observation safaris and see how much you can learn about the behaviors of different animals.

★ On a vacation, visit interesting geological places and/or museums and together work to understand how things got formed.

★ Get to know and appreciate the various plants of a place you're visiting on a first-hand basis, and understand why they exist here and how they're used.

★ Play a game to see how many repeating or recurring patterns you can find in a natural setting, then think about where else you find these same patterns.

STAGE 3: STRATEGIC UNDERSTANDING

Not only do I know about the eight intelligences, but I know when and how to use each one most effectively.

At the strategic level of understanding the eight ways of knowing, we move to the conscious use of the different intelligences to help us with problem solving and meeting the challenges faced in daily living. This is where children should become aware of the vast "kitbag" of intelligence tools, techniques, and methods they have at their disposal as near as their own brains. To strategically use the different ways of knowing involves learning how to make an intelligence produce, or work, in a given situation. This also means learning to trust and interpret the intelligences in actual knowing, learning, and understanding tasks.

The strategic level involves helping children develop sufficient knowledge about the intelligences—the capacities and skills involved, how to trigger them, and how to strengthen and enhance them. Then they will develop confidence in knowing how to employ the different ways of knowing on a regular basis to enhance their learning, expand their creativity, and improve their problem-solving abilities, both in themselves and in others. This is the ability to use the intelligences with intention.

At this level, part of the task is to teach children how to use each of the intelligences to gain knowledge and achieve certain learning objectives. From the standpoint of parents who are concerned about their children's success in school, this may be the most important level. However, as parents, we must re-educate ourselves on what school is all about. We have been told by our culture that school is about educating our children in the Three Rs. I agree with this. However, I believe that school is about much more, for children can learn the Three Rs and still not be equipped to live in his or her times.

As I have mentored my daughters through their schooling, I must confess that I have been far more excited by those teachers who focused on "timeless methods for living" than those who were preoccupied by the content of a particular subject. In our current society, which has been described as a knowledge explosion, a large percentage of the content we require our children to learn today will have significantly changed by the time they graduate. Learning how to learn seems to me to be the more important task. When the content changes, as it will, our children will then know how to learn again. It's a bit like an old Chinese proverb: *Give a man a fish, and it will feed him for a day; teach him how to fish to feed him for a lifetime.* I want my daughters to be educated for a lifetime.

What this means is that we must use the current content, which is the best we've got. Through it we can teach our children how to be as intelligent on as many levels, using as many different approaches, as they (and we) can find. Yes, they must master certain content areas, and they must be able to produce on the various examinations our culture deems important. But how they master this assigned material must be given equal weight as the material itself. This prepares them to live in the 21st century.

As a father, this is one of the reasons I am excited about and committed to the theory of multiple intelligences. When this way of teaching and learning is actively employed in the classroom and at home, more of our children can succeed in school more of the time.

Application suggestions in this section are focused on helping your children with their homework using the eight ways of knowing. However, with some slight adjustments, they could be adapted to other aspects of family life as well. All of these suggestions assume that you are actively involved in your children's schooling and learning. Try some of these suggestions with your children, and encourage their teachers to learn about and use multiple intelligences in their teaching.

Activities to Support the Strategic Use of the Intelligences

Verbal/Linguistic

★ Experiment with nontraditional ways to study English: learning the parts of speech or punctuation through drawing, physical actions, and music.

★ When your child has written an essay/report, for example, take the opposite side and ask him or her to defend what was written.

★ Encourage your child to think on his or her feet, by asking unexpected questions about things he or she has been studying.

★ Ask your child to create a sequel to a history lesson or tell it as a modern day story; for example, say, "What would have happened if . . . ."

Logical/Mathematical

★ Create a set of "good homework practices" and have your child evaluate himself or herself at the end of doing each assignment.

★ Once your child has completed an assignment, have him or her do something creative and fun with what has been learned.

★ Devise ways for your child to use what he or she is studying at home; for example, dividing a pizza so each family member gets two pieces, or integrating vocabulary words into the dinner conversation.

★ Help your child use graphic organizers to analyze and understand what he or she is studying; for example, a character attribute web, a compare-and-contrast Venn diagram for math processes, or a classification matrix for parts of speech.

Visual/Spatial

★ Help your child prepare for a test by drawing pictures of the concepts and/or visually mapping relationships between things he or she is studying.

★ Ask your child to draw a symbol or image to go along with the homework or what he or she has been studying.

★ In math, help your child visualize alternative solutions to story problems.

★ Have your child enter into an imaginary conversation with some person, thing, or concept in a lesson.

★ In history, social studies, or literature lessons, lead your child in "pretend you are there" imagination exercises.

Bodily/Kinesthetic

★ Help your child learn foreign language vocabulary words by using physical actions movements.

★ In American history, role-play key concepts your child must learn; for example, the three branches of our government, or the Bill of Rights.

★ When your child is studying another culture in social studies, have him or her help prepare food, dress in costumes, and create decor from that culture.

★ Help your child understand math concepts and operations (for example, work with fractions) physically by subtracting two family members, or dividing the family into halves, then into thirds.

Activities to Support the Strategic Use
of the Intelligences

(continued)

Musical/Rhythmic

★ Have your child experiment with playing different kinds of music as a background for homework from different subject areas.

★ Help your child create raps/songs (like the "ABC Song") to memorize various facts, such as states and capitals, the major food groups, multiplication times tables, and classification of living things.

★ When your child is studying a period of history or another culture in social studies, play music from that period and help him or her learn folk songs from that culture.

★ Work with your child to illustrate with sound; for example, the sound of different punctuation marks (ala Victor Borge's phonetic punctuation), the sound of math operations (such as +, =, >, ÷, x), the sounds that should accompany a story, and so on.

Naturalist

★ Make something for dinner using only things gathered from nature (such as vegetables, berries, an animal or fish, churned butter, ground maize, and so on).

★ Do an analysis of your family's environmental friendliness and create conservation plans where needed, such as recycling, planting, water usage, and so on.

★ Engage in your own weather predictions using a barometer, or radar pictures on the Internet, for example, then check the accuracy of your predictions.

★ Set up a mini-greenhouse and experiment with growing some of your own food year-round and/or with creating plant hybrids.

★ Try to apply various animal and plant behaviors to problems faced by human beings, such as how they care for their young, how they gather food, how they fend off predators, and so on.

Intrapersonal

★ Buy your child a special notebook for keeping track of his or her thinking and learning; for example, write about the main idea of a lesson, or tell what he or she finds interesting and boring about this lesson, and so on

★ In science, have your child pretend he or she can become what the class is studying and learn about it from the inside out; for example, become a plant to learn about photosynthesis, imagine being an insect and tell what life is like, or pretend to be an organ in the body and describe a typical day.

★ Provide a chance for your child to speak into a tape recorder about "Questions I'm thinking about," "New understandings about life," or "Things I feel," as a result of something assigned.

★ Before your child starts his/her homework, have him/her make a list of application questions related to the homework; after completing the homework, have him or her look at the questions again and make corrections as appropriate.

Interpersonal

★ Divide a homework assignment into sections, with each family member learning one part, then teaching it to the others; give a quiz to make sure each person "got it."

★ For a research project in any subject, help your child map out a research plan; then help your child create a multimodal report for the class.

★ Create a game in which the whole family helps a child prepare for a test; for example, "Mammals Trivia," "Parts-of-Speech Bingo," "Math-Operations Jeopardy," or "Dates-in-History Wheel of Fortune."

★ When a child has a paper to write, ask the family to brainstorm ideas. The child writes it, using whatever ideas seem appropriate. The family gives feedback and asks questions.

STAGE 4: "REFLECTIVE" UNDERSTANDING

I am learning how to use all eight ways of knowing to help me in my daily life.

The purpose of the reflective level of teaching and learning about the eight ways of knowing is to help children approach the task of daily living on more levels using their multiple intelligences. This involves encouraging them to use all of their intelligence capabilities to improve their effectiveness in dealing with the issues, challenges, and problems they face in everyday life. This means approaching these situations on multiple levels, using a variety of problem-solving methods which use different intelligences, integrating the intelligences into their repertoire for living. Children should learn the *appropriate* applications of the intelligences to situations encountered in the world beyond the classroom. The goal is for the intelligences to become a regular part of their cognitive, affective, and sensory coping with life.

In the learning process, we often learn something in one situation but fail to see how it applies in another. When I was a child I took more than nine years of music lessons learning to play the piano and bassoon. I enjoyed this very much, but saw little application of it beyond my own enjoyment. It was not until I was in college that a math professor helped me see some helpful connections between my music and math. I was just barely making my way through a required algebra course when my professor, a very skilled musician, showed me how math and music are alike:

"In math," he said, "you learn numbers. In music, you learn notes. They are both abstract and symbolic representations of something else— quantity on the one hand and tones on the other. In math, you learn certain operations and processes, that link numbers in different meaningful patterns. In music, you learn to link the notes in certain specified ways to make a tune."

He then pointed out that math has its special jargon—ratio, square root, proportion, and so on—which tells you what to do with a set of numbers. Music has its special jargon as well—clef signs, flats, sharps, rhythm, and so on—which tells you what to do with a set of notes. Suddenly, I had a new way to approach my math class using something in which I was confident and which I liked. Now, I didn't get an A in the class, but my performance did improve, as did my enjoyment of the class.

In working with the reflective level of the intelligences, we need to help children make connections between their intelligence skills/capacities and other parts of their lives. I believe this can happen very quickly in the classroom situation, where an intelligence skill learned in one subject area can quite easily be bridged or transferred into another subject area. However, helping students take their intelligences beyond the classroom into everyday life is a task that no one can do like a parent. The following activities are intended to give you a starting place to help your child "make the connections" between his or her eight ways of knowing and daily living. Once you have tried a few of these, I'm sure you will begin to come up with many much better ideas on your own.

Activities to Support the Reflective Use of the Intelligences

Verbal/Linguistic

★ When a child has a firm opinion on something, ask him or her to create and deliver a convincing argument for the opposite position.

★ List things about which your child has a strong opinion or a special interest; then, have him or her create an explanation for others about items on the list.

★ Develop your child's debating skills (that is, defending his or her thinking) by disagreeing with him or her, forcing him or her to explain his or her position.

★ Work with your child to help him or her understand such things as cartoons or comic strips in the newspaper, puns, and punch lines to jokes.

Logical/Mathematical

★ Help your child become aware of various behavior patterns; both ones that work well for him or her and ones that cause difficulty.

★ Work with your child to establish certain healthy routines for his or her daily lives, including eating.

★ Teach your child how to set goals and then work backward from a goal to arrive at logical steps that will help him or her get there.

★ Work with your child to learn such applied intelligence skills as balancing a checkbook, making a calendar, planning a party, and so on.

Visual/Spatial

★ When your child experiences some problem or difficulty, have him or her draw pictures or images of the difficulty, then explain what the picture means. Explore solutions by adding images to the picture.

★ Teach your child how to use his or her imagination to plan for or deal with a challenge.

★ Teach your child to mentally rehearse for an important task he or she has to perform; in the mind's eye" he or she pictures doing the task perfectly.

★ Help your child learn various techniques to keep from getting lost when he or she is visiting a new place (including, reading maps, sighting landmarks, and so on).

Bodily/Kinesthetic

★ Help your child learn how to act out his or her emotions or feelings about things happening in his or her life.

★ Play "Body-Language Jeopardy" (one person does a gesture, the other tells what it means and/or the feelings it conveys). Talk about use of appropriate body language in everyday communication.

★ Work with your child to develop "multi-tracking" skills needed in daily life. Multi-tracking is the ability to do several things at the same time, such as cooking, listening to the news, and watching the baby.

★ Practice dramatic enactment of an idea or opinion your child has about something.

★ Show your child how to make appropriate hand gestures or body movements to go along with a story as it is being read.

Activities to Support the Reflective Use of the Intelligences

(continued)

Musical/Rhythmic

★ Work with your child to create ridiculous songs about certain problems or issues. Also make up verses about possible solutions.

★ Help your child learn how to use various kinds of music to change his or her mood, such as using music to relax a stressful situation, or to improve his or her performance in various tasks (using music to help a person develop a steady rhythm in typing is one example).

★ Brainstorm different kinds of music your child could play to help with various tasks (such as cleaning his or her room, doing homework, exercising, and so on).

★ Help your child learn to listen to the different sounds in different situations and learn what they signify (for example, sound of the traffic, sounds from nature, sounds other people make, and so on).

Interpersonal

★ Have the whole family give input on a personal decision a member is facing; then prioritize the different suggestions together.

★ Experiment with a family council in which individuals air complaints, share difficulties, celebrate successes, plan, or share ideas.

★ Teach your child how to do reflective listening, where he or she listens and then paraphrases what has been said, asking the other person about his or her feelings, making observations about body language, and so on.

★ Give your child a list of various interpersonal relationship skills and then target time to work on one skill per week as a family.

Intrapersonal

★ Have your child start keeping a diary or journal in which he or she writes or draws about things that happened during the day, including the emotions felt.

★ Teach your child how to have an imaginary conversation with someone or something that was upsetting from the day, speaking about feelings he or she had, and how to resolve these feelings.

★ Help your child imagine projecting himself or herself into a future situation and to plan how he or she will handle difficulties and/or challenges.

★ Work with your child on different techniques for building positive self-esteem and esteem for others; affirmation exercises, writing paragraphs about "What's Right with Me," creating personal symbols of possibility, and so on.

Naturalist

★ Use the patterns and events of the natural world to help reflect on your own life experience and journey as a family.

★ Take the family out of doors to a natural setting and ask everyone simply to sit and experience all this setting has to offer (sights, sounds, tastes, textures, and so on), then compare your experiences.

★ Create a family nature album in which you place things that are important to each member of the family: objects gathered from nature, nature photographs, and so on.

★ Teach your child how to use the natural world as a place for renewal, rebalancing, and gaining perspective on difficult issues or challenges he or she may be facing.

=2=

Exercises for Tacit
Use of the Intelligences

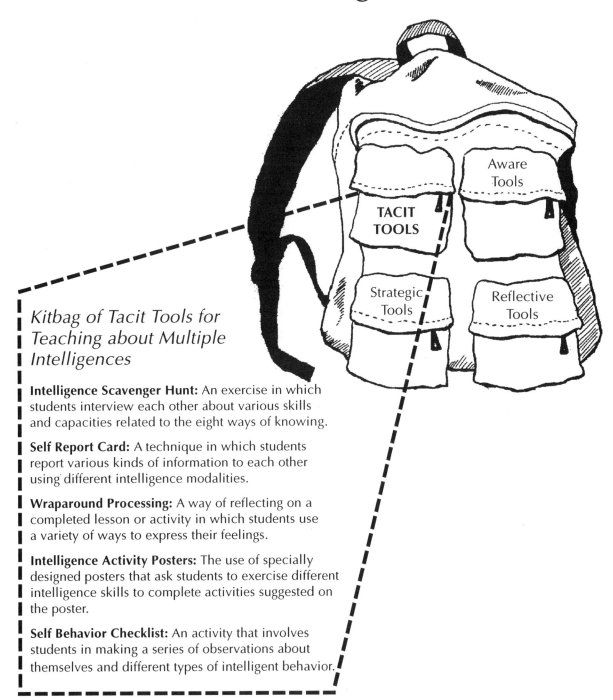

*Kitbag of Tacit Tools for
Teaching about Multiple
Intelligences*

Intelligence Scavenger Hunt: An exercise in which
students interview each other about various skills
and capacities related to the eight ways of knowing.

Self Report Card: A technique in which students
report various kinds of information to each other
using different intelligence modalities.

Wraparound Processing: A way of reflecting on a
completed lesson or activity in which students use
a variety of ways to express their feelings.

Intelligence Activity Posters: The use of specially
designed posters that ask students to exercise different
intelligence skills to complete activities suggested on
the poster.

Self Behavior Checklist: An activity that involves
students in making a series of observations about
themselves and different types of intelligent behavior.

Billy was a third-grade student who was not doing very well in school. He had some strange ideas and some strange ways of behaving in the classroom. He rarely succeeded at assigned classroom work, on tests, or on his homework. He did not have many friends because the other children thought that he was dumb and some kind of a "weirdo."

Billy's teacher had received training in working with the multiple intelligences in the classroom. She decided to share these eight ways of knowing with the class by having the students work in small groups on an Intelligence Activities poster (see pp. 72–80). Suddenly Billy came alive; he was able to do some of the things on the poster that others in his group could not. The teacher told the class that all of the ideas on the poster are the different ways we are smart. Billy's hand shot up immediately.

He said, "These are things that I do every day. I usually feel like I'm kind of dumb. But I was really good at some of the things on the poster! I never thought of these things as making me smart in a different way!"

The teacher asked Billy's team to share some of their thoughts about and experiences of working on the poster. Some of the comments follow:

> *We would have failed if Billy hadn't been in our group. He could do some of the things none of the rest of us could!*

> *Everyone in the group could do something, but no one could do everything.*

> *I could sort of do everything on the poster, but some people were really good!*

> *I'm glad I didn't have to do it alone!*

Other groups shared similar reflections.

Needless to say, this simple activity had a dramatic impact on the class. Suddenly their perception of what makes someone smart had changed. And, what is more important, their perception of Billy and Billy's perception of himself had changed.

Pathways of Learning © 2000 Zephyr Press, Tucson, Arizona • 800-232-2187 • http://zephyrpress.com

EXPLORATION AND DISCOVERY BASE EXERCISE: INTELLIGENCE SCAVENGER HUNT

Exercise Procedures

1. Create eight interview questions that students will use to ask each other about the eight intelligences (see examples on the work sheets on pp. 54–56).
2. Have each student secretly decide which two activities on the Scavenger Hunt work sheet he or she performs best.
3. Give your students the following instructions before the Scavenger Hunt actually begins:

   > Get up out of your seats. Each of you will find eight different people who can each do the activity in one of the boxes. When you find someone who can do the activity, have that person sign your work sheet. You need only one name per box, but you cannot repeat a name; you are to get eight different names.
   >
   > When you are talking with the other students, do not take their word that they can do the activities listed in the boxes. Make them prove it to you by performing! Once each person has demonstrated the skill, have him or her sign your work sheet in the appropriate box.
   >
   > Watch yourself and watch each other as you are involved in the activity. See what you can learn about yourself and about each other.

4. Ask the class if they have any questions about the assignment. If not, then tell them to begin going about the classroom, looking for students who meet the criteria on the work sheets. Give students ten to fifteen minutes to do the activity, depending on how you sense things are going as you walk around.
5. While the students are doing the Scavenger Hunt, watch them carefully and make notes about what you observe. You may want to share some of these observations with them later.

Intelligence Scavenger Hunt

INTRODUCTION

This exercise is a great strategy for helping students learn about the eight intelligences from others' experience. Students interview each other, looking for different skills and capacities in fellow classmates. Some students have called it a "human treasure hunt."

OBJECTIVE

The purposes of this exercise are to help students become aware of, appreciate, and enjoy the differences that exist among them and to become aware of their own skills and capacities, including their strengths and preferences in certain areas.

DISCUSSION

Further applications of the Scavenger Hunt strategy are limited only by your imagination. Remember that this is a learning process, and the key is to have students discover information and knowledge by asking each other questions. It is important that you have the whole class reflect on what they learned while they did their Scavenger Hunt. You may also want to collect their work sheets, especially if you are using the work sheets to help you assess students' comprehension of a lesson or unit or to evaluate their academic progress.

6. When the students have finished the activity, have them return to their seats and lead them in the following discussion:

- *Which activity was the easiest to find someone for? (Ask who signed that box and what he or she said or did.)*
- *Which activity was the hardest to find someone for?*
- *What did you find interesting? What surprised you? Excited you?*
- *What did you learn about yourself? What did you learn about each other? (You might also share any observations you made.)*
- *What are some of your ideas about how we could use the Scavenger Hunt again?*
- *How could we use some of the skills you discovered in the Scavenger Hunt in our classroom work?*

Parallel Curriculum Interface

INTELLIGENCE SCAVENGER HUNT

Personal Exploration and Discovery

The various Scavenger Hunts you design should be easy and fun learning experiences in which students have an opportunity to discover and celebrate the intelligences in each other. When students find a person who meets one of the criteria, that person gets to sign the other's Scavenger Hunt paper. Several guidelines can help make this a greater learning and discovery exercise: (1) no can sign one person's paper more than once, (2) no one is allowed to sign their own, and (3) to sign another's paper a person must demonstrate that he or she can indeed perform the given skill, task, or activity.

Personal Exploration and Discovery Exercises

➤ **Intelligence Capacities Scavenger Hunt.** Design a Scavenger Hunt for each of the intelligences respectively. The questions should allow students to explore the various capacities and/or skills of different intelligences in each other. (See Capacities Summary Wheels on pp. 261–262).

➤ **Getting Acquainted Scavenger Hunts.** Use the Scavenger Hunt exercise at the beginning of the year to help students get to know each other on more levels. Be sure to include questions that will allow all students to brag about stuff they can do. This can also a very powerful bonding experience for the new class.

➤ **After the Holidays Reporting.** After any period of time away from the classroom, such as the summer vacation period, December holidays, spring break, and so on, create Scavenger Hunts which let students report on their holiday or vacation. Be sure to include questions and categories that require use of the eight ways of knowing to report.

Commentary: Personal MI Exploration and Discovery

The *Intelligence Scavenger Hunt* is ideally suited to introduce students to the eight intelligences at the tacit level. As students participate in various kinds of intelligence-based scavenger hunts their appreciation of the skills and capabilities of their classmates is dramatically expanded. The key to success with this exercise is to get students started. They may be hesitant at first; however, once you get them started it may be hard to get them to stop. Remember, it is very important to have students reflect on their learning and discoveries from the experience of each Scavenger Hunt.

INTELLIGENCE SCAVENGER HUNT

Academic Exploration and Discovery

When using the Scavenger Hunt strategy with your academic content, provide students with ample opportunities to continue getting to know the intelligences as they work with various curricular material. Structure the Scavenger Hunt learning experience so that students experiment with using the different intelligences to enhance their learning. As much as possible, they should mirror the base exercise, using the different ways of knowing with the content at hand.

Academic Exploration and Discovery Strategies

➤ **Unit or Chapter Review.** Create a Scavenger Hunt in which students must find people who know the answers to various questions about a completed unit of study. Make sure that the questions give options for answering using the eight intelligences.

➤ **New Learning.** Put students into expert groups, which are responsible for mastering new concepts, processes, definitions, and so on. Each group must learn its assigned piece and then teach it to others using the eight intelligences during the Scavenger Hunt activity.

➤ **Homework Processing.** Use a Scavenger Hunt to have students discuss the previous night's homework, correct it, and check for understanding. Create questions that are related to the specifics of the homework assignment as well as to the intelligences. Students must find others who know and can show the answers using several intelligences.

➤ **Post-Test Relearning.** At the conclusion of an examination, create a Scavenger Hunt with wrong answers from the test. Students must find others who can explain why the answer is wrong and demonstrate how to get the right answer using as many of the intelligences as possible. After this activity, let them take the test again.

Commentary: Multiple Intelligences and the Learning Process

As students are being asked to access more ways of knowing, they may find themselves uncertain about what is required and how they can succeed. Early on, a great deal of teacher modeling will be required. The more connections students are able to find and make on their own, however, the greater will be their beginning understanding of the intelligences and how they can be used.

INTELLIGENCE SCAVENGER HUNT

Beyond-the-Classroom Exploration and Discovery

The goal of these suggestions is to help students take their learning and discoveries about multiple intelligences into their relationships with others beyond the classroom. The trick here may be convincing students that something they do in school has relevance in life beyond school. You may want to ask students to give you their input on other situations where they could use the Scavenger Hunt strategy. Have them brainstorm with their peers.

Beyond-the-Classroom Exploration and Discovery Applications

➤ **Family Scavenger Hunt.** Have students create Scavenger Hunts they could use to explore the intelligences in different members of their family.

➤ **TV Scavenger Hunts.** Have students create Scavenger Hunts to examine the eight intelligences in the characters of TV programs they are watching.

➤ **Club/Organization Scavenger Hunts.** Have students create a Scavenger Hunt to try out in a club or organization of which they are a part.

➤ **My Relationships Inventory.** Have students create Scavenger Hunts in which they hunt, within their relationships with other people, for each of the intelligences (for example, who provides me with visual/spatial intelligence insights/feedback, and so on).

Commentary: Multiple Intelligences and Everyday Life

The Scavenger Hunt exercises here give students a new set of eyeglasses for looking at and understanding other people beyond the formal school setting. Initially, these may need to be homework assignments. Eventually you will want to move the use of this strategy to something less structured. For example, explain that during the next six weeks students should design and conduct at least three different Scavenger Hunts in three different situations where you think it would be interesting to learn more about other people. Always make sure that you provide opportunities for them to reflect on and learn from their experience of using the Scavenger Hunt strategy beyond school.

Intelligence Scavenger Hunt
(Elementary)

Find someone who . . .

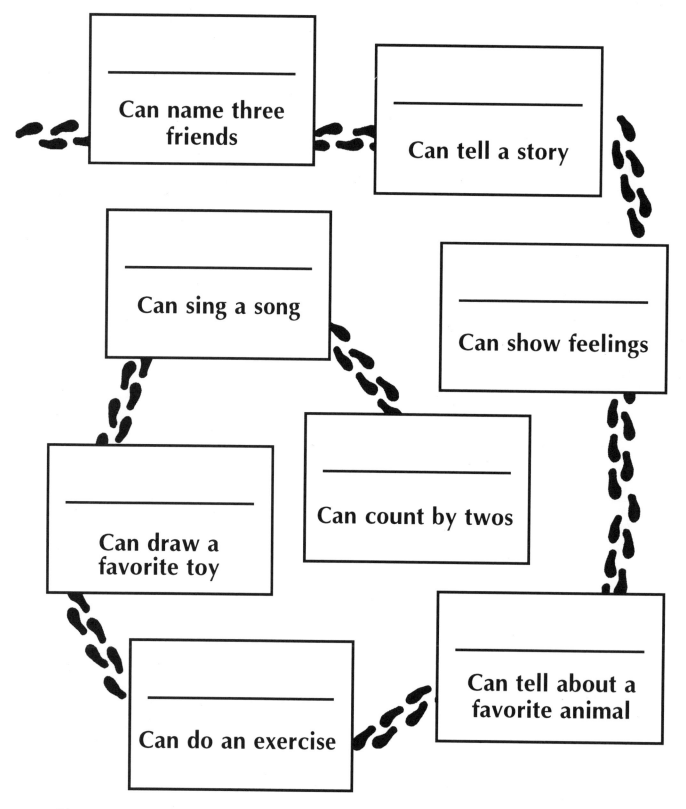

Intelligence Scavenger Hunt
(Middle School)

Find someone who . . .

_____
Can list three things that help her or him learn.

_____
Can draw a picture of his or her favorite food.

_____
Can tell what it's like to be on a team.

_____
Has a physical game she or he likes to play.

_____
Likes to read or write or has a good joke to tell.

_____
Loves being near plants and animals.

_____
Likes to solve puzzles or is good at math.

_____
Will sing part of a favorite song.

Intelligence Scavenger Hunt
(Secondary)

Find someone who . . .

_____
Sings in the shower
and with the radio
when riding in a car.

_____
Can solve a variety of math
problems (including getting
the correct change).

_____
Has some special thing
she or he does to relax
and renew her- or himself.

_____
Can tell about a powerful
experience in nature
or with an animal.

_____
Can draw a picture
about what kind of day
he or she is having.

_____
Can list at least five different
ways people learn, know,
and understand.

_____
Loves to dance or is involved
in some type of daily
physical exercise.

_____
Loves to read and write
and is good at expressing
him- or herself in words.

Pathways of Learning © 2000 Zephyr Press, Tucson, Arizona • 800-232-2187 • http://zephyrpress.com

Teacher's Personal Reflection Log

INTELLIGENCE SCAVENGER HUNT

I have the following thoughts/insights about the Intelligence Scavenger Hunt strategy:

I feel that the Intelligence Scavenger Hunt strategy can help me in my teaching in the following ways:

As a learning process, the Intelligence Scavenger Hunt strategy includes the following benefits for my students:

I have the following specific ideas for using the Intelligence Scavenger Hunt strategy in my classroom in the near future:

I think the Intelligence Scavenger Hunt strategy can be used beyond the classroom and school in the following ways:

Self Report Card

INTRODUCTION

The Self Report Card is a wonderful activity for making students aware of their own intelligence "comfort zones." The process asks students to share things about themselves in the different intelligence areas that the students like.

OBJECTIVE

The goal of this exercise is to make students aware that they have all eight ways of knowing, but that they are more comfortable with and probably better at some than at others.

DISCUSSION

The Self Report Card strategy asks students to be slightly introspective because they have to be aware of which intelligences they prefer. Initially, however, they will not know that the things about which you are asking them to report are intelligences. They become aware on the tacit level when you reflect on the lesson, helping them to see and appreciate the fact that we are different. The gimmick of having them exchange report cards with each other and asking about things on the card makes them more willing to risk, since the card appears to be the point of dialogue, not the person.

EXPLORATION AND DISCOVERY BASE EXERCISE: SELF REPORT CARD

Exercise Procedures

1. Pass out a large index card and some colored marking pens to each student.
2. Tell the students that they are each going to create a report card to evaluate themselves and some of the things they can and like to do. Choose seven areas, such as those on the model report card on the work sheet (see p. 63). Project the questions on an overhead or write them on the board.
3. Give students several minutes to record their answers to the questions in the spaces on their index cards.
4. Explain the task to the class:

   > In a moment I am going to ask you to get out of your seats and start sharing your report cards with each other. Find one other person with whom to exchange report cards. Choose one or two things that especially interest you from your partner's report card and ask her or him to tell you about it and do it for you. For example, if someone says she can make a funny face, have her do it. If someone says he can sing a song, have him sing it.
   >
   > After each of you has had a chance to share at least two things on your report card, get your own card back and move to someone else. Your goal is to see how many people you can talk with in ten to fifteen minutes. Watch yourself and each other and see what you can learn about these different skills.

5. Ask if there are any questions. If not, tell the students to begin. Watch them carefully so that you can give feedback during the discussion time.
6. After the allotted time has elapsed, call the class back together and lead them in the following discussion:

Pathways of Learning © 2000 Zephyr Press, Tucson, Arizona • 800-232-2187 • http://zephyrpress.com

- *Without mentioning any names, what was the most interesting thing you found someone else could do?*
- *What did you find out that was surprising? That was not surprising?*
- *What were your feelings about doing the Self Report Card activity? What did you like? What did you not like?*
- *What did you learn about yourself? About each other?*

On the board or overhead list ideas about how to use these different capacities in schoolwork.

Parallel Curriculum Interface

SELF REPORT CARD

Personal Exploration and Discovery

The various Self Report Cards you design should be easy and fun learning experiences, that cause students to think about and recognize the eight intelligences in their own lives. As you create different kinds of report card exercises, make sure that each causes some level of introspection, either at the outset when students are creating their initial report, or retrospectively, as they reflect on the use of various kinds of report cards.

Personal Exploration and Discovery Exercises

➤ **Intelligence Focused Reports.** Create a Self Report Card based on the capacities or skills of the different intelligences; for example, a visual/spatial report card, an intrapersonal report card, a naturalist report card, and so on. (Refer to the Capacities Summary Wheels on pp. 262–263 for help.)

➤ **MI Affective Reports.** In the various corners of the Self Report Card, have students express their feelings on a topic such as favorite food, a pet, a magical place, and so on, using the eight intelligences. For example, write a word/phrase, draw a symbol or picture, be able to make a sound/sing a song, do a physical gesture or make a body movement, and so on.

➤ **Special Event Report Cards.** Ask students to share their experiences of some kind of special event in the different corners of the report card, such as a wedding, a vacation, a funeral, and so on. Structure the report card so students must report on the event using all eight intelligences.

Commentary: Personal MI Exploration and Discovery

The Self Report Card exercises introduce students to the eight intelligences primarily within themselves and, secondarily, in each other. As students participate in various kinds of self-reflection, that the report cards cause, they gain new levels of understanding about their own multiple intelligences skills and capabilities. When you ask them to share their report cards with each other, you instantly create an occasion for students to brag about things they can do, and also an opportunity for them to appreciate some of the capacities of their fellow students.

SELF REPORT CARD

Academic Exploration and Discovery

These kinds of Self Report Cards should provide students with opportunities to continue reflecting on lessons or units using their eight ways of knowing. As you design academic uses of the Self Report Card strategy, make sure you ask students to report and/or demonstrate their learning using the eight intelligences. The meta-intelligence goal is to get students to recognize and appreciate multiple intelligences in themselves and each other.

Academic Exploration and Discovery Strategies

➤ **Key Learnings Report Card.** At the conclusion of a unit of study create a Self Report Card which asks students to share different things from the unit or lesson that have been significant for them in the different intelligence areas.

➤ **Report Card "Jeopardy."** For each part of the report card, give students a multiple intelligence-based answer; for example, a picture or image, a song, a quote, and so on, to a question that could be on a test about the unit or lesson you are studying. They are to write a question for the answer.

➤ **Applications Report.** As a way to help students with the transfer or bridging of classroom learning beyond the classroom, design a Self Report Card on potential applications of a lesson or unit—Where has it been applied in the past? Can you think of a place to use it today? Does it have possible applications in the future?

➤ **Connections Report Card.** On their Report Cards have students list one cross-discipline connection they see between the current lesson/unit and things they are learning in other classes or subjects. They should try to think of one such connection on each corner of the card.

Commentary: Multiple Intelligences and the Learning Process
The key to each of these suggestions is designing Report Cards that sort the different parts of the curricular concepts you are studying into the different intelligence areas. This reinforces students' learning about the reality of multiple intelligences in themselves. It also helps them process the required material on more levels of the brain, mind, body system, thus promoting greater retention and understanding of the material.

SELF REPORT CARD

Beyond-the-Classroom Exploration and Discovery

These extensions represent ways that students can become more aware that the multiple intelligences are already a regular part of their daily experience—they may not have ever considered this. Your goal in creating these exercises is to find ways to bring a level (or rather, eight levels) of reflection to bear on students' lives outside of the classroom. Ask them to brainstorm other ways to utilize this exercise.

Beyond-the-Classroom Exploration and Discovery Applications

➤ **MI Reflective Journals/Diaries.** Design a journal entry process in which students reflect on a day, week, experience, and so on, using all eight of their intelligences, for example, "Today I felt like (what animal) . . .," "This week's theme song is . . .," and so on.

➤ **MI Strategies Used in the Past.** Ask students to think about difficult times in the past and to analyze how the various intelligences were part of those occasions.

➤ **Anticipating Future Multiple Intelligences Possibilities.** Ask students to brainstorm a list of difficult or challenging situations they will likely face in the future. Then ask them to brainstorm ways the intelligences might help deal with these situations.

Commentary: Multiple Intelligences and Everyday Life
These kinds of Self Report Card extensions can give students a new story about their own capacities as human creatures and dramatically increase their self-esteem. Students feel bad about themselves in precisely those ways in which they have been put down by others. When you provide them with an occasion to think about all the things they can do, this process can be reversed.

Self Report Card
(All Grades)

Name _____

Name an animal you like and hate.

Write a big word.

Draw your house.

Sing a song or say a rhyme.

How high can you count?

Do something funny.

"I'm happy when . . ."

Name _____

List things you like to do out in nature.

Name something you read recently (outside of schoolwork).

Write down a favorite song that you are able to sing.

List three words that express your feelings about math.

Write down a physical exercise that you are able and willing to do.

Draw your bedroom as it looks now.

Finish the sentence: "When I'm alone I like to . . ."

Name _____

Fill in the blanks: "My favorite place in nature is ____ because ____ ."

Name something you read recently that was important to you.

Draw a symbol to show your feelings about today.

Write down a favorite song or type of music. (You must be able to perform it.)

On a scale of 1 to 10, rank your math problem-solving ability.

Write down a physical feat you can and would perform.

What do you do for personal renewal?

Teacher's Personal Reflection Log

SELF REPORT CARD

I have the following thoughts/insights about the Self Report Card strategy:

I feel that the Self Report Card strategy can help me in my teaching in the following ways:

As a learning process, the Self Report Card strategy includes the following benefits for my students:

I have the following specific ideas for using the Self Report Card strategy in my classroom in the near future:

I think the Self Report Card strategy can be used beyond the classroom and school in the following ways:

EXPLORATION AND DISCOVERY BASE EXERCISE: WRAPAROUND PROCESSING

Exercise Procedures

1. At the conclusion of a lesson or activity, give students time to think about their individual responses to the lesson or activity using the eight intelligences (see "stem" examples on the work sheet, p. 70).

2. After students have had time to do their own thinking, have them each turn to a partner and share their eight responses to the lesson or activity. They are not only to talk about their responses; they are to show each other images, do gestures, make sounds, sing a few bars of their songs, and share their ideas about the importance of the lesson for our times and themselves. Tell the students to pay close attention to the various ways in which their partners respond, for they will be asked to reproduce what their partners do later.

3. Now have each student turn to a different partner and share by doing the previous partner's responses to the lesson or activity.

4. After the class has had time to share in this manner, call them back together. Lead them in the following discussion, making a list of the responses on the overhead or board:

   - *What are some of the words you heard others say that expressed their feelings about the lesson or activity?*
   - *What kind of thinking did this lesson cause us to use?*
   - *Have several students come to the board and draw images that express some of the feelings about the lesson or activity. The images should be ones they learned from one of their partners. Ask the students, "What common patterns or designs do you see as you look at all of the images?"*

Wraparound Processing

INTRODUCTION

You can use the Wraparound Processing technique (also known as a "stem") at the end of any lesson or activity to help students reflect on and share their feelings about the lesson or activity. This activity is a great "instant thermometer" that quickly reveals how the students feel about and what they have learned.

OBJECTIVE

The goal of this exercise is to help students realize that there are many ways to reflect on and process their feelings and thoughts about a classroom lesson or activity.

DISCUSSION

In some ways, the processing of a lesson is the most important part. During the processing, the knowing of the lesson is cemented in the brain/mind/body system. The keys to successful wraparound processing are (1) having "stems" that students want to answer, (2) accepting every answer that is given (there are no wrong answers), and (3) going around the room with the expectation that everyone will have an answer, allowing (but not encouraging) students to pass if they choose. You can often learn more about the impact a lesson has on students through the wraparound processing technique than through any other method.

- *On the count of three, everyone makes a gesture that expresses feelings about the lesson or activity. The gestures should be ones they learned from a partner. Have students look around the room and ask them, "What common things do you see?"*
- *Choose ten students to stand. Have each of them take turns making the sounds or singing the song that one of their partners would play as a background for the lesson or activity. Then, as if you were a conductor, randomly point to the different students and create a symphony of the "background music." Ask the class, "What does this sound or music tell us about the lesson?"*
- *Have several students relate ideas they heard from one of their partners about the importance of the lesson for people living in our times.*
- *Give students a few minutes to rewrite their statements about how they can use the information from this lesson or activity beyond the classroom (number 7 on the worksheet), incorporating ideas they got from their partners. Ask for several volunteers to share what they have written.*

5. Ask students, "How has this way of reflecting on a lesson or activity helped you appreciate the lesson? What other ideas do you have for using the eight ways of knowing to reflect on and discuss our lessons?"

Parallel Curriculum Interface

WRAPAROUND PROCESSING

Personal Exploration and Discovery

The various Wraparound Processing exercises with which you experiment should be novel, creative, and unconventional ways for students to express their feelings, thoughts, and opinions about things going on in their lives and our world using the eight intelligences. The goal is to begin to recognize the many different levels on which one can experience almost any life experience.

Personal Exploration and Discovery Exercises

➤ **Mural Wraparound.** Students go to a wall covered with newsprint and create a mural expressing their feelings about something the whole class has experienced. Have students talk with those on either side of them so that their contributions blend in with what others are creating.

➤ **Tableaux Wraparound.** Place students in groups of five. They are to turn themselves into "human sculptures" to express emotional responses, which are drawn from a hat. Each group presents itself to the rest of the class, which tries to guess the emotion.

➤ **Sound Wraparound.** Each student thinks of a sound to accompany common class experiences. Have them make the sound and find others who are making a similar sound. Pretend that the class is an orchestra. Point to different groups and have them make their sound on your cue. Afterwards, have students reflect on what these sounds tell us about the experience.

➤ **"Piggy-back" Wraparound.** Each student creates a three- to five-word phrase about his or her response to something in the news or a TV show, for example. One volunteer shares his or her phrase. The next student must piggy-back his or her own phrase on what the previous student said.

Commentary: Personal MI Exploration and Discovery

Wraparound Processing exercises introduce students to the eight intelligences as ways of more fully experiencing, reflecting on, and appreciating almost everything in their lives. As students experiment with processing their feelings, thoughts, ideas, and opinions using the eight intelligences, they gain new levels of understanding of the reality of the intelligences within themselves.

WRAPAROUND PROCESSING

Academic Exploration and Discovery

The Wraparound Processing strategy can provide you many insights into students' comprehension of material you are teaching. They often have learned (or are learning) much more than they can express limited to the more traditional verbal/linguistic or logical/mathematical modes. When you employ Wraparound Processing with specific lessons and/or units, you provide students with opportunities to reflect on and express their feelings and/or learning about certain curricular material using the eight intelligences.

Academic Exploration and Discovery Strategies

➤ **Capacities Wraparound.** Design your Wraparound Processing stems around the specific capacities of an intelligence. For example, if you have been emphasizing musical/rhythmic intelligence in the lesson, you might have students beat out a rhythm, make vocal sounds, hum a popular tune, write a simple song, imagine different environmental sounds, and so on.

➤ **Wraparound by Groups.** At the end of a lesson, have students quickly huddle with three or four other students. Together they discuss their individual responses to the lesson using the Wraparound Processing stems. They are to reach a consensus on one response that most accurately represents the feelings of the team for each stem. All team members must agree and be able to explain the team's response.

➤ **Content-Specific Stems.** Match the various aspects of the concepts you are teaching to the different intelligences. Create the processing stems using both the content and the intelligences; for example, in social studies, you could use the music, drama, poetry, or art of a culture as the basis for reflecting on other aspects of this culture.

Commentary: Multiple Intelligences and the Learning Process

The key to effectively using Wraparound Processing with academic content is to weave them together in such a way that the content is enhanced and amplified by processing it using all the intelligences. Processing stems can help students understand the material on many more levels, while continuing to help them recognize the eight intelligences in themselves and in their classmates. Given the relative newness of multiple intelligences (and the terminology), you will likely need to get students started doing this kind of processing by giving them some examples from your own reflections on the material. However, with just a little jump-starting of their thinking, this strategy will usually carry itself.

WRAPAROUND PROCESSING

Beyond-the-Classroom Exploration and Discovery

These extension exercises represent ways that students can begin to use their newfound awareness about multiple intelligences as a regular part of their daily experience. This gives them another level of reflection on things they are already doing. Again, as with all the tacit-level exercises, you want students to see that multiple intelligences are already an unconscious part of their daily lives. You are simply asking them to bring the concept to consciousness.

Beyond-the-Classroom Exploration and Discovery Applications

➤ **Family Discussion Wraparounds.** Create a series of processing stems for use in different family-life situations, such as reflecting on a movie together, problem solving, dealing with difficult situations, and so on Make sure you tap all the intelligences as you create the stems.

➤ **"Dear Diary" or Journaling.** Adapt the Wraparound Processing stems for use as a means of processing your experience of a day, week, year, and so on. Examples include: "If today were an animal it would be . . ." or "The colors of my week were . . ."

➤ **Experience Processing.** Use the stems to help reflect on and deepen your experience of a special event, such as a birthday or anniversary, special trip or vacation, key accomplishment, and so on.

Commentary: Multiple Intelligences and Everyday Life
The suggested extension exercises can help students gain a new awareness of many dimensions of their own capacities for experiencing almost anything on many different levels of their brain, mind, body system. When we move any experience "beyond the head," it often becomes much more meaningful. Students will discover the vast reservoirs of untapped feelings to draw on in their life, using Wraparound Processing.

Wraparound Processing
(All Grades)

Elementary: Do each part with the whole class; have individuals make suggestions that the class performs.

Middle: Have students work through the steps with a team and share with the whole class.

Secondary: Have students work through the steps individually, then share with a partner or with the whole class.

1. **Write three words about the lesson.**

2. **What kind of thinking did the lesson cause you to do?**

3. **Draw an image or picture about the lesson.**

4. **Make up a body movement or gesture about the lesson.**

5. **What sound or song would you play as background to the lesson?**

6. **Discuss with a partner how the information from the lesson is important and can be applied today.**

7. **Finish the sentence: "This lesson is important to me because . . . "**

8. **Name animals or plants that this lesson makes you think about.**

Teacher's Personal Reflection Log

WRAPAROUND PROCESSING

I have the following thoughts/insights about the Wraparound Processing strategy:

I feel that the Wraparound Processing strategy can help me in my teaching in the following ways:

As a learning process, the Wraparound Processing strategy includes the following benefits for my students:

I have the following specific ideas for using the Wraparound Processing strategy in my classroom in the near future:

I think the Wraparound Processing strategy can be used beyond the classroom and school in the following ways:

Intelligence Activity Posters

INTRODUCTION

This exercise engages students in a group exploration of their various intelligence skills or capacities. The posters provide a variety of fun and engaging activities. To complete the posters, students must help and learn from each other.

OBJECTIVE

The goal of the exercise is to reveal the importance of honoring and utilizing the unique gifts and skills of each member of a group.

DISCUSSION

Although this exercise relies heavily on visual/spatial intelligence, it can move students very effectively into a tacit awareness of the other intelligences as well. Obviously, the posters do not have to be as well developed or as sophisticated as the ones in the examples. The posters could even be made into activity sheets. Remember, however, the more intriguing and fun you can make the posters, the more you will hook students on doing the activity and the greater the discoveries they will make.

EXPLORATION AND DISCOVERY BASE EXERCISE: INTELLIGENCE ACTIVITY POSTERS

Exercise Procedures

1. Divide students into groups of four and give each group a copy of a poster from the work sheets (see pp. 77–79).

2. Give the groups the following assignment:

> Look at the poster together and make sure you understand the various tasks or activities it is asking you to perform. You may ask me questions about anything you do not understand.
>
> Before beginning work on the poster, plan your strategy for completing the poster. Write down your plan and why you chose each part of the plan. Remember that there are no "right" reasons for your decisions. The only right is knowing the "why" for each step you decide to take.
>
> You have fifteen to twenty minutes to work on the poster and execute your plan.

Observe the groups carefully as they work, making sure that you are available to answer questions and to help them through any difficulties.

3. After the students have completed their work, have each group join with another group to share what they have done. Make sure that they don't just talk about their work, but have them lead the other group in an experiential report of their work; that is, have them try to learn the tongue twister, try to guess the number pattern, try the exercise routine, and so on.

4. After the groups have completed their sharing, bring the class back together. Lead them in the following discussion:

> • What are some of the things that happened as you were working on the poster with your group?

Pathways of Learning © 2000 Zephyr Press, Tucson, Arizona • 800-232-2187 • http://zephyrpress.com

- *What are some of the things that happened when you shared your work with another group?*
- *What are some of the feelings you experienced as you worked with your group? What was easy? What was hard?*
- *What surprised you? What was fun? Exciting? Frustrating?*
- *What did you learn about each other as you worked on the poster? What did you learn about yourself?*
- *What did we learn in this activity that will help us in our daily classroom work? What did you learn that will help you with your homework?*

Parallel Curriculum Interface

INTELLIGENCE ACTIVITY POSTERS

Personal Exploration and Discovery

The Activity Posters students create should include activities that involve the actual utilization of the different intelligences and their related capacities. It is important that the posters be intelligent-appropriate; that is, within the unique cognitive process and domain of each of the different ways of knowing. The students' activities indicated on the posters must access the modality of the target intelligence.

Personal Exploration and Discovery Exercises

➤ **One Poster per Intelligence.** Have students use the various capacities of the eight intelligences (see Capacities Summary Wheels, pp. 262–263), to create an Activity Poster that is based on exploring each of the intelligences.

➤ **Personal Strength Reporting.** Have students create an Activity Poster to report to their classmates on which of the eight intelligences they feel is their strongest. The poster must show many dimensions and aspects of the strength.

➤ **Intelligence Like/Dislikes Posters.** For each of the intelligences, students must show what they like or dislike about using the intelligence, using the unique language of the intelligence to demonstrate their feelings.

➤ **Favorite Activities Posters.** Have students create Activity Posters which share a hobby or a favorite afterschool activity. The posters must somehow represent the hobby or activity using all the intelligences. These could also be related to movies or TV shows.

> **Commentary: Personal MI Exploration and Discovery**
> The most difficult part of creating Activity Posters is to make sure the various activities on the posters take students beyond merely discussing the intelligences and their capacities. Do not allow the form and structure of the poster to limit the possibilities for how students use it. Have them work in groups to do the posters so they can encourage each other to explore the various intelligence-related activities. This will also heighten their appreciation for their classmates and some of the things they can do.

INTELLIGENCE ACTIVITY POSTERS

Academic Exploration and Discovery

The Activity Posters you employ with lessons and/or units should provide students with ample opportunities to explore academic concepts using the eight intelligences. Your goal is to come up with learning tasks in the different parts of the posters that ask students to explore and represent their understanding of the curriculum using the eight intelligences.

Academic Exploration and Discovery Strategies

> ➤ **Concept Extension Posters.** Have students create an Activity Poster that explores a key concept using the eight ways of knowing; for example, write about it, draw it, make up a song about it, act it out, analyze it, discuss it with others, and meditate on it.

> ➤ **Application Posters.** Have students create an Activity Poster that applies certain things from a lesson to everyday life situations; for example, dividing a cake into equal pieces to serve all people at the table, writing a persuasive argument for one's parents regarding use of the car on the weekend, and so on. Ask students to cover all the intelligences in the activities' design.

> ➤ **Curriculum Integration Posters.** In the center of a poster write a key concept or idea from a lesson that "reverberates across the curriculum." Have students make connections to other subjects or content areas. Make sure to cover all curriculum areas; such as history, science, math, language arts, health, social studies, fine arts, family/consumer science, industrial technology, and P.E.

> ➤ **"Stump the Class" Posters.** In groups of three to four, have students create an Activity Poster of their own based on concepts and ideas from a completed lesson. Have them randomly draw a concept from a hat, then create an Activity Poster based on it. Each team presents its poster and the class tries to guess the concept behind the poster.

Commentary: Multiple Intelligences and the Learning Process

The first few times you apply Activity Posters to the content you are teaching, you will probably need to give students examples about how to respond to the different items on the different kinds of posters. One very effective way to do this is to complete a poster yourself related to some personal, nonacademic, or school-related content, such as baking something, something you've read recently, and so on. Your goal is to introduce students to the idea that they can indeed express their learning and understanding of what they are studying in a wide variety of ways.

INTELLIGENCE ACTIVITY POSTERS

Beyond-the-Classroom Exploration and Discovery

The extensions suggested here represent ways that students can make awarenesses about their own multiple intelligences more of a regular part of their daily experience and reflections. By creating and using the Activity Posters exercise outside the classroom, students begin to recognize the intelligences in other aspects of their lives. Invite them to come up with as many additional poster ideas as possible.

Beyond-the-Classroom Exploration and Discovery Applications

➤ **Introducing Multiple Intelligences.** Have students create a poster that would help a friend or family member understand the eight intelligences. Design a poster for use with young children, teenagers, and adults. Try them out on these people.

➤ **MI Challenge Posters.** Have students create posters that involve asking others to perform tasks or challenges which require utilizing the capacities of the various intelligences in their performance.

➤ **Exploring Personal Goals.** Have students create posters in which they express, via the eight intelligences, some of the things they want to accomplish in their lives beyond the school setting, such as friendship or family goals, material possessions, spiritual goals, and so on.

Commentary: Multiple Intelligences and Everyday Life

When students create Activity Posters to use with other people, it takes students to new levels of their own awareness about the intelligences. Posters also help students interiorize their understanding of the intelligences in their own lives (which is what the tacit level is all about). This exercise also tends to move students toward a more conscious use of multiple intelligences in daily living.

Multiple Intelligence Activity Poster

(Elementary)

Can you count to 10?

1 _ _ _ _ _ _ _ _ 10

Can you add to 10?

1+2+3+4+5+6+7+8+9+10=

A B C D E

Can you make all the letters in the alphabet with your body? Try it!

I like to sit alone and think about . . .

Tell a friend about a pet.

8
Ways of Knowing

What makes a good friend?

1.
2.
3.

Make a pattern with the colors you like most!

Make up a song about your family.

Tell a story about . . .

your family
a party
an old person
water
a trip

Multiple Intelligence Activity Poster
(Middle School)

Can you figure out the pattern of the following numbers?

| 1, 2, 4, 8, 16, 32, 64, 128, 256, 512 |

Make a number pattern of your own to stump your friends.

Can you make sounds for these things?

- **Rush-hour traffic**
- **Something scary about to happen in a movie**
- **Anger, contentment, excitement, and sadness**
- **Spring, winter, summer, and autumn**
- **Getting up in the morning**

TEAMWORK	GIVING SUPPORT

Can you describe the social skills in the 4 corners?
(Use the T-chart)

Looks like . . . | Sounds like . . .

ENCOURAGING	LISTENING

8
Ways of Knowing

Make a graph of your moods during the day.

High point

Low point

Draw a picture of how you feel about today.

Fill in this chart:

	Animal	Plant	Spot in Nature
My Favorite			
Why			

Make a limerick about something that happened today. Example:

A pretty young girl named Rae,

Was having a wonderful day,

Until she went into math

Where her test she got back.

Now she has no idea what to say.

 Pathways of Learning © 2000 Zephyr Press, Tucson, Arizona • 800-232-2187 • http://zephyrpress.com

Multiple Intelligence Activity Poster
(Secondary)

List 10 examples of "math in everyday life."

1.
2.
3.
4.
5.
6.
7.
8.
9.
10.

Rank the list from most to least important to you.

?

What's it all about? My big questions about life are . . .

Write an exciting, fun paragraph about something very mundane, such as the examples that follow:

- **BRUSHING YOUR TEETH**
- **DOING THE LAUNDRY**
- **EATING A HAMBURGER**
- **WALKING THE DOG**

Make it sound as if it is the most important thing that ever has and ever will happen in human history.

Make up a physical game related to each of your subjects in school.
Examples:

Science soccer
Math marathon
Social studies skating
Language arts archery

8
Ways of Knowing

Make the appropriate back-ground music or rhythm for the following:

- **Standing in the checkout line at the store**
- **Getting ready to go on a date, being on the date, after the date**
- **Doing the homework you get for each of your subjects**
- **Explaining a bad grade to your parents**
- **Being caught in rush-hour traffic**

What objects, persons, or animals can you find in this design?

List at least 10 ways nature impacts you:

1	2	3	4	5
6	7	8	9	10

Teacher's Personal Reflection Log

INTELLIGENCE ACTIVITY POSTERS

I have the following thoughts/insights about the Intelligence Activity Posters strategy:

I feel that the Intelligence Activity Posters strategy can help me in my teaching in the following ways:

As a learning process, the Intelligence Activity Posters strategy includes the following benefits for my students:

I have the following specific ideas for using the Intelligence Activity Posters strategy in my classroom in the near future:

I think the Intelligence Activity Posters strategy can be used beyond the classroom and school in the following ways:

Pathways of Learning © 2000 Zephyr Press, Tucson, Arizona • 800-232-2187 • http://zephyrpress.com

EXPLORATION AND DISCOVERY BASE EXERCISE: SELF BEHAVIOR CHECKLIST

Exercise Procedures

1. Give each student a small notebook or have students create notebooks that will be their "intelligence tracking" logs for one week. The models on pp. 86–88 give examples of how the logs could be set up.
2. Give students a few moments each day of the week to record things they have noticed about themselves under each of the categories of their logs.
3. At the end of the week, place students in groups of three. Have each group use the following criteria to create a three-way Venn diagram on a piece of newsprint that can be posted later. Have the students compare and contrast their logs with others using the Venn diagrams.

   1. things that were unique to each person
   2. things I had in common with one other person in the group
   3. things that we all had in common

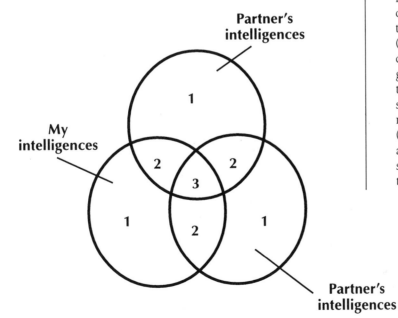

Self Behavior Checklist

INTRODUCTION

This exercise asks students to track or pay attention to a number of their taken-for-granted behaviors and activities during the course of a normal week. As the week progresses students will find more and more skills they have rarely considered to be intellectually significant.

OBJECTIVE

The goal of the exercise is to help students recognize and name their "intelligent behavior" beyond the classroom and in activities that are not usually thought of as intelligence related.

DISCUSSION

Of all of the exercises in this chapter, the Self Behavior Checklist strategy requires the highest degree of introspection from your students. In some ways this activity requires students to be like detectives, seeking intelligence clues within taken-for-granted behavior patterns. Keys to the success of this strategy include (1) elevating it to the level of homework you expect students to complete during the week; (2) reminding students everyday to check their self behavior, maybe giving them a few minutes in class to work on their checklists (doing so will demonstrate your seriousness about the assignment); and (3) discussing how the checklists are coming, addressing difficulties students are experiencing in doing the assignment.

4. Have the groups post their Venns on the walls around the room. Have each group visit the other Venns and note the similarities and differences among their Venns and those of the other groups.

5. Call the class back together for a discussion of what they have learned about their eight ways of being intelligent. On the overhead or board list the items they recorded on their Venns at the three-way intersections for each intelligence. Ask them the following questions:

  • *Is there anything that surprises you about this list?*
  • *What ideas do you have about how you could create an even greater awareness of how you use the eight intelligences in your daily life?*
  • *What could we do in this class to make ourselves more aware of the seven intelligences and how we use them everyday?*

6. Give students time to create a symbol that will remind them to be aware of the eight intelligences in their everyday lives. Ask the students to post their symbols on their walls at home and to draw the images in their notebooks in places where the students will see them often.

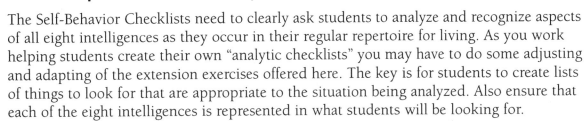

Parallel Curriculum Interface

SELF BEHAVIOR CHECKLIST

Personal Exploration and Discovery

The Self-Behavior Checklists need to clearly ask students to analyze and recognize aspects of all eight intelligences as they occur in their regular repertoire for living. As you work helping students create their own "analytic checklists" you may have to do some adjusting and adapting of the extension exercises offered here. The key is for students to create lists of things to look for that are appropriate to the situation being analyzed. Also ensure that each of the eight intelligences is represented in what students will be looking for.

Personal Exploration and Discovery Exercises

➤ **Intelligence Capacities Checklists.** Have students create separate checklists of behaviors to watch for in themselves that are focused on the capacities or skills of each intelligence on its own. Make sure the checklists are both developmentally and intelligence appropriate.

➤ **Analyzing Pastime Activities.** Ask students to make a list of several things they like to do after school, on weekends, or during vacation. They are then to use the multiple intelligences checklists to analyze what is involved in these activities. Which intelligences are more related to which of the activities?

➤ **MI and My Relationships.** Have students create two columns. In the first column ask students to list all of the people who have some kind of effect on them, including family, friends, casual acquaintances, and so on. In the second column, have them analyze these people in terms of the multiple intelligences roles they play in their lives. Notice which intelligences are dominant and which are lacking.

Commentary: Personal MI Exploration and Discovery

Your goal with the Self Behavior Checklists is for students to realize that their eight intelligences are already, consciously or unconsciously, part of their daily lives. The checklists help students make explicit these intelligence behaviors and/or aspects. The trick of working with any introspective exercise is to encourage students to be honest in their analysis of themselves. Continually remind them that there is really no good, bad, right, or wrong. Instead, use language that is more developmental, such as *more developed intelligences, emerging intelligences,* or *intelligences that are in various states of latency.*

SELF BEHAVIOR CHECKLIST

Academic Exploration and Discovery

The Self Behavior Checklist strategy can be applied to almost any concept if, in your own mind, you "anthropomorphize" it (that is, imagine it is human and possesses human personality traits, characteristics, and qualities). A second technique is to ask students to imagine that they can "pass over" into the material they are studying; for example, have them go inside of a plant and experience, from the inside out, what it is like. While this may seem a little bizarre at first, it can really be a great deal of fun and can unearth some powerful discoveries about the material.

Academic Exploration and Discovery Strategies

➤ **Lesson Reaction Checklist.** Create a checklist of possible reactions to a lesson, making sure that you include reactions for each intelligence. At the beginning of a lesson, hand out the checklist and ask students to watch themselves during the lesson, checking off anything on the list that is true of their experience of the lesson.

➤ **Academic Subjects Checklist.** Have students list the subjects they study in school. Create a checklist comprised of the capacities or skills of the different intelligences using the Capacities Summary Wheels (pp. 262–263). Ask students to carry the checklist with them for a week, matching the various intelligence capacities or skills with the different subjects.

➤ **Curricular "Stuff" Analysis.** Make Self Behavior Checklists to go along with content you are teaching; for example, a checklist to analyze historical figures or characters in a story, a checklist to analyze aspects of a story problem in math, or a checklist to describe aspects of a scientific process.

➤ **Connections to the Future Checklists.** Have students create individual checklists that illustrate potential future uses for particular concepts and ideas you are teaching. Make sure the checklists ask them to consider the future from the perspective of all eight intelligences Ask them to think of ways a particular concept will or may be useful and necessary 100 years from today.

➤ **Connections to the Past Checklists.** Have students create checklists that illustrate past uses and the importance of particular ideas you are teaching in a unit. Have them talk with their parents and other adults for examples, as well as examining their own lives from birth till the present. Make sure they ask these people to consider the future from the perspective of all eight intelligences.

Commentary: Multiple Intelligences and the Learning Process

The Self Behavior Checklists are a powerful tool for helping students make personal connections between themselves and material they are studying through various lessons in the classroom. One of the big pluses of introducing multiple intelligences into the meaning-creating process is that it allows students to make connections with the curriculum throughout their entire brain, mind, body system, thus taking learning beyond "head knowledge" alone.

SELF BEHAVIOR CHECKLIST

Beyond-the-Classroom Exploration and Discovery

These kinds of Self Behavior Checklists give students a new set of eyeglasses for looking at and understanding the behaviors of other people they meet on a daily basis. Ask students to brainstorm situations in which it would be interesting to create and use various kinds of multiple intelligences checklists. Have them try out the checklists they create, then report on the results, their findings, and what they are learning about multiple intelligences by doing the exercise.

Beyond-the-Classroom Exploration and Discovery Applications

➤ **Life Experience Checklist.** Have students create a checklist which compares and contrasts their use of the eight intelligences in different stages of their lives up till the present moment.

➤ **Other People Checklist.** Using the base Self Behavior Checklist exercise, assign students to watch for intelligent behavior in people they know outside school; for example, in their family, a church youth group, an after-school club, and so on.

➤ **TV Show or Movie Watching Checklists.** Have students design a checklist for analyzing the behavior of characters in various TV sitcoms, detective shows, soaps, or when they go to the theater to see a movie.

Commentary: Multiple Intelligences and Everyday Life
These kinds of Self Behavior Checklist exercises require students to apply their knowledge of multiple intelligences with other people that they encounter outside of the school setting. The checklists can become an additional layer of reflection to deepen students' understanding of, appreciation for, and empathy with the behaviors of other people. As students gain a new view of themselves and their many capacities, they also gain a new understanding for and appreciation of others and their many capacities.

Self Behavior Checklist
(Elementary)

What did you do today?

☐ **Drew a picture**

☐ **Counted**

☐ **Sang a song**

☐ **Wrote something**

☐ **Played with an animal**

☐ **Talked to a friend**

☐ **Thought**

☐ **Played a game**

☐ **Touched a plant**

Self Behavior Checklist
(Middle School)

What did you do today?

Mark an "X" in the box beside each thing you did today.

- ☐ Had contact with an animal
- ☐ Had an interesting conversation with someone
- ☐ Spent some time alone, thinking
- ☐ Listened to music
- ☐ Did some drawing
- ☐ Played a game that required me to use my body
- ☐ Used math to figure something out
- ☐ Did some singing (even in the shower!)
- ☐ Wrote something outside of assigned schoolwork
- ☐ Smelled a flower
- ☐ Made something with my hands
- ☐ Got some exercise
- ☐ Spent some time just relaxing
- ☐ Watched a television show or a movie
- ☐ Expressed my feelings
- ☐ Read something interesting outside of my schoolwork
- ☐ Learned something new about another person
- ☐ Spent time enjoying nature

Self Behavior Checklist
(Secondary)

What did you do today?

Look back on your day and put an "X" in the box
beside each behavior or activity that you did.

☐ I took time to appreciate the natural world.

☐ I doodled during a lesson.

☐ I learned something new about myself.

☐ I had a great conversation with someone.

☐ I had an enjoyable experience listening to music.

☐ I used "applied math."

☐ I wrote something that pleases me.

☐ I got some physical exercise.

☐ I expressed myself using gestures and other body language.

☐ I was aware of colors.

☐ I read something outside of schoolwork that was interesting.

☐ I saw a pattern or design that I found interesting.

☐ I caught myself singing or humming a tune.

☐ I was aware of my feelings about something.

☐ I resolved a disagreement with another person.

☐ I learned something from a picture or a visual aid.

☐ I spent time alone just thinking about things.

☐ I drew a picture or diagram to aid me in communication
with others.

☐ I spent time with an animal.

Pathways of Learning © 2000 Zephyr Press, Tucson, Arizona • 800-232-2187 • http://zephyrpress.com

Teacher's Personal Reflection Log
SELF BEHAVIOR CHECKLIST

I have the following thoughts/insights about the Self Behavior Checklist strategy:

I feel that the Self Behavior Checklist strategy can help me in my teaching in the following ways:

As a learning process, the Self Behavior Checklist strategy includes the following benefits for my students:

I have the following specific ideas for using the Self Behavior Checklist strategy in my classroom in the near future:

I think the Self Behavior Checklist strategy can be used beyond the classroom and school in the following ways:

= 3 =
Exercises for Aware Use of the Intelligences

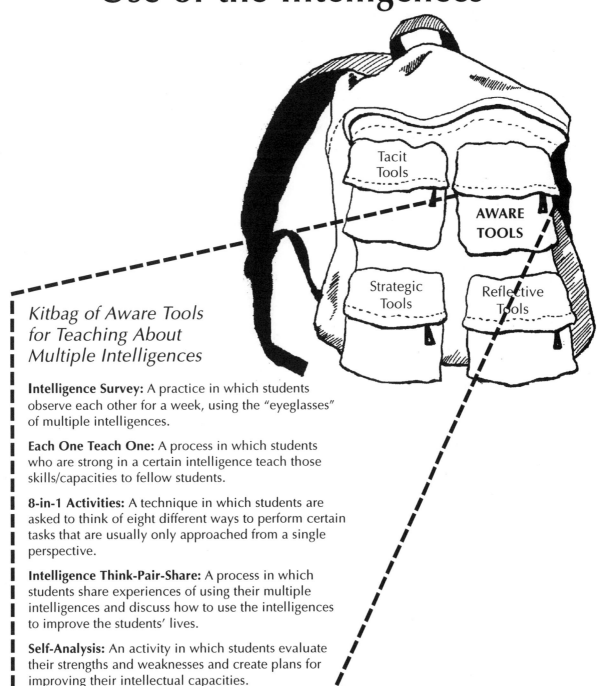

Tacit
Tools

AWARE
TOOLS

Strategic
Tools

Reflective
Tools

Kitbag of Aware Tools for Teaching About Multiple Intelligences

Intelligence Survey: A practice in which students observe each other for a week, using the "eyeglasses" of multiple intelligences.

Each One Teach One: A process in which students who are strong in a certain intelligence teach those skills/capacities to fellow students.

8-in-1 Activities: A technique in which students are asked to think of eight different ways to perform certain tasks that are usually only approached from a single perspective.

Intelligence Think-Pair-Share: A process in which students share experiences of using their multiple intelligences and discuss how to use the intelligences to improve the students' lives.

Self-Analysis: An activity in which students evaluate their strengths and weaknesses and create plans for improving their intellectual capacities.

Sandra was a middle school student. During the past year her teacher had been teaching the class about multiple intelligences. Sandra was intrigued with the idea that she has multiple ways of knowing but was hesitant to try using those at which she wasn't very skilled. She was afraid that other students would laugh at her.

The teacher was working with the students to help them learn how to improve and strengthen all of their ways of knowing. He created a list of skills for the different intelligences. The assignment was for each student to choose an intelligence in which he or she felt confident. In groups, the students were to create a plan and an activity that would help to strengthen the skills of the rest of the class. Sandra was pleased that she would get a chance to work in an intelligence area with which she was comfortable, but she was also excited that she would have an opportunity to practice using other intelligence skills in a safe environment, where everyone was learning and trying new things.

When the groups had completed their planning, each group reported to the class by demonstrating their skills and the practice activity they had designed. The teacher set aside a brief time each day for students to practice one or two of the intelligences. The expert groups led the class in the practice sessions.

After two weeks, the teacher asked the class to discuss their feelings about the intelligence practice sessions. Sandra was one of the first to respond: "When I was asked to do things I'm not very good at, I was scared and uncomfortable at first. But when I saw that others also weren't good at all the skills, I was able to relax and get into it a little. I'm still not very good at the body stuff and the drawing, but at least I'm not afraid to try anymore!"

During the quarter, the practice sessions continued and students were pleased to notice that their skills in using the eight intelligences had definitely improved and that they felt more "at home" trying to use the skills to enhance learning.

EXPLORATION AND DISCOVERY BASE EXERCISE: INTELLIGENCE SURVEY

Exercise Procedures

1. Group students into observation teams of three. Tell them they will be working with their teams for a week to observe teachers and other students in their class, and in the school as a whole, using the eight intelligences. Following is a list of what you and your students will be doing:

   - Use the Intelligence Survey Checklists (see examples, pp. 98–100), or even better, create your own checklist with the students. Students are to observe their fellow students and their teachers for a week and log each instance of the behaviors they see.
   - To log an instance, students are to go up to someone they see manifesting one of the behaviors on the checklist and say, "I caught you using your _____ intelligence!"
   - The students have that person sign his or her name on the intelligent behavior checklist.
   - At the end of the week you will tally the observation logs and create a bar graph. You want to find out which intelligent behaviors seem to occur more often than others and why.

2. Ask if all students understand the assignment. The first task of the team is to plan its observation strategy; for example, the team might decide to divide up the intelligences so that each person is specializing in looking for behaviors for two or three intelligences, or team members may want to assign each other various territories and groups of the school to cover.

3. Each day during the week give students a few minutes to share stories from their observations, to handle any difficulties they are experiencing, and to ask you any questions they may have.

Intelligence Survey

INTRODUCTION

This strategy is designed to help students appreciate the differences that exist among us in our various ways of knowing. It is designed also to give students a set of eyeglasses for seeing intelligence skills in others so that the students might learn to broaden their own perspectives when approaching an issue, challenge, or problem.

OBJECTIVE

The goal of this exercise is to help students recognize, first in others and then in themselves, different intelligences as those intelligences manifest themselves in the course of daily living.

DISCUSSION

This strategy is obviously not only beneficial to the students who are conducting the survey; it also makes other students aware and interested in the eight intelligences. The strategy involves taking small risks, but if you can get your students to try it even a couple of times they will start to have a great deal of fun with the exercise and will learn an immense amount. Not only must they recognize the intelligences in others, but they will have to explain the eight ways of knowing as well. Before students begin the survey, it would be a good idea for you to discuss with them what they should say when someone asks them about the intelligences.

4. At the end of the week, have each team tally the numbers for each behavior on the checklist. After the teams have their numbers, create a master tally of the numbers from all of the teams.

5. Use the following questions to lead the students in a discussion:

- *What immediately grabs your attention as you look at these numbers?*
- *What do you find surprising? Confusing? Exciting? Disturbing?*
- *Why do you think these were the results?*
- *What factors might have produced different results?*
- *What have you learned about your own intelligences by doing this survey?*
- *What new ideas did you get for how you might use all the ways of knowing in your schoolwork?*

6. Get one volunteer from each group to work as part of a team. The team will create a bar graph that shows the composite results of the survey. Have the team be imaginative and create something that you can display for the rest of the school to see.

Parallel Curriculum Interface

INTELLIGENCE SURVEYS

Personal Exploration and Discovery

The Intelligence Surveys help students realize that our multiple ways of knowing literally shape almost every aspect of life. As you design the surveys, let your own creativity be your guide. See how many different kinds of surveys you can conceive. Ask students to brainstorm other places and/or situations where they would like to create and use Intelligence Surveys. Remember, each potential survey situation will require a specially designed or adapted survey.

Personal Exploration and Discovery Exercises

➤ **Specific Capacities Surveys.** Design a survey around the specific capacities or skills of each intelligence. Ask students to name people in the larger community whom they think exhibit strength in particular intelligence areas; for example, artists, people in the theater, athletes, counselors, writers, computer programmers, bankers, and musicians. Assign them to survey two or three such people and report their findings.

➤ **Cross-Culture Surveys.** Have students make up a survey for analyzing how different cultures approach life using multiple intelligences; for example, the importance of music, kinds of visual art and its role in the culture, nature of interpersonal relationships (family, peer, social), knowledge and enjoyment of folk dances, spiritual/religious practices, and so on.

➤ **Male/Female Surveys.** Invent a survey around such things as how men and women process information, solve problems, and meet challenges in their daily lives. Assign students to interview ten men and ten women to see what specific differences they can discover in how each gender group uses the eight ways of knowing.

Commentary: Personal MI Exploration and Discovery
Students initially may be hesitant to survey fellow students, however, once they get started it may be hard to get them to stop! Not only do the Intelligence Surveys help the surveyors recognize the intelligences in others. Students also have to explain and teach multiple intelligences to the surveyees, thus deepening their own awareness of multiple intelligences. Part of the goal of the surveys is to help students become aware of how much the intelligences shape many of the taken-for-granted aspects of daily life.

INTELLIGENCE SURVEYS

Academic Exploration and Discovery

When using the Intelligence Surveys strategy with various academic content, a certain amount of personalization must occur. You must pretend that you can interview certain people, places, and things that you are studying. If you are using a survey with something beyond the human species, or something that is inanimate, you must help students stretch their imaginations so they can converse with such things.

Academic Exploration and Discovery Strategies

➤ **Historical Surveys.** Survey past periods of history using the eight intelligences. Ask students to analyze various periods, trying to get a glimpse of differing emphases on the eight intelligences at different times; for example, Ancient Greece and the Middle Ages, or America at the time of independence, or during the Great Awakening.

➤ **Literature Character Surveys.** When you are studying a piece of literature, have students conduct an ongoing survey of the various characters and their use of the eight intelligences as the story or play unfolds.

➤ **Surveys in Math.** Have students pretend that they can have a conversation with several math operations. For example, a student could chat with the process for converting a fraction to a decimal or finding the hypotenuse of a right triangle.

➤ **Surveys in Science.** Have students pretend that they can converse with different scientific processes to help learn more about them, such as the immune system, the process of photosynthesis, and so on.

Commentary: Multiple Intelligences and the Learning Process

When students are asked to interact with various academic content as if it were present and available for an interview, many personal connections can be made with the material. In order to conduct these kinds of surveys, students will have to move to the "higher-order thinking realms" of Bloom's now-famous taxonomy (1956). The surveys will likely create a certain amount of empathy between the students and the concepts being interviewed. Even more important, the surveys can help students invest the material with their own personal meaning.

INTELLIGENCE SURVEYS

Beyond-the-Classroom Exploration and Discovery

The more encouragement you can give students to look
for multiple intelligences beyond the formal school setting
the more they will find that multiple intelligences are
really a very important part of everyone's daily experience,
whether or not they have the terminology of MI to talk about it. When students
begin to recognize people's use of the different intelligences, they will also gain new
levels of awareness of the role the eight intelligences play in their own lives.

Beyond-the-Classroom Exploration and Discovery Applications

➤ **Family Surveys.** Have students create surveys to interview different members of their immediate families to see what they can learn about how the eight intelligences have shaped the family. They could include such things as who plays musical instruments, who writes poetry, who is really good at mathematical problem solving, who likes to dance, who is good at sports, and so on.

➤ **Special Groups Surveys.** Help students create a survey to analyze the different ways of knowing for a group of which they are a part. For example, How are meetings run? Does the group have a symbol/emblem? A song? What do members like to do for celebration? How do they handle disagreements? Each student is to pick five such groups to observe for a month and then report the findings to the class.

➤ **TV/Movie Surveys.** Have students create a survey for analyzing various characters they encounter when watching TV sitcoms, soaps, detective shows, and/or when going to a movie.

Commentary: Multiple Intelligences and Everyday Life
The goal of these kinds of surveys is to help students begin to look at other people and their relationships with them through the eyeglasses of the multiple intelligences. When we can learn to look at other people and our relationships with them using multiple intelligences, our understanding of those around us increases, as does our appreciation for their unique gifts and capacities. It can also help us raise our tolerance level for certain behaviors that we may find annoying.

Intelligence Survey Checklist
(Elementary)

I'm looking for . . .

1. Someone who "talks" with her or his body.

2. Someone who is drawing.

3. Someone who is singing or humming as he or she works.

4. Someone who is talking to other people.

5. Someone who is alone and thinking.

6. Someone who is using numbers.

7. Someone who is reading or writing.

8. Someone who is showing interest in an animal or a plant.

Intelligence Survey Checklist
(Middle School)

Try to catch someone . . .

1. Having a good discussion with someone else.

2. Using body language to express her- or himself.

3. Humming or singing while doing something else.

4. Drawing pictures or images to communicate.

5. Trying to solve a problem.

6. Making a "speech" to convince others he or she is right about an idea.

7. Being alone and appearing to be deep in thought.

8. Giving directions to someone else for getting someplace.

9. Taking notes on something (not in a classroom!).

10. Listening to music as he or she works or exercises.

11. Arguing.

12. Using math to solve an everyday, real-life problem.

13. Showing someone else how to do something through body movement.

14. Expressing "inner feelings" about something.

15. Caring for a plant.

16. Telling about an experience with an animal.

17. Talking about the weather.

Intelligence Survey Checklist
(Secondary)

*How many of these behaviors
can you find in other people?*

1. Two or three people are talking and "good listening" is clearly going on.

2. Someone is expressing her- or himself through gestures and physical movement.

3. The tone of someone's voice is communicating how he or she feels about something (maybe even more than *what* he or she is saying!).

4. Someone is giving someone else directions to get somewhere (maybe drawing a map as well!).

5. Someone is using metaphors, similes, and analogies to communicate ideas.

6. Someone is analyzing or evaluating the thinking patterns she or he used to make a recent decision.

7. Someone is using mathematical concepts to solve an everyday problem.

8. Someone is giving someone else positive support, encouragement, or feedback.

9. Someone is expressing ideas, opinions, or concepts through drawing (or any kind of visual media).

10. People are telling jokes or stories or debating an idea with one another.

11. Someone is using music as a background for some task he or she is trying to perform.

12. Someone is "acting out" his or her feelings, ideas, or opinions on some topic.

13. Someone is relating a powerful experience of the natural world (such as the weather, an earthquake, an encounter with a wild animal, and so on).

14. Someone has written a letter, poem, or an essay on a topic she or he feels strongly about.

15. People are sharing their problem-solving strategies (including creative approaches to homework!) with one another.

16. People are expressing their religious views, their thoughts on the "meaning of life," or sharing their feelings about themselves.

17. Someone is expressing her- or himself through a song, rap, or a rhythmic pattern.

18. Someone is involved in the act of caring for a plant or animal.

19. Someone's walk or posture catches your attention and you sense it is communicating something about how that person is feeling.

Pathways of Learning © 2000 Zephyr Press, Tucson, Arizona • 800-232-2187 • http://zephyrpress.com

Teacher's Personal Reflection Log
INTELLIGENCE SURVEY

I have the following thoughts/insights about the Intelligence Survey strategy:

I feel that the Intelligence Survey strategy can help me in my teaching in the following ways:

As a learning process, the Intelligence Survey strategy includes the following benefits for my students:

I have the following specific ideas for using the Intelligence Survey strategy in my classroom in the near future:

I think the Intelligence Survey strategy can be used beyond the classroom and school in the following ways:

Each One Teach One

INTRODUCTION

This exercise focuses on students helping each other learn specific skills that will enable the students to use all the intelligences more comfortably in the classroom. Current educational research shows that when peers teach something to peers, the learning often increases dramatically.

OBJECTIVE

The goal of the exercise is to expand students' intelligence skill base and to make them aware that intelligence can be practiced, improved, and fun.

DISCUSSION

The Each-One-Teach-One process is a very powerful learning strategy. William Glasser (1986), the renowned educational researcher, has stated that we learn approximately 10 percent of what we read, 20 percent of what we hear, 30 percent of what we see, 50 percent of what we see and hear, 70 percent of what we discuss with others, 80 percent of what we experience personally, and 95 percent of what we teach to someone else. In using this process, students not only reinforce and deepen their own skills, they also help fellow students hear, see, discuss, and experience the eight ways of knowing, thus learning how to use the full spectrum of their intellectual capabilities.

EXPLORATION AND DISCOVERY BASE EXERCISE: EACH ONE TEACH ONE

Exercise Procedures

1. Review the Multiple Intelligences Capacities Inventory Wheels (see pp. 262–263). Remind the class of the various skills and capacities that are part of each intelligence.

2. Have students spend a few minutes thinking individually about how they feel about the eight intelligences. Post the following statements on an overhead or the board and have students complete each of the statements, selecting things from the examples. Remind students to consider all of the intelligences when they complete these sentences. Encourage them to venture beyond the safety of verbal/linguistic and logical/mathematical intelligences.

   • Three things I know how to do and am good at are . . .
   • Three things I don't like to do and am not very good at are . . .
   • Three things I would like to learn how to do better are . . .

3. Have students place an asterisk by the item in the first list that is the capacity they know how to do best or enjoy doing the most. Have them place another asterisk by the item in the third list that they most want to learn.

4. Pass out two index cards to each student and have the students write their strongest or favorite capacity on one card and the capacity they want to learn on the other.

5. Divide the class into two sections. Ask one half to tape the want-to-learn cards to their chests, and ask the other half to tape the know-how-to-do cards to their chests. Have each half of the class sort itself into intelligence groups with others who have chosen "want-to-learn" or "know-how-to-do" capacities from the same intelligence.

6. Have the want-to-know and the know-how-to-do groups for each intelligence get together. Students in the know-how-to-do group are to teach the want-to-know skills to as many students as possible in the allotted time. Suggest that students use the following pattern to teach the skills:

   - Demonstrate the skill.
   - List the steps involved in performing the skill.
   - Go through one step at a time, helping the learners succeed at each step.
   - Put all the steps together.
   - Tell the learners several simple things they can do to practice the skill.

7. After a reasonable amount of time, have the class return to the two groups they formed in step 5. Have them switch roles: the second group tapes their want-to-know cards to their chests and the first group tapes their know-how-to-do cards to their chests. The first group now teaches the second group. You may have to do this part of the lesson on another day, depending on the amount of time you can give to the exercise.

8. After all students have had the opportunity to experience both roles, call the class back together and lead them in a discussion based on the following questions:

   - *What was this exercise like for you? What happened?*
   - *Which role did you like best—learner or teacher? Why?*
   - *What new discoveries did you make?*
   - *What new ideas did you get for improving your intelligences, especially those in which you feel weak?*
   - *What would have to happen in the classroom to encourage you to practice and use all of your intelligences every day? What things need to change?*

Parallel Curriculum Interface

EACH ONE TEACH ONE

Personal Exploration and Discovery

Most Each One Teach One exercises place students in the role of teacher or facilitator to help others develop a fuller range of their multiple intelligence capacities. Students must first become aware of their own intelligence profile; namely which of their intelligences are more developed and where they need help. Build on this knowledge, capitalizing on the more-developed intelligences, as well as working on the less-developed ones.

Personal Exploration and Discovery Exercises

➤ **Intelligence Skill-Building Tutorials.** For eight weeks, focus on teaching students the specific capacities/skills of the eight intelligences (one intelligence per week). Each day, teach a new skill using the transfer model of instruction. Have students practice using the skill as many different ways as possible during the day.

➤ **Intelligence Skill Relays.** Students work in teams of five members and are paired with another team. Each member of the team draws an intelligence skill from a hat. Each team learns the set of skills it has drawn. Then the first team sends one member to the second team to teach the skill. When the second team has performed the skill to the satisfaction of the first team, reverse the process.

➤ **Grade-Level Exchange Program.** At least once a week have children from the upper grades in the school travel to lower-grade classes for the purpose of helping the younger children develop their eight intelligences. Put younger students in groups of four or five with two upper-grade students. Target specific skills for each training session, and coach upper-grade students in specific activities to help them teach the skills.

> **Commentary: Personal MI Exploration and Discovery**
> The Each One Teach One type of exercise gives every student a chance to shine. This is a real self-esteem booster and it boosts students' esteem for each other. The Each One Teach One process gives students opportunities to become aware of the full spectrum of their own intelligence capacities. It also provides a chance to experiment with using them, making them part of their lives, and teaching them to others.

     Pathways of Learning © 2000 Zephyr Press, Tucson, Arizona • 800-232-2187 • http://zephyrpress.com

EACH ONE TEACH ONE

Academic Exploration and Discovery

The use of this strategy with your academic content really should probably be called "each one teach one, or two, or three, or four!" The teacher must come up with different kinds of assignments, projects, reports, and so on which require students to not only use their various intelligence skills to complete the assignment, but, ideally, to also incorporate the various media of the different intelligences into the final product.

Academic Exploration and Discovery Strategies

➤ **Intelligence Apprentice Projects.** Place students in groups with one student who exhibits some definite strength in a particular intelligence area. Place others in a group that want to develop their own skills in that area. Give them an academic project to complete in which they must use the particular intelligence to the hilt. The "master" in the intelligence is to train and work with the "apprentices" to produce the final product.

➤ **Eight-Layered Assignments.** Give students an assignment that must be completed in cooperative groups and must include all eight intelligences. Students may help by recruiting group members who have some skill in a needed intelligence area. Each member of the group must agree to find a way to incorporate his or her skill into the assignment and to train others in the group how to do it.

➤ **Intelligence Reports.** Assign students to make a report on something read, researched, a lab experiment, and so on. The report must include as many of the intelligences as possible. They are to find classmates who can help them do this.

Commentary: Multiple Intelligences and the Learning Process

The various intelligences can help us with almost any task we perform in our lives, problems we must solve, or challenges that must be met. One of the benefits of the Each One Teach One strategy is that the students begin to realize the many possibilities and benefits of using multiple intelligences. When utilizing this strategy to increase students' transfer of multiple intelligences beyond academics, be sure to have some time for reflecting on uses of the intelligences as an aid to learning.

EACH ONE TEACH ONE

Beyond-the-Classroom Exploration and Discovery

As you brainstorm possibilities for this part of the multiple intelligences parallel curriculum, look for many ideas that will challenge students to take the teaching-and-exposing-others-to-multiple-intelligences process beyond the classroom. The more you can get them to experiment in this regard, the more you will see their awareness of and belief in the validity of multiple intelligences grow.

Beyond-the-Classroom Exploration and Discovery Applications

➤ **Family Intelligence Training.** Assign students the task of teaching their families about the eight intelligences. Help them first learn how to explain the eight ways of knowing concept. Then brainstorm with them at least one experiential exercise for each intelligence that they could use at home to illustrate the different ways of knowing. It's a good idea to forewarn parents about this assignment and ask for their cooperation.

➤ **Eight Ways of Knowing Videos.** Create a video presentation to inform parents or other classes about the eight ways of knowing. Work with students to write a script that explains the eight intelligences. Brainstorm ideas and decide on a demonstration activity for the video that illustrates what it is like to use the eight intelligences in everyday life.

➤ **Intelligence Mentoring.** Ask students to find at least one person outside of school with whom they would like to help explore the different intelligences. Work with students to help them come up with ideas on how to do this.

Commentary: Multiple Intelligences and Everyday Life
One of the goals of the exercises suggested here is to get students involved in teaching other people about multiple intelligences. When we do this, their own awareness and understanding of their own multiple intelligences is enhanced. I call the second benefit the "transfer quotient"—namely, students' self-awareness of how much multiple intelligences can be part of one's regular repertoire for living. The more you can get your students to do these kinds of exercises, the more they will understand the value of multimodal living.

Examples of Each-One-Teach-One Tasks
(Elementary)

Verbal/Linguistic
- tell a story
- write words/sentences
- read a sentence/paragraph

Logical/Mathematical
- count by twos
- solve a problem
- see/explain patterns

Visual/Spatial
- draw objects
- make shapes in clay
- read simple maps

Bodily/Kinesthetic
- understand gestures
- imitate body movement
- act out a feeling or scene

Musical/Rhythmic
- reproduce a tune or beat
- make expressive sounds
- recognize sounds

Interpersonal
- listen to a partner
- encourage others
- play social roles

Intrapersonal
- tell feelings
- name a goal
- tell who you are

Naturalist
- describe animal behaviors
- recognize different plants
- explain weather patterns

Examples of Each-One-Teach-One Tasks
(Middle School)

Verbal/Linguistic
- make up and write a story
- tell a joke or understand a pun
- comprehend reading

Logical/Mathematical
- describe thinking patterns
- perform regular math operations
- understand math symbols

Visual/Spatial
- draw in perspective
- use accurate visual memory
- find a location on a map

Bodily/Kinesthetic
- teach a physical skill
- role-play or dance an idea
- play physical games

Musical/Rhythmic
- grasp music symbols
- be aware of different beats
- know musical sounds

Interpersonal
- be able to paraphrase
- take steps to build friendships
- take steps to develop empathy

Intrapersonal
- take steps to build self-esteem
- set personal goals
- be aware of likes and dislikes

Naturalist
- train a pet
- grow a plant
- understand natural patterns

Pathways of Learning © 2000 Zephyr Press, Tucson, Arizona • 800-232-2187 • http://zephyrpress.com

Examples of Each-One-Teach-One Tasks
(Secondary)

Verbal/Linguistic
- be able to debate or speak on an issue
- write creatively (poetry/stories)
- understand figures of speech
- analyze language for meaning

Logical/Mathematical
- be aware of own thinking patterns
- make logical connections
- solve problems beyond school
- use math in everyday life

Visual/Spatial
- create unique art forms
- design things
- use complex internal imagery
- create accurate maps

Bodily/Kinesthetic
- show creative dramatic ability
- show creative dance ability
- be an inventor
- do a physical exercise routine

Musical/Rhythmic
- enjoy various forms of music
- express self in music
- perform music
- grasp music language

Interpersonal
- build consensus
- build cultural sensitivity
- show skill in group processes
- communicate well

Intrapersonal
- begin an identity quest
- establish a personal belief system
- control emotions
- understand symbols

Naturalist
- use nature appropriately
- conserve/care for nature in personal life
- see/understand the self in nature
- live in harmony with nature

Teacher's Personal Reflection Log

EACH-ONE-TEACH-ONE STRATEGY

I have the following thoughts/insights about the Each-One-Teach-One strategy:

I feel that the Each-One-Teach-One strategy can help me in my teaching in the following ways:

As a learning process, the Each-One-Teach-One strategy includes the following benefits for my students:

I have the following specific ideas for using the Each-One-Teach-One strategy in my classroom in the near future:

I think the Each-One-Teach-One strategy can be used beyond the classroom and school in the following ways:

Pathways of Learning © 2000 Zephyr Press, Tucson, Arizona • 800-232-2187 • http://zephyrpress.com

EXPLORATION AND DISCOVERY
BASE EXERCISE: 8-IN-1 ACTIVITIES
Exercise Procedures

1. On the overhead or board write the following riddle:

   How many intelligences does it take to change a light bulb?

   Can you name them and tell how each would approach the task?

   Ask students to suggest strategies from each intelligence that would accomplish the task.

2. Tell your students, *"Anything and everything can be approached using the eight intelligences. All it takes is stretching your creativity a bit to figure out how. In this lesson you will have a chance to make this stretch!"*

3. Place students into groups of three or four. Pass out copies of the Multiple Intelligence Toolbox (pp. 116–117) to students. Say,

   The toolbox gives us strategies for using the eight intelligences. In this lesson your group will randomly select a topic from a set of cards (see pp. 118–120) for ideas). Your task is to choose one strategy from each intelligence that you think would help you learn about that topic. You are to record your ideas on a piece of newsprint so we can put them up on the wall and learn from your group's ideas.

4. Ask the groups if they have any questions about the assignment. Then take the stack of cards to each group and have one person draw a card. The topic on the card is the focus of the group's planning.

   If a group wants to draw another card because students can't figure out what to do with the card they got, allow them to do so. It is very important that you monitor the groups closely, helping them come up with ideas.

8-in-1 Activities

INTRODUCTION

This lesson will help students learn to think about life and their school-work in new and more effective ways. It involves activating more intelligence capacities than one normally uses in any situation. Students will be asked to use all eight ways of knowing to deal with a single activity.

OBJECTIVE

The goal of the lesson is to help students get in touch with the well-springs of their own creativity by accessing and using all eight ways of knowing.

DISCUSSION

One of the most exciting and revealing ways to make students aware of the possibilities of the eight ways of knowing is through 8-in-1 Activities. The essence of this lesson is to take specific concepts, ideas, or tasks and to force yourself to use all eight intelligences to deal with them. Possibly more than any other technique in this book, this one evokes the greatest creativity in students and provides them with a clear demonstration that learning can be a great deal of fun! While I believe that anything can be taught and learned in eight ways, it is probably best, at least initially, to have students deal with some of the topics in which the ways to apply the eight intelligences are more obvious.

5. After the groups are finished with their planning, have each join two other groups and share their ideas. Then have each group post its work in a part of the room set aside for the purpose.

6. Call the class back together and reflect on the lesson using the following questions:

- *What happened as you worked on this assignment? What things did you notice?*
- *What was easy? What was hard? What did you like? What did you not like?*
- *What surprised you? What excited you?*
- *In one sentence, how would you tell someone who was not here today what we did in this lesson?*
- *Think about lessons that we have done in the past week. What strategies could we have used that would have made the lessons better for you?*

Pathways of Learning © 2000 Zephyr Press, Tucson, Arizona • 800-232-2187 • http://zephyrpress.com

Parallel Curriculum Interface

8-IN-1 ACTIVITIES

Personal Exploration and Discovery

The exercises suggested here can instantly move students to the higher-order realms of each of the intelligences. Your goal should be to find unexpected, unusual, even bizarre ways of utilizing the intelligences. The more fun students are having trying to figure out how to apply the intelligences to anything, the more they will be learning about the many possibilities inherent in the different intelligences. Try out ideas on yourself first so that you can coach students on possibilities as they are involved in the various 8-in-1 extensions.

Personal Exploration and Discovery Exercises

➤ **Eight Ways of Knowing Party.** Work with students to plan a celebration around the theme of the eight intelligences. Have them work in eight teams, each representing one of the intelligences. They are to create costumes for themselves that communicate the intelligence they are representing, an intelligence game for the rest of the class to play, a snack that represents their intelligence, and a decoration for the room.

➤ **Designing the MI School.** Group students in teams of five. They are to pretend that they are multiple intelligence architects. Their task is to create a school environment that supports and nurtures the eight ways of knowing. Students should consider such things as the decor, space arrangement, supplies and materials, equipment, music, time schedule, and so on Each group is to draw the blueprint of what this new, multimodal school would look like.

➤ **Intelligence Games.** Have students get into eight groups, one for each intelligence. Each group makes a list of games and puzzles that require the use of their assigned intelligence; for example Scrabble™ for verbal/linguistic, Pictionary™ for visual/spatial, or hopscotch for bodily/kinesthetic. The groups then invent a new game, that accesses the capacities and skills of their assigned intelligence. Over the next several weeks, allow each group to lead the class in playing its new game.

Commentary: Personal MI Exploration and Discovery

The 8-in-1 Activities promote an amplified awareness of multiple intelligences and the many possibilities for using them consciously. These kinds of exercises will definitely stretch students beyond their comfort zones. Therefore, it is important that you create a safe, relatively risk-free environment in which to experiment with these exercises. Frequently remind students that some of the intelligences are more developed than others in all of us, and that any less developed intelligence can be strengthened.

8-IN-1 ACTIVITIES

Academic Exploration and Discovery

One of the most exciting ways to make students
aware of the possibilities of the eight ways of
knowing is to force the use of all of the intelligences in learning specific curricular concepts,
ideas, or tasks. This may not work equally well for all concepts you have to teach.
Make your own empirical judgments about when this is appropriate. Be careful
that you don't let your own biases, comfort zones, or more developed intelligences
rule out the creative possibilities here.

Academic Exploration and Discovery Strategies

➤ **Round Robin Intelligence.** Put students in groups of eight, with each student representing one of the intelligences (preferably self-chosen). Assign the
groups to learn a particular concept or idea from the current lesson. Each
person in the group must help the total group learn the assigned material
using the intelligence he or she is representing.

➤ **Illustrating a Story or Reading.** Break students into eight groups, one for
each intelligence. Read them a story or article and have the groups brainstorm various ways that the story could be "illustrated" using the media appropriate to their assigned intelligence; for example, sounds, music, and
rhythm; colors, images, textures, and designs; or physical gestures, movement, and dance. Read the story or article again, this time with each group
performing its "illustration."

➤ **Multilayered Homework.** Create homework assignments that require students to use all eight intelligences. Discuss the assignment with the class and
be prepared to answer their questions and/or give examples of how they
might complete the various tasks.

Commentary: Multiple Intelligences and the Learning Process
This strategy will stretch both you and your students to look at the
traditional academic content in very new and creative ways. Begin
by having students deal with easier topics where the connection to
the eight intelligences is more obvious. Then, systematically move
to explore less obvious connections and possibilities. In this process,
whole new levels of understanding and excitement about learning
may emerge. You may even find that you are learning new things
about content whose meaning you thought you had exhausted!

8-IN-1 ACTIVITIES

Beyond-the-Classroom Exploration and Discovery

The Latin-American philosopher, Ortega y Gasset, once remarked that so many things fail to interest us simply because we do not approach them on a sufficient number of planes. In the language of multiple intelligences, I would amend his insight by saying that we don't approach them using all of our potential intelligences. The use of the 8-in-1 Activities can instantly help us move almost anything in our lives to many more levels of our brain/mind/body system, thus amplifying our experience of living.

Beyond-the-Classroom Exploration and Discovery Applications

➤ **"Juicing-Up" Daily Living.** Have students make a list of things that bore them in their lives beyond school. Assign them to create a plan, using the eight intelligences, for injecting some multimodal interest into these situations. Then have them implement their plans and report on the results to the rest of the class at a later time.

➤ **Amplifying My Interests.** Ask students to list things that interest them outside of school; for example, hobbies, after school activities, and so on. Then ask them to use an 8-in-1 Activities exercise to discover new aspects of these areas of interest.

➤ **Communication Times Eight.** Ask students to experiment with using all eight intelligences to enhance their communication with others when they are trying explain something to someone else. Have them try this with several different people then report the results to the class.

Commentary: Multiple Intelligences and Everyday Life

Contemporary brain/mind/body research has documented that a multisensory approach to living enlivens the brain (it helps grow dendrites!), and also engages the totality of our beings in whatever we are doing. When we consciously tap into the eight intelligences, we are virtually assured of accessing this full range of possibilities. Awareness of multiple intelligences and the various strategies gives one a relatively easy checklist of possible ways to explore and/ or experience any aspect of daily life.

Logical/Mathematical
- Outlining
- Graphic organizers
- Numbers
- Problem solving
- Pattern games

Verbal/Linguistic
- Reading
- Writing
- Poetry
- Telling jokes
- Storytelling

Visual/Spatial
- Painting
- Drawing
- Finding pictures
- Pretending
- Sculpting
- Pictures

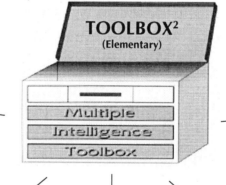

TOOLBOX²
(Elementary)

Multiple Intelligence Toolbox

Intrapersonal
- Silent reflection
- Thinking strategies
- Feelings awareness
- Self-esteem practice
- Concentration skills

Musical/Rhythmic
- Making music and beats
- Humming
- Making sounds
- Playing music
- Singing

Interpersonal
- Giving feedback
- Understanding others' feelings
- Division of labor
- Receiving feedback

Naturalist
- Growing things
- Collecting natural stuff
- Raising animals
- Classifying nature
- Using things from nature

Bodily/Kinesthetic
- Dancing
- Role-playing
- Physical gestures
- Body language
- Physical exercise

2. Adapted from Lazear, David. *Eight Ways of Knowing*. Palatine, Ill.: Skylight, 1998.
Pathways of Learning © 2000 Zephyr Press, Tucson, Arizona • 800-232-2187 • http://zephyrpress.com

Verbal/Linguistic
- Reading
- Vocabulary
- Formal speech
- Journal or diary keeping
- Creative writing
- Poetry
- Oral debate
- Impromptu speaking
- Humor or telling jokes
- Storytelling

Logical/Mathematical
- Abstract symbols and formulas
- Outlining
- Graphic organizers
- Number sequences
- Calculation
- Deciphering codes
- Forcing relationships
- Syllogisms
- Problem solving
- Pattern games

Visual/Spatial
- Guided imagery
- Active imagination
- Color schemes
- Patterns and designs
- Painting
- Drawing
- Mind mapping
- Pretending
- Sculpture
- Pictures

Intrapersonal
- Silent reflection methods
- Metacognition techniques
- Thinking strategies
- Emotional processing
- "Know thyself" practices
- Mindfulness practices
- Focusing and concentration skills
- Higher-order reasoning
- Complex guided imagery
- "Centering" practices

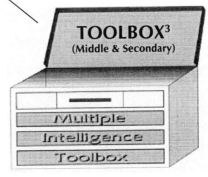

TOOLBOX[3]
(Middle & Secondary)

Multiple
Intelligence
Toolbox

Musical/Rhythmic
- Rhythmic patterns
- Vocal sounds and tones
- Music composition and creation
- Percussion vibrations
- Humming
- Environmental sounds
- Instrumental sounds
- Singing
- Tonal patterns
- Music performance

Interpersonal
- Giving feedback
- Intuiting others' feelings
- Cooperative learning strategies
- Person-to-person communication
- Empathy practices
- Division of labor
- Collaboration skills
- Receiving feedback
- Sensing others' motives
- Group projects

Naturalist
- Archetypal pattern recognition
- Caring for plants/animals
- Conservation practices
- Environmental feedback
- Hands-on labs
- Nature encounters/field trips
- Nature observation
- Natural world simulations
- Species classification (organic/inorganic)
- Sensory stimulation exercises

Bodily/Kinesthetic
- Folk or creative dance
- Role-playing
- Physical gestures
- Drama
- Martial arts
- Body language
- Physical exercise
- Mime
- Inventing
- Sports

3. Adapted from Lazear, David. *Eight Ways of Knowing.* Palatine, Ill.: Skylight, 1998.
Pathways of Learning © 2000 Zephyr Press, Tucson, Arizona • 800-232-2187 • http://zephyrpress.com

8-In-1 Exercises
(Elementary)

Activity Cards

Tie your shoes.	**Brush your teeth.**
Pick up your room.	**Wash your face and hands.**
Care for a pet.	**Use good table manners.**

 Pathways of Learning © 2000 Zephyr Press, Tucson, Arizona • 800-232-2187 • http://zephyrpress.com

8-In-1 Exercises
(Middle School)

Activity Cards

Meet people at a party.

Order food at McDonald's.

Shop for a new pair of shoes.

Make up after an argument.

Tell parents about your day.

Meet your friends at the mall.

8-In-1 Exercises
(Secondary)

Activity Cards

Ask someone for a date.	**Fill out a job application.**
Think about college opportunities.	**Tell a friend about a problem.**
Plan a party with your friends.	**Say "NO" to drugs in different ways.**

Teacher's Personal Reflection Log

8-IN-1 ACTIVITIES

I have the following thoughts/insights about the 8-in-1 Activities strategy:

I feel that the 8-in-1 Activities strategy can help me in my teaching in the following ways:

As a learning process, the 8-in-1 Activities strategy includes the following benefits for my students:

I have the following specific ideas for using the 8-in-1 Activities strategy in my classroom in the near future:

I think the 8-in-1 Activities strategy can be used beyond the classroom and school in the following ways:

Intelligence Think-Pair-Share

INTRODUCTION

This exercise asks students to share their everyday experiences of using the eight ways of knowing to help each other find applications of the intelligences in their lives beyond school. The sharing will provide new insights and new ideas for all students regarding possible uses for the eight intelligences.

OBJECTIVE

The goal of the exercise is to allow students to exchange information regarding their intelligences and how the intelligences are part of everyday living.

DISCUSSION

This particular learning strategy is one of the best for teaching students the social skill of listening to another person. Having to paraphrase what their partners said is the acid test of whether they were really listening. After the first round of think-pair-share, brainstorm a list of ideas, based on this experience, that students could use to be better listeners. Then give them an opportunity to work with different partners and do the exercise again, this time trying to improve their listening by applying some of the suggestions from the list.

EXPLORATION AND DISCOVERY BASE EXERCISE: INTELLIGENCE THINK-PAIR-SHARE

Exercise Procedures

1. Project the grade-appropriate work sheet on an overhead or write it on the board (see pp. 127–129). Address each question in turn and give students a minute to think of an experience they have had or a time they used the particular intelligences implied in the questions. Have them make a few notes to themselves to use later in the exercise when they share their experiences with partners.

2. After you have been through all of the questions, have students choose a partner, one who they don't know too well—not a good friend in the class.

3. Have the pairs decide who will be person A and who will be person B.

   • Person B quickly shares his or her list of times when he or she used the intelligences.
   • Person A listens carefully to what person B shares. When person B is finished, person A takes a few moments to ask person B questions or to ask for more details on anything person A found particularly interesting.
   • Now person A is to try to remember the eight things person B shared. Person B may coach person A.
   • Repeat the process with person A sharing and person B listening.

4. Have each pair join with another pair. Each person, in turn, is to share with the foursome what his or her partner shared in as much detail as he or she can remember. The former partners may amend and clarify as necessary.

5. After all four people have shared their partners' experiences with multiple intelligences, have each person write his or her answers to the following questions:

- *How did hearing about others' experiences with multiple intelligences help you?*
- *What new ideas for using the intelligences did you get from each other?*

6. After students have completed the think- pair-share as a foursome and have answered the discussion questions, pull the class back together and lead them in the following reflection:

   - *What was the most interesting thing you heard from someone else about how he or she uses or has used the multiple intelligences?*
   - *How does this kind of sharing make you feel? What did you like? Not like?*
   - *Ask several groups to share their answers to the two questions in number 5.*
   - *Quickly go around the class and have each person complete the sentence "One new intelligent thing I plan to try is . . ."*

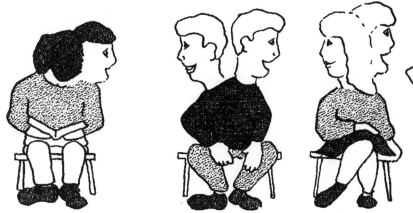

Parallel Curriculum Interface

THINK-PAIR-SHARE

Personal Exploration and Discovery

At the heart of any Think-Pair-Share exercise is the development of students' listening skills and genuine comprehension of what is being communicated by another person. This particular learning strategy is one of the best for teaching students the social skill of listening. Having to paraphrase what their partner said is the acid test of whether they were really listening. When one brings all the intelligences to bear on this task, new levels of comprehension appear.

Personal Exploration and Discovery Exercises

➤ **Paraphrased Interviews.** Assign students to create questions for an interview based on the use of and feelings about particular intelligences. After the interviews, each student is to write a brief summary about what their partner communicated in the interview via various intelligences. Have students check the accuracy of their summaries with the appropriate partners.

➤ **Listening between the Lines.** Have each student get with a partner that they do not know well. Each partner is to have "air time" to tell about an important event in their life; for example, a family vacation, the birth of a sibling, and so on. As one person tells a story, the other is to listen to the verbal telling. At the same time, the partner must listen to the nonverbal signals used to communicate the story: for example, body language, voice tone and sounds, breathing patterns, visible emotions, and so on.

➤ **Tattle-Tale Conversations.** Have each student find a partner and discuss how he or she uses the eight intelligences in their daily lives. This pair then joins another pair and each member of this foursome tells about his or her former partner and what was learned about their partner's daily use of the intelligences.

Commentary: Personal MI Exploration and Discovery

The listening that is developed in and through the use of the Think-Pair-Share strategy helps students learn to trust the different intelligences and the unique way each knows. It helps them interpret the information received from each intelligence, only one of which communicates in words. It also helps them learn to express their own emotions, thoughts, ideas, concerns, and feelings in different ways. Often the things that matter the most to us simply cannot be adequately expressed in words alone.

 Pathways of Learning © 2000 Zephyr Press, Tucson, Arizona • 800-232-2187 • http://zephyrpress.com

THINK-PAIR-SHARE

Academic Exploration and Discovery

As you design academic extensions for the base Think-Pair-Share process, make sure that you create tasks that require students to *listen through the unique cognitive modality* of each of the eight intelligences. Allow for a wide range of expressive forms and interpretive possibilities. In your instructions, help students understand how each intelligence expresses its knowing and the media each employs.

Academic Exploration and Discovery Strategies

➤ **Multimedia Reporting.** In groups of three or four, students are to listen carefully to an audiotape of a famous speech, and then create a multimodal report on what they heard. For example, create an image to go along with the report; decide on a musical introduction; make up appropriate body gestures or physical movements to interpret the spoken words; or share the feelings the report evoked.

➤ **Intelligence Communication Clues.** Have several students read a serious, short piece of poetry to the class. Students then turn to a partner and experiment with changing the meaning of the poem through tone of voice, body posture, gestures, facial expressions, and so on.

➤ **Conversations from the Past.** Ask students to write the name of a historical or literary figure you have been studying. Have students get with a partner to imagine they are the figure they listed. Assign a question to discuss "in character;" that is, saying and doing what their figure would say and do.

Commentary: Multiple Intelligences and the Learning Process

One of the qualifying criteria for the intelligences in Howard Gardner's original research was its potential to be encoded in some symbolic notational form (1983). Each intelligence has its own very special language, jargon, vernacular, and *modus operandi*. The key to Think-Pair-Share exercises is to help students crawl inside the various intelligences, and to listen and/or express themselves using its unique cognitive modality. Encourage them to trust the information they receive from the different intelligences as well as their own intuitions.

THINK-PAIR-SHARE

Beyond-the-Classroom Exploration and Discovery

In our daily lives, we often find ourselves stuck because we can think of only one way to solve a problem or deal with a difficult situation. The Think-Pair-Share strategy can help us break through these stuck places and find solutions and/or directions. The key to this "destuckification" is to process things on as many levels as possible. The conscious use of multiple intelligences can rapidly take us into these alternative ways of looking at a problem or challenging situation we are experiencing.

Beyond-the-Classroom Exploration and Discovery Applications

➤ **Think-Pair-Share at Home.** Have students brainstorm a list of situations where the Think-Pair-Share strategy might work: a family discussion where there are different points of view; as a way to debrief each other on the events of the day; or as a mediation strategy when there is disagreement. After making the list, have students work in groups of three or four to help each other think of how they could adapt the strategy for each situation.

➤ **Think-Pair-Share Problem Solving with a Friend.** Ask students to create a plan for solving a problem or dealing with a difficult challenge. It must involve processing the information related to the challenge using all of the intelligences; for example, not only talking about the problem, but drawing it, acting it out, singing about it, and so on.

➤ **Think-Pair-Share with Imaginary Partners.** Ask students to imagine what it would be like if they could discuss problems, issues, or challenges with their favorite TV, movie, or literary characters. Have them experiment having an imaginary conversation with this partner, thinking about what this character might say to them, and what they would say to the character.

Commentary: Multiple Intelligences and Everyday Life

At the heart of this process is accessing the full cognitive potential of each intelligence. As students think about and anticipate situations in which the use of multiple intelligences might help them, they are reinforcing and deepening their own awareness of these potentials within themselves. They should be encouraged to find someone outside of school, with whom they can engage in the Think-Pair-Share exercise—both for expressing ideas and getting intelligent feedback in at least eight different ways.

Think-Pair-Share
(Elementary)

Answer these questions:

1. What do you like to read?

2. When do you use numbers?

3. What do you like to draw?

4. What games do you like to play?

5. What music do you like?

6. Do you like to talk to others?

7. What do you do when you're alone?

8. What is your favorite animal or plant?

Think-Pair-Share
(Middle School)

Can you think of a time when . . .

1. You read something outside of school that was really interesting to you?

2. You used math to help you in your everyday life?

3. You drew something to help you communicate with someone else?

4. You played a game in which you used your body a lot?

5. You listened to music to help you relax or to help you be more creative?

6. You asked a friend for advice on a personal problem or challenge you were facing?

7. You spent some time alone just thinking?

8. You especially enjoyed being out in nature, away from the humanly created world?

Think-Pair-Share
(Secondary)

When have you experienced the following situations?

1. **You read something that was important or meaningful to you and you discussed it with someone else.**

2. **You used math concepts or processes to help you solve a problem in your everyday life.**

3. **You used drawing, painting, or sculpture to express something you were feeling or thinking.**

4. **You used body language, physical gestures, or role-playing to help you communicate.**

5. **You used music to change how you were feeling or to improve your performance in an activity.**

6. **You were part of a successful team and could talk about the factors that contributed to its success.**

7. **You learned something new about yourself: how you think, how you feel, what you believe, or what you think is really important.**

8. **You learned something about yourself from the natural world or you felt "at one with nature."**

Teacher's Personal Reflection Log

INTELLIGENCE THINK-PAIR-SHARE

I have the following thoughts/insights about the Intelligence Think-Pair-Share strategy:

I feel that the Intelligence Think-Pair-Share strategy can help me in my teaching in the following ways:

As a learning process, the Intelligence Think-Pair-Share strategy includes the following benefits for my students:

I have the following specific ideas for using the Intelligence Think-Pair-Share strategy in my classroom in the near future:

I think the Intelligence Think-Pair-Share strategy can be used beyond the classroom and school in the following ways:

Pathways of Learning © 2000 Zephyr Press, Tucson, Arizona • 800-232-2187 • http://zephyrpress.com

EXPLORATION AND DISCOVERY BASE EXERCISE: SELF-ANALYSIS

Exercise Procedures

1. Tell students that in this exercise they will analyze the relative strengths and weaknesses of their own eight ways of knowing. The first part of the lesson is an individual task.

2. Project the appropriate self-analysis chart from the examples (pp. 136–138) on the overhead or draw it on the board. Have students reproduce the chart on a piece of blank paper. They will analyze their intelligences. Ask students to do their analyses in silence, trying to be as honest as they can about their feelings. Encourage them to trust their first instinct or to go with their first impression of what their responses should be. Now explain how it works:

   - **Elementary.** For each question on the chart, have students draw the face that expresses how they feel about the question. If they need to draw a different face from those at the top of the chart, they may.

   - **Middle.** For each way of knowing, there are three items listed. In the columns at the far right, have students rank themselves based on how much they like to do and how good they are at each component. They will use the plus and minus scale at the top of the page as their ranking guide. Each of the twenty-four items should have a mark beside it when the students are finished.

   - **Secondary.** Students will evaluate how well they use the skills or capacities listed under each of the eight intelligences. The students will use the scale at the top of the page as a guide. Each item should have a number between 0 and 10 beside it. When students have answered each of the questions, they will total the numbers by each intelligence and place the figure in the column at the right.

Self-Analysis

INTRODUCTION

In this exercise, students have an opportunity to take a good look at themselves and to evaluate their intelligence strengths and weaknesses. Students will also create an initial plan for improving any weaknesses they discover.

OBJECTIVE

The goal of this exercise is to provide students with a chance to get to know themselves and their intelligences better. It also helps them discover that they can be proactive in the development of their intelligence capacities.

DISCUSSION

The trick to being successful with this strategy is to get students to be honest in their analysis of themselves. One of the keys to achieving this honesty is to make sure they understand that the analysis contains no judgments of good or bad. We are all strong in certain intelligences and weak in others. The good news about doing this kind of self-analysis is that as soon as we are aware of certain strengths and weaknesses, we can capitalize on the strengths and work to improve the weaknesses.

3. Now have each student turn to a partner and compare his or her responses with that partner's. Have students ask themselves the following questions:

- *What immediately strikes you as you look at your charts?*
- *What surprises you? Intrigues you? Bothers you? Confuses you? Pleases you?*
- *What does this activity tell you about yourself?*

4. Have students make two lists with their partners:

- *List at least five things you can do to capitalize on and use your own intelligence strengths more fully in your daily classroom work.*
- *List at least five things you can do to stretch your intelligence weaknesses to create a greater balance and use all eight ways of knowing.*

5. Call the class back together and lead them in a brief general discussion using the following. Ask for several volunteers to share what happened.

- *What did you discover as you did your self-analysis?*
- *What are some of the ideas you and your partner thought of to help you use your stronger intelligences more?*
- *What are some ideas you had for stretching your weaknesses?*
- *How can we use this information to help us create a more interesting classroom where we are using all intelligences for teaching and learning? Make a list of ideas on a piece of newsprint.*

You might consider having students choose something each day from their lists to try and implement while they are in your class, on the school grounds, or in the cafeteria with their friends.

Parallel Curriculum Interface

SELF-ANALYSIS

Personal Exploration and Discovery

As you design different Self-Analysis exercises, make sure to give equal weight to each of the intelligences and/or to all of the capacities of a single intelligence, if this is the focus of the analysis. Also make sure that the various analyses are growth-oriented, as opposed to evaluating strengths and weaknesses as good and bad. The point of each analysis should be gaining more awareness of one's own intelligence profile.

Personal Exploration and Discovery Exercises

➤ **Intelligence Instant Replay.** Ask students to individually make lists of at least three recent situations in which they had to make a decision. Have them reconsider each decision from the perspective of the eight intelligences, pretending they can do an "instant replay" of the decision. As it replays, they can change anything that occurs to them as they think about the eight intelligences. Then have them share other suggestions with a partner.

➤ **Intelligence Safari.** Ask students to track their use of the eight ways of knowing in a notebook. Choose three consecutive weeks for students to list which intelligences they were most aware of using during the day, including when and where descriptions. At the end of each week have them hunt for a weekly pattern. Which intelligences were used most? Least? Have students then create a plan for using more intelligences the next week.

➤ **Multimodal Communication.** Have each student make a list of recent experiences of trying to communicate an idea or thought to someone else. Ask them to analyze how the effectiveness of their communication could have been improved if they had used the eight intelligences; for example, using visuals (appropriate body language and gestures), variations of voice tone, pitch, and other sounds. Now have them get with a partner and replay their earlier communication, incorporating their ideas.

Commentary: Personal MI Exploration and Discovery

The trick to success with this strategy is to get students to be honest in their analysis of themselves. Make sure they understand that the analysis contains no judgments of good or bad. We are all strong in certain intelligence areas and weak in others. As we are aware of certain strengths and weaknesses, we can do something about them, intentionally capitalizing on the strengths and working to improve the weaknesses.

SELF-ANALYSIS

Academic Exploration and Discovery

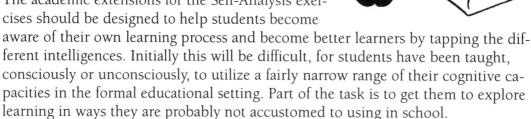

The academic extensions for the Self-Analysis exercises should be designed to help students become aware of their own learning process and become better learners by tapping the different intelligences. Initially this will be difficult, for students have been taught, consciously or unconsciously, to utilize a fairly narrow range of their cognitive capacities in the formal educational setting. Part of the task is to get them to explore learning in ways they are probably not accustomed to using in school.

Academic Exploration and Discovery Strategies

➤ **Your Intelligence Comfort Zones.** After completing a lesson in which you employed the eight ways of knowing, have students rank themselves on a continuum regarding the affective or feeling aspects of the different intelligences: for example, "I felt like a fish in water" (very comfortable, felt at home) to "I felt like I had landed on another planet" (very foreign to me). Then have them work in pairs to compare rankings, discussing the reasons for their responses.

➤ **The Homework Connection.** Ask each student to list all the homework assignments he or she can remember from the past week. For each, they should name the intelligence that was predominant. Then go back through the list and write down things they could have done that would have made the homework more interesting, fun, or easier, and might have helped them learn more by using all of the intelligences.

➤ **MI Analysis of Others.** Design an exercise which asks students to use the eyeglasses of multiple intelligences to analyze the actions of a character in literature, a historical figure, social or economic factors which shaped society, scientific discoveries or inventions, aspects of another culture, people in the news, and so on.

Commentary: Multiple Intelligences and the Learning Process
The more students know about the teaching and learning process, the more active and responsible learners they become. We should keep no secrets from our students about the teaching and learning process. Self-Analysis exercises may help students get to know their own learning process intimately via the intelligences. By doing the Self-Analysis exercises, students can often become advocates for themselves and their own learning.

SELF-ANALYSIS

Beyond-the-Classroom Exploration and Discovery

Provide students with an ongoing, easy-to-adapt process of thinking about and reflecting on their life experience using multiple intelligences. Your job is to help them think of many ways to introduce and incorporate multiple intelligences analysis into their regular, daily routine.

Beyond-the-Classroom Exploration and Discovery Applications

➤ **Self-Analysis Journal Writing.** Create a journaling process which asks students to reflect on a day, week, event, experience, and so on. They are to analyze their use of the different intelligences during a specified time period or in a certain situation.

➤ **Analysis of Human Encounters.** Have students create an analysis which asks for reflection on an encounter—positive or negative—with another person. The categories of the analysis should explore the intelligences that were used during the encounter as well as those intelligences that might have been employed to improve communication, deepen the experience, and so on.

➤ **MI Analysis of "Tough Times."** Ask students to think about difficult times in their lives. Have them analyze how they have used the different intelligences during those times and what they can do in the future to use more of the intelligences to help them cope more effectively with life's challenges.

Commentary: Multiple Intelligences and Everyday Life
Improving the self-reflective capacities is the main benefit of making the Self-Analysis exercise a regular part of the daily experience. Pre-planning and scheduling such exercises can help make this kind of self-awareness almost an automatic part of one's daily experience.

Self-Analysis
(Elementary)

What Do I Like?		
:)	:(	:|
Reading and writing		
Working with numbers		
Drawing and painting		
Body stuff		
Singing		
Working with others		
Being alone		
Being out in nature		

Pathways of Learning © 2000 Zephyr Press, Tucson, Arizona • 800-232-2187 • http://zephyrpress.com

Self-Analysis
(Middle School)

What do I like and what am I good at?		
+++ = "super!" – – – = "ugh!" ++ = "okay" – – = "fair" + = "so, so" – = "so, so"	**Pluses**	**Minuses**
Verbal/Linguistic:		
reading		
writing		
speaking		
Logical/Mathematical:		
working with numbers		
solving problems		
thinking logically		
Visual/Spatial:		
pretending and using the imagination		
drawing/painting/working with clay		
finding my way		
Bodily/Kinesthetic:		
playing roles		
playing physical games		
exercising my body		
Musical/Rhythmic:		
singing or playing music		
sounding rhythm or beats		
recognizing different sounds		
Interpersonal:		
listening to others		
encouraging and supporting others		
being part of a team		
Intrapersonal:		
talking positively to myself		
being aware of my feelings		
liking to do some things alone		
Naturalist:		
growing things		
raising/training animals		
recognizing patterns in nature		

Self-Analysis
(Secondary)

What am I good at?		
10 = WOW! **10 9 8 7 6 5 4 3 2 1 0** 0 = UGH!	Individual Capacity Ranking	Totals
Verbal/Linguistic: 1. Reading and understanding what I've read 2. Communicating through writing something I'm thinking 3. Making a speech or giving a report		
Logical/Mathematical: 1. Doing math in my head 2. Knowing that I've received the correct change at the store 3. Figuring out how to solve everyday problems		
Visual/Spatial: 1. Finding my way using a map 2. Drawing an object or scene on paper 3. Pretending or imagining things		
Bodily/Kinesthetic: 1. Playing charades or roles (as in drama) 2. Dancing or playing games that require body movement 3. Exercising my body for better body performance		
Musical/Rhythmic: 1. Being able to hum a tune I've heard on the radio or a tape 2. Recognizing different recorded instruments and sounds 3. Using music to alter my feelings and moods		
Interpersonal: 1. Listening to others' opinions and feelings (even when I disagree) 2. Doing my part when I'm part of a team project 3. Giving encouragement and positive support to other people		
Intrapersonal: 1. Spending time alone thinking things through 2. Being aware of and dealing with my own feelings 3. Evaluating my own thinking patterns and improving them		
Naturalist: 1. Classifying different plants and animals. 2. Knowing how to use things from nature 3. Understanding patterns in the natural world		

Teacher's Personal Reflection Log

SELF-ANALYSIS

I have the following thoughts/insights about the Self-Analysis strategy:

I feel that the Self-Analysis strategy can help me in my teaching in the following ways:

As a learning process, the Self-Analysis strategy includes the following benefits for my students:

I have the following specific ideas for using the Self-Analysis strategy in my classroom in the near future:

I think the Self-Analysis strategy can be used beyond the classroom and school in the following ways:

Exercises for Strategic Use of the Intelligences

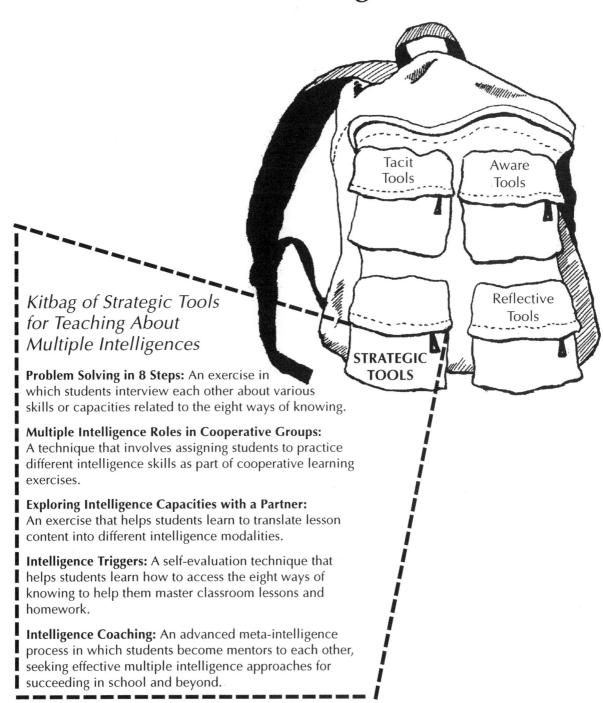

Kitbag of Strategic Tools for Teaching About Multiple Intelligences

Problem Solving in 8 Steps: An exercise in which students interview each other about various skills or capacities related to the eight ways of knowing.

Multiple Intelligence Roles in Cooperative Groups: A technique that involves assigning students to practice different intelligence skills as part of cooperative learning exercises.

Exploring Intelligence Capacities with a Partner: An exercise that helps students learn to translate lesson content into different intelligence modalities.

Intelligence Triggers: A self-evaluation technique that helps students learn how to access the eight ways of knowing to help them master classroom lessons and homework.

Intelligence Coaching: An advanced meta-intelligence process in which students become mentors to each other, seeking effective multiple intelligence approaches for succeeding in school and beyond.

It was the day after the big unit test in Mr. Boggs's high school chemistry class. As a whole, the class had not done well. And it was doubly distressing to Mr. Boggs because the very students he thought understood the material best did poorest on the test. He decided to talk with the class and ask them what went wrong.

Some of the comments he got follow:

> *I don't know what went wrong. When we are in the lab and I can be doing chemistry, I understand it perfectly. It's when I have to write about it that I seem to lose it all.*

> *The test was fake. Where in real life would we ever have to go off by ourselves and answer a bunch of dumb ol' questions? In class we could talk to each other. We could ask you questions. We could relate. I know a lot more than I could show you on the test!*

> *Chemistry is seeing stuff happen, like when you mix things together and the solution changes color, or starts to smoke, or makes a bad smell. When you taught us you used all kinds of cool drawings to help us imagine what was going on in a chemical reaction. How come we couldn't draw on the test?*

These and other comments came like a bolt of lightning to Mr. Boggs. He had been using multiple intelligences to teach chemistry for some time and had discovered that students not only enjoyed his class more, but they seemed to understand the material better.

The tragic flaw was that he had expected them to make the transfer of learning suddenly from a full-blown "multi" intelligence teaching and learning situation to a "mono" intelligence paper-and-pencil test.

This experience caused Mr. Boggs to move in several new directions in his classroom. First, he started helping students develop bridging or transfer strategies for classroom activities in which the students were engaged. Second, he placed students in multiple intelligence coaching teams and gave them the written test again. This time, however, they were allowed to help each other "translate" the verbal/linguistic stuff into other intelligence modalities, which gave all the students a chance to win and use all their intelligences on the test itself. Third, on future tests Mr. Boggs offered a variety of ways from which students could choose to demonstrate what they knew; he also required everyone to use at least three different intelligences in addition to the verbal/linguistic.

Needless to say, all Mr. Boggs's students were much more successful on the next test, which made Mr. Boggs much happier.

EXPLORATION AND DISCOVERY BASE EXERCISE: PROBLEM SOLVING IN 8 STEPS

Exercise Procedures

1. Lead students in a preliminary discussion of what they usually do when they have a problem to solve.

   - Have each student list two to three problems he or she has solved recently. Get a random sampling of the kinds of problems the students listed.
   - Have them individually list the steps they went through to find a solution.
   - Have each student turn to a neighbor and compare and contrast problem-solving approaches.
   - On the overhead list some of the steps students used to solve problems. Try to get a cross-section of the variety of approaches different individuals used.

2. Place students into cooperative groups of three to four. Assign each group one of the problem scenarios from the examples (see pp. 148–150). The students' task is to find eight different ways to approach solving their assigned problem. Have them figure out the intelligence-appropriate steps to use for solving the problem. Once they have mapped out these steps, have them role-play the situation using the intelligence steps they have created and see what happens.

   Make sure students know that they can do anything they want to find a solution. Also make sure that a wide variety of media are available for their use: colored markers, paints, clay, musical and percussion instruments, and so on. Proposing creative solutions that use the eight intelligences is more important than finding the "right" answer.

3. Allow time for each team to share the variety of things they did to find a solution to their assigned problem.

Problem Solving in 8 Steps

INTRODUCTION

This exercise involves students in problem-solving tasks that bring all eight intelligences to bear on a single problem. When we use more of the brain's full intellectual potential on a single problem we can often find more and better solutions.

OBJECTIVE

The goal of the exercise is for students to learn how they can use the eight intelligences in any situation that presents a problem or a challenge and for them to discover that using all the intelligences creates a deeper, richer, and more varied approach to the task of living.

DISCUSSION

Problem Solving in 8 Steps involves learning to use the eight intelligences to amplify possibilities and options to solve problems and meet life's challenges. The same results can happen when all eight intelligences are brought to bear on the learning and processing of daily classroom material. While I am not suggesting that every lesson should be an 8-in-1 exercise, I believe that it is important that students (and teachers) realize that anything and everything can be taught and learned in eight different ways. The more levels on which a lesson is taught and learned, the more integrated the knowing and learning experience becomes for students.

4. After each team has given its report, lead your class in the following discussion of the lesson:

- *What happened as you tried to use all eight intelligences to solve a single problem?*

- *What happened to your understanding or perception of the problem?*

- *What was helpful to you? What was not helpful?*

- *What have you learned that you think can help you when you have everyday problems to solve or new challenges to meet?*

Pathways of Learning © 2000 Zephyr Press, Tucson, Arizona • 800-232-2187 • http://zephyrpress.com

Parallel Curriculum Interface

PROBLEM SOLVING IN 8 STEPS

Personal Exploration and Discovery

As you work to design additional exercises for the Problem-Solving in 8 Steps strategy, your goal should be to amplify students' possibilities and options in problem solving and meeting life's challenges using their multiple intelligences. Create activities and tasks that require students to access all of the intelligences. Also make sure they understand these goals—they will rise to the challenge.

Personal Exploration and Discovery Exercises

➤ **School Issues Debate.** Make a list of students' issues or concerns about their school. Divide students into groups of three or four, assigning each group one issue. Each group is to create a plan for approaching the issue using the eight intelligences; for example, posters, slogans, songs, dance routines, interviews with teachers and students, personal opinion polls, and so on. Have each group share its plan and discuss possible next steps.

➤ **Intelligence on TV.** Pre-record a slice of a soap opera, sitcom, or drama and show it to the class. At a critical turning point, stop the action and brainstorm eight possible decisions (based on the eight intelligences) that could be made. Then start the video again and see what decisions were made and what happened as a result. Discuss the pros and cons in light of the possible decisions brainstormed earlier.

➤ **Solving Scintillating Scenarios.** On several pieces of paper create a series of scenarios that involve problems, challenges, or issues that are age-appropriate for your students. Divide the class into teams and put the scenarios in a hat. Teams draw one out of the hat and try to be the first team to come up with eight different, viable ways to solve the problems.

Commentary: Personal MI Exploration and Discovery

When students are asked to move their thinking about problems onto more planes than usual, surprising solutions to seemingly unsolvable issues often emerge. The Problem Solving in 8 Steps exercise will get them started. Once they get into it, the exercise will tend to carry itself. Make sure you are available to help students if they get stuck with any of the intelligences.

PROBLEM SOLVING IN 8 STEPS

Academic Exploration and Discovery

Every lesson does not need to incorporate all eight intelligences. Nevertheless, I strongly believe that anything and everything can be both taught and learned eight different ways. At the heart of this strategy is research which supports the concept that the more sensory and cognitive levels that can be brought to bear on the teaching and learning process, the more integrated the knowing/learning experience is for students.

Academic Exploration and Discovery Strategies

➤ **Alternatives to World Problems.** As a whole class, study a contemporary issue facing humanity across the globe. In eight small groups (each group assigned to one of the intelligence areas), have students think of alternatives that should be explored to find an answer to the issue from the perspective of their assigned intelligence. Hold a mock United Nations meeting in which each group presents its recommendation.

➤ **History/Literature Decisions Audit.** Place students in cooperative groups of three to four students. Ask them to analyze key decisions from history or literature using the eight intelligences. Have them discuss the decision using such questions as: "What was the governing intelligence behind this decision?" "What other decisions might have been made if other intelligences had been brought to bear on the decision?" "How might have the outcomes been different or similar had a multiple intelligence approach been used?"

➤ **Review Questions Variety Show.** Divide students into eight groups, each representing one of the eight ways of knowing. Give the groups a set of review questions at the end of a lesson or unit. Each group is to brainstorm appropriate answers to the questions for the group's assigned intelligence area. They are then to prepare a presentation to the rest of the class where they share their answers in the modality of their assigned intelligence.

Commentary: Multiple Intelligences and the Learning Process
The more ways in which we know something, the more we really know (and understand) it. This type of exercise asks students to explore subject content on as many intelligence levels as possible. Not all the intelligences will work equally well for all students (nor with all content). However, almost all of them will find a much greater interest in and many new connections with the content using this approach.

PROBLEM SOLVING IN 8 STEPS

Beyond-the-Classroom Exploration and Discovery

We frequently approach solving problems or meeting challenges on only one or two levels. We then often get stuck, and miss many of the creative solutions that may be available by using all of our intelligences. This exercise blasts through this monomodal approach by asking students to bring the creativity of all the intelligences to bear on solving problems and/or meeting the challenges of their normal daily lives.

Beyond-the-Classroom Exploration and Discovery Applications

➤ **Intelligent Approaches to Personal Problems.** Ask students to think of a challenge they are facing. For their particular problem/issue/challenge, ask them to list one possible approach to the problem for each intelligence. Now have them share their approaches with a partner, making helpful suggestions of additional approaches that occur to them. (*NOTE: The focus of this activity is finding a variety of possible problem-solving approaches, not psychological analysis.*)

➤ **8-in-1 Problem-Solving in the Family.** Have students list several issues, challenges, and/or problems with which their family is currently wrestling. Ask students to work with a partner to create a plan for taking multiple intelligence strategies home to help their family look at these issues, challenges, or problems in a new way.

➤ **Peer Problem-Solving Strategy Planning.** Ask students to list difficult situations that often arise with their friends, such as misunderstandings, jealousy, lack of agreement on activities, and so on. Then have them use the eight intelligences to plan strategies to try next time these kinds of difficulties arise.

> ### Commentary: Multiple Intelligences and Everyday Life
> The goal of these kinds of exercises is to help students discover how the intelligences can help deal more creatively with situations, problems, concerns, issues, and so on that they face as part of the task of daily living. Learning to think about these things using all of our intellectual capabilities and prowess can not only help us find solutions for those problems, concerns, and issues but also make living itself a lot more interesting!

Problem Solving in 8 Steps
(Elementary)
Get eight ideas for each of the following suggestions.

What could you do to help if someone has . . .

An argument

Lost money

A sick friend

A broken window

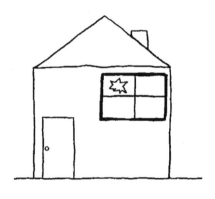

A broken toy

Been left out

Pathways of Learning © 2000 Zephyr Press, Tucson, Arizona • 800-232-2187 • http://zephyrpress.com

Problem Solving in 8 Steps
(Middle School)
Choose three of the situations that follow and see if
you can think of eight "intelligent" responses for each!

What could you do if . . .

You have an argument with a good friend	**You feel misunderstood by a parent**
You lose something that is important to you	**You are accused of something you didn't do**
Someone double-crosses you	**You get some bad news**
You run out of allowance money before the end of a week	**You can't find the homework that you did**
A plan you made for something doesn't work	**You get left out of an activity by your friends** 

Problem Solving in 8 Steps

(Secondary)
Choose a partner, then together choose two
of the scenarios that follow and discuss them.

Can you solve these problems using the eight intelligences?

Scenario 1

Don, a high school junior, comes home from school to discover that his parents have grounded him for something he didn't do. In the past he has not always been totally honest with his parents, so there is a "trust gap" between them. Think of eight "intelligent" ways Don can approach this situation.

Scenario 2

Mary Jo, a high school senior, is planning on going into a business career. She has been rejected by her top three college choices, however, due to the low grades she made in several subjects during her last two years of high school. What are your eight "intelligent" suggestions about what she should do?

Scenario 3

Katrina has recently started to drive. The first time she is allowed to take the family car out by herself, she has a minor accident. She is struggling with how to tell her parents. What are eight "intelligent" ways she could break the news to them?

Scenario 4

Juan is a new student from Mexico. He is shy and doesn't speak English very well. Other students are making fun of him because he is different. See if you can come up with eight "intelligent" ways of helping other students understand and accept Juan.

Scenario 5

You have just discovered that one of your good friends has a serious, life-threatening disease. You want to reaffirm your friendship and your support. Make a list of at least eight "intelligent" ways you could communicate your support.

Scenario 6

Eric, a high school junior, comes from a classic disadvantaged family. For much of his schooling he has been in special education classes. He is considering going to college but is not sure he can make it. Think of eight "intelligent" ways you could encourage him to give it a try.

 Pathways of Learning © 2000 Zephyr Press, Tucson, Arizona • 800-232-2187 • http://zephyrpress.com

Teacher's Personal Reflection Log

PROBLEM SOLVING IN 8 STEPS

I have the following thoughts/insights about the Problem Solving in 8 Steps strategy:

I feel that the Problem Solving in 8 Steps strategy can help me in my teaching in the following ways:

As a learning process, the Problem Solving in 8 Steps strategy includes the following benefits for my students:

I have the following specific ideas for using the Problem Solving in 8 Steps strategy in my classroom in the near future:

I think the Problem Solving in 8 Steps strategy can be used beyond the classroom and school in the following ways:

Multiple Intelligence Roles in Cooperative Groups

INTRODUCTION

This exercise helps students learn how to use their multiple intelligences strategically to add excitement, depth, and breadth to a learning activity. Students will have an opportunity to play roles that embody the various intelligences to assist a cooperative learning group.

OBJECTIVE

The goal of the exercise is for students to learn the skill of playing different roles that will help a group succeed in its task.

DISCUSSION

This exercise is a multiple intelligence adaptation of one of the key strategies of cooperative learning: assigning students roles to play in groups. Multiple intelligences and cooperation go together like a hand and glove. Is it any surprise that cooperative group learning can provide a major boost to students' understanding of and willingness to use their eight ways of knowing? When students are allowed to play a role and everyone knows they are only playing a role, they often can transcend some of their inhibitions and weaknesses. When we actively and vividly imagine something to be real, the brain believes what we actively imagine. It does not know the difference. Think, for example, of what happens when you actively and vividly imagine your favorite food! In this exercise students have a chance to imagine that they are experts in performing various intelligence capacities or skills, the very capacities and skills that, when students are "just themselves," they may not be able to perform.

EXPLORATION AND DISCOVERY BASE EXERCISE: MULTIPLE INTELLIGENCE ROLES IN COOPERATIVE GROUPS

Exercise Procedures

1. Think of an upcoming lesson that lends itself nicely to a cooperative learning structure: a set of vocabulary words that students will need to learn, a reading assignment with distinct parts that individuals could study and teach to others, a set of math problems that students could help each other solve, and so on.

2. Have students get into teams of four. Carefully explain the academic task of the exercise (that is, what students are assigned to do, accomplish, and learn). Ask if there are any questions about the task.

3. After making the assignment and answering any questions, say, "One of our concerns in this exercise is to make sure that we are using our multiple intelligences to help us with the learning goals. Therefore I am going to assign different intelligence roles to each of you so that you can help your group be as intelligent as possible during the lesson." For possible roles you might assign, see the examples that follow this exercise (pp. 157–159).

   Students probably will not need to use eight roles in one lesson, so assign the four that you think are most appropriate. Students will need help in defining the "looks like" and "sounds like" behaviors associated with each role you have assigned. You will also need to decide if you are going to assign the roles randomly or if you will allow each group to make their own assignments.

4. Ask if there are any questions about the role assignments. If not, tell the groups they may go to work, but make sure that you monitor their work carefully, intervening as necessary to ensure that each group is successful.

5. When the time you have allotted for students to complete the assignment is up, have each

team get together with another team and share how they approached the lesson; that is, students will show their visual recordings, do their gesture or physical movements, and talk about what they did to encourage and support each other in the exercise.

6. After they have had time to share their work with the other groups, lead the whole class in the following discussion:

- *What was it like to use the different intelligences consciously to do this exercise?*
- *Which of the intelligence roles did your group like the most? Why?*
- *Which was most difficult? Why?*
- *What have you learned about how the different ways of knowing can enhance a lesson?*
- *How did this way of approaching a lesson help you?*
- *What things do you want to try again in future exercises?*

Parallel Curriculum Interface

MULTIPLE INTELLIGENCE ROLES IN COOPERATIVE GROUPS

Personal Exploration and Discovery

When assigning multiple intelligence roles, you are moving beyond simply developing the social skills necessary for effective group work into helping students develop their own intelligences through the roles they assume in the process of the group's assignment. Therefore, design exercises which stretch students to play the assigned role to the hilt.

Personal Exploration and Discovery Exercises

➤ **"What's My (Intelligence) Line."** Create multiple intelligence role cards which describe a role that might be helpful in a group situation. Have one student draw a role card out of a hat and study the description of the role for a moment. The rest of the class tries to guess the role by asking yes-or-no questions.

➤ **Intelligence Roles Scenarios.** Create several problem scenarios that occur in the typical school classroom and could be helped by various intelligence roles being played. Assign students to work in groups of five, each having a different scenario to work with. The groups discuss the scenarios, deciding what multiple intelligence roles are needed and create a dramatization of the situation.

➤ **The MI Roles Catalogue.** Brainstorm a list of all the possible roles the class can think of related to the eight ways of knowing. Have them get into small groups and write a five-point description of the roles, selecting one role for each intelligence from the brainstorm. Have each group present a dramatic enactment of their favorite role.

Commentary: Personal MI Exploration and Discovery

As you assign various multiple intelligences roles to students, provide examples of what the role entails. The charts on pp. 157–59 should give you a starting place for this. Always check for understanding and/or confusion regarding the specific duties of each role. When you first use this strategy it is probably best to let students choose the roles they want to play. However, don't let them always play the same or most comfortable role. You want everyone to learn to play as many different roles as possible.

MI ROLES IN COOPERATIVE GROUPS

Academic Exploration and Discovery

Cooperative or collaborative learning is probably one of the most important instructional strategies to hit education in the last thirty years. The Multiple Intelligences Roles in Cooperative Groups strategy puts students into groups to learn certain material you are teaching. As they work in groups, they must actively embody and utilize the different intelligences to help them (and their group) with the learning at hand.

Academic Exploration and Discovery Strategies

➤ **Intelligent Figures from History.** Conduct a rapid brainstorming session in which students name figures from history whom they associate with each of the intelligence areas. Place the historical figures' names in eight groups, according to the intelligence they represent. Each student chooses one historical figure from the list and pretends to be that person, discussing a modern-day issue that you assign. Make sure all intelligences are represented in the figures they choose.

➤ **The "Remake" of Classical Stories.** As a class, discuss and analyze a story or play you have been studying in terms of the different intelligences. Ask: "What is the dominant intelligence portrayed? Which is weak or almost absent? What new roles or characters would you add to bring about more of an intelligence balance? What changes in the plot might this achieve?" In groups of five, have students act out the story or play adding the multiple intelligence roles. See how the plot changes.

➤ **MI Roles in Science Labs.** When students are involved in hands-on science labs, have them work in teams with each person having a special role to play. Name the roles so they are appropriate to the lab and the content with which they are working, but also make sure they understand the relationship of the roles to multiple intelligences.

Commentary: Multiple Intelligences and the Learning Process
In order for this strategy to be successful, you may have to do a fair amount of modeling how to play the roles which the different intelligences suggest and/or what contribution each intelligence could make to a given situation. Move slowly at first until students master the art of the role-playing. However, once students understand the task, get out of the way. You may be pleasantly surprised by where they go with this, how much fun it is, and what they learn in the process.

MI ROLES IN COOPERATIVE GROUPS

Beyond-the-Classroom Exploration and Discovery

In *All's Well That Ends Well,* William Shakespeare wrote: "All the world is a stage, and all the men and women merely players..." When students take this strategy beyond the classroom, they begin to experience the real difference multiple intelligences can make when they become part of daily life. In a sense, they become multiple intelligence players, acting various multiple intelligences-related roles that may bring light to difficult situations they and others are facing.

Beyond-the-Classroom Exploration and Discovery Applications

➤ **"Different Strokes for Different Folks" (or Situations).** In groups of three or four, have students think about their lives beyond the classroom and make a list of group situations in which they often find themselves. Ask them to think of times when playing certain multiple intelligence roles could help move a difficult situation along; for example, a club trying to make a difficult decision, or handling conflicts in an organization.

➤ **MI Roles in the Family Group.** Ask students to analyze their family using multiple intelligences: Which intelligences are currently dominant in the family? Who most often plays the roles of each intelligence? Which intelligences seem to be underutilized or lacking? Students are then to experiment with the multiple intelligences roles they feel will help the family.

➤ **MI and My Peers.** Ask students to examine their relationships with their peers and to notice multiple intelligence behavior patterns that may be present or lacking. Also have them create a pluses/minuses list regarding bringing the different intelligences into those relationships. Ask them to experiment for several weeks by playing the multiple intelligences roles they believe are needed to improve and/or deepen these relationships.

Commentary: Multiple Intelligences and Everyday Life

The learning about and understanding of multiple intelligences that can occur when students use these exercises can be very profound. These exercises promote the application stage of teaching students *about* multiple intelligences. From the students' perspective, each exercise places them in the role of a facilitator of change in situations in which they decide to play multiple intelligences' roles, thus, some risk is involved. Therefore, your assistance in helping students plan successful strategies is crucial. Allow time to debrief and reflect as well.

Multiple Intelligence Roles in Cooperative Groups
(All Grades)

Verbal/Linguistic Roles

★ **Reader** is responsible for reading the written material that is necessary to complete a lesson the group is working on.

★ **Secretary** takes notes on the group's work and does any writing the lesson requires.

★ **Speller** checks all of the group's products for correct spelling.

★ **Reporter** communicates the results of the group's work to the rest of the class.

★ **Historian** keeps a record of key events that occur while the group is working.

★ **Poet** writes poems or limericks about the group and the work it has done in a lesson.

★ **Comedian** entertains the group with jokes, puns, and humorous comments about the lesson.

★ **Memory-jogger** helps the group create "remembering gimmicks" for a lesson.

★ **Debater** takes an opposing position in a discussion to promote thinking and discussion.

★ **Storyteller** tells others stories about the high and low points that occurred as the group worked on a task.

Logical/Mathematical Roles

★ **Checker** makes sure each group member understands the content and answers of the lesson.

★ **Scientist** helps the group create step-by-step procedures for an assigned task.

★ **Fortune-teller** makes predictions about the outcome of the group's work.

★ **Numbers expert** checks any math the group performs and the numbers it uses.

★ **Problem solver** suggests different ways to deal with a problem the group is to solve.

★ **Detective** looks for answer clues as the group works on solving the problem.

★ **Timekeeper** watches the clock during timed tasks and adjusts the pace as needed.

★ **Calculator** performs math operations for the group.

★ **Thinker** helps the group remember, evaluate, and improve its thinking steps.

★ **Patterns expert** looks for connections to other subject areas, both in and beyond the classroom.

Visual/Spatial Roles

★ **Architect** helps the group create a "blueprint" or master plan for the final product.

★ **Colorizer** suggests color ideas to express the group's feelings and ideas in the final product.

★ **Drawer** produces images or pictures to illustrate different parts of an assigned lesson.

★ **Visualizer** helps the group think in images and pictures using the "eyes of the mind."

★ **Shapes expert** makes any abstract design and patterns to go along with the team's work.

★ **Locator** makes sure the group is at the right place on a page or can find its way on a map.

★ **Sculptor** helps the group express its ideas and feelings through manipulatives, such as clay.

★ **Cutter** does any paper cutting or tearing the group needs done.

★ **Symbolizer** creates symbols and images of the group's identity or any key ideas.

★ **Dreamer** helps the group use its active imagination to understand a lesson more fully.

Multiple Intelligence Roles in Cooperative Groups
(All Grades)

Bodily/Kinesthetic Roles

★ **Actor** helps the group think of role-playing ideas for acting out parts of a lesson.

★ **Dancer** suggests creative physical movements that could be part of the group's report.

★ **Coach** helps a group learn physical movement routines to embody what the group learns.

★ **Inventor** creates new steps, procedures, and active ways to do old things.

★ **Choreographer** helps the group plan its staging of a report or presentation.

★ **Gesture manager** suggests body language to communicate group feelings about a lesson.

★ **Athletic coordinator** thinks of physical games to play that are related to a lesson or task.

★ **Mimer** creates nonverbal ways to show what the group has learned in a lesson or activity.

★ **Stage director** helps the group practice and perfect an upcoming presentation.

★ **Props manager** helps the group find any presentation props it needs.

Musical/Rhythmic Roles

★ **Drummer** makes up rhythmic patterns to match the "beat" of the stages of the group's work.

★ **Singer** thinks of popular songs or tunes about the group and the specific task it is doing.

★ **Sound director** helps the group plan appropriate background sounds for a report.

★ **Composer** makes up words for songs about the group and the assignment it is doing.

★ **Volume controller** ensures the group's noise does not rise above an appropriate level during a cooperative task.

★ **Music coach** rehearses the group in the musical parts of a report that is to be presented.

★ **Rapper** helps the group create raps and jingles about itself and its work.

★ **Rhythm coordinator** cues the group when it is to perform various rhythmic patterns.

★ **Choral director** leads the group in any musical or rap parts of a presentation or report.

★ **Instrument manager** gathers or creates the noise and sound makers the group needs.

Naturalist Roles

★ **Flora analogist** connects to the plant kingdom related to a lesson.

★ **Fauna analogist** suggests connections to the animal kingdom related to a lesson.

★ **Hot air balloonist** teaches scientific principle of hot air rising as it relates to a science lesson.

★ **Weatherman** explains how different cloud patterns signal changing weather patterns.

★ **Environmental designer** suggests ideal natural setting for the lesson.

★ **Conservationist** ensures that supplies are used in an "earth-friendly" way.

★ **Waste management manager** discusses the importance of personal recycling, reusing, and recovery to the environment.

★ **Nutritionist** cooks meal for the group using all locally grown ingredients, describing nutrients for a health lesson.

★ **Nursery person** describes how we require the oxygen plants give off and plants require our carbon dioxide exhales to survive.

Multiple Intelligence Roles in Cooperative Groups
(All Grades)

Intrapersonal Roles

★ **Worrier** is concerned about whether the group is doing what it is supposed to be doing.

★ **Reflector** helps the group think about the significance and implications of a task.

★ **Processor** leads the group in evaluating its thinking and cooperative behavior.

★ **Quality controller** ensures that the group is doing its best possible work and that the final product is good.

★ **Creativity manager** helps the group think of unique and fun approaches to an assigned task.

★ **Feelings watcher** pays attention to and helps the group discuss its affective responses to a task.

★ **Learning-awareness catalyzer** helps the group be conscious about what it is learning.

★ **Connection maker** helps the group see links with other subjects, both in and beyond the classroom.

★ **Concentration technologist** suggests ways the group can maintain its focus on an assignment.

★ **Philosopher** raises questions about values and beliefs that emerge as the group works.

Interpersonal Roles

★ **Organizer** helps the group plan and agree on strategies for approaching an assigned task.

★ **Encourager** provides positive support and encouragement for the members of the group.

★ **Motivator** finds ways to keep each group member excited about an assignment.

★ **Counselor** advises the group on how to deal with any problems or issues that may arise.

★ **Interpreter** explains the meaning of any parts of the group's work that others don't understand.

★ **Involvement manager** ensures that each group member contributes to the final product.

★ **Task master** helps the group stay on task and makes sure all parts of a task are completed.

★ **Consensus maker** makes sure that all members agree on and understand the final product.

★ **Communications watcher** guards the group's interaction processes (listening, hearing, and so on).

★ **Paraphraser** repeats what various members of the group are saying to help all understand.

Teacher's Personal Reflection Log

MULTIPLE INTELLIGENCE ROLES IN COOPERATIVE GROUPS

I have the following thoughts/insights about the Multiple Roles in Cooperative Groups strategy:

I feel that the Multiple Roles in Cooperative Groups strategy can help me in my teaching in the following ways:

As a learning process, the Multiple Roles in Cooperative Groups strategy includes the following benefits for my students:

I have the following specific ideas for using the Multiple Roles in Cooperative Groups strategy in my classroom in the near future:

I think the Multiple Roles in Cooperative Groups strategy can be used beyond the classroom and school in the following ways:

EXPLORATION AND DISCOVERY BASE EXERCISE: EXPLORING INTELLIGENCE CAPACITIES WITH A PARTNER

Exercise Procedures

1. Have students get into groups of two or three using grouping criteria that provide maximum heterogeneity.

2. On the overhead or board display the appropriate work sheet from pp. 166–168. Say, *"Each group will randomly select one of these items and plan a presentation for the rest of the class."* Following are several random selection methods each group can use to choose an item from the work sheet:

   - Use the sixth digit in the telephone number of the tallest person in the group.

   - Each member puts one hand behind his or her back, holds up a number of fingers, and then brings the hand out; add the numbers.

   - Each person rolls a number on some dice; the group adds up its members' numbers, then divides the sum by the number of members in the group.

   - The group takes the average of their shoe sizes.

   - Use the number of people in the family of the group member with the largest family.

   - Use the number of letters in the name of the person with the curliest hair.

3. Give the groups ten to fifteen minutes to work out their presentations. Carefully monitor the groups as they work, intervening as necessary to ensure that each group succeeds at its assigned task.

4. When the groups have completed their assignments, have each group make its presentation to the whole class.

Exploring Intelligence Capacities with a Partner

INTRODUCTION

In this exercise students have an opportunity to learn how to "translate" various verbal/linguistic or logical/mathematical lesson content into the unique "language" or modality of the different intelligences. Most of the material we have to teach is prepackaged in a verbal/linguistic or logical/mathematical form. This lesson helps students go beyond these constraints.

OBJECTIVE

The goal of the exercise is to teach students how to reconceptualize a task in terms of all eight ways of knowing and how to see the multiple ways in which students can approach their schoolwork.

DISCUSSION

One of the presuppositions of this exercise is that students often learn better, more willingly, and more quickly from their peers than from an outside authority figure. The exercise capitalizes on this phenomenon by asking students to figure out with a partner how to perform certain tasks. This approach not only provides the needed peer support, but also allows students to build new levels of trust and a willingness to risk. The key to success in the exercise is for students to know that there is no right answer or right way of performing the skills they select. What you are after is having them stretch themselves beyond their usual and comfortable ways of operating. Make sure that the list of tasks is slightly outrageous and fun.

5. Lead the whole class in the following discussion about the exercise:

    • *What do you remember from these presentations? (This is a group "remembering" reflection.)*

    • *What were your feelings as you worked with your group?*

    • *What were your feelings as you made your presentation to the class?*

    • *What were your feelings as you watched the different presentations?*

    • *What ideas do you have about how we could incorporate what we have done in this intelligence exercise into our daily classroom work?*

Parallel Curriculum Interface

EXPLORING INTELLIGENCE CAPACITIES WITH A PARTNER

Personal Exploration and Discovery

As you use these exercises (or design your own), make sure that students are given ample opportunity to work with their more comfortable intelligences and that the stretch to the less comfortable intelligences occurs in a risk-free environment. If they're not having fun and enjoying these explorations, something is wrong.

Personal Exploration and Discovery Exercises

➤ **Random Capacities Draw.** Have students create a set of tasks to perform which stretch students to use their different intelligences, such as giving instructions for doing or making something by drawing pictures, acting out an inanimate object, creating a soundtrack to accompany different parts of the day, and so on.

➤ **Round-Robin Capacities Demonstration.** Students get with a partner to create a set of tasks to perform, such as showing how to brush their teeth or make cookies. They choose one intelligence and write each of its capacities (with a brief explanation) on a card. Each student pair selects one of the capacities from the target intelligence to demonstrate with an assigned task.

➤ **MI Capacities Scramble.** This exercise is modeled after the childhood game "Fruit Basket Upset." Each student secretly selects an intelligence. Write the capacities for each intelligence on separate index cards and put them into eight different hats. Students stand in a circle and you call out the name of an intelligence. A student representing that intelligence comes to the center, draws a capacity from the appropriate hat, and leads the rest of the class in doing the capacity.

> **Commentary: Personal MI Exploration and Discovery**
>
> The Exploring Intelligence Capacities with a Partner exercises will expand students' repertoire of capacities in the different intelligences. They will be encouraged to tap a wider range of their full intellectual potential than is usually required in the course of normal living. These exercises suggest that using all our intellectual capacities is the normal way humans can (and should) operate. However, many of these capacities have not either been fully developed or may have been squashed into various states of latency. These exercises can quickly call on these intelligences to once again become part of one's normal daily living.

EXPLORING INTELLIGENCE CAPACITIES WITH A PARTNER

Academic Exploration and Discovery

Your goal in utilizing these kinds of exercises with your content is to ask students to stretch their conceptualization and understanding of the material beyond what is given in the book. Each of these suggestions, as well as others you will create, help to amplify and expand students' involvement with and understanding of the material being studied.

Academic Exploration and Discovery Strategies

➤ **Subject Area Theatre.** Create a list of the basic skills that students need to be able to perform as part of a given subject area. Using the same random selection processes outlined in the base exercise, have them work with a partner to create an everyday-life demonstration showing the skills they have chosen.

➤ **Stop the Action and Respond.** Have one student start telling a well-known story, historic event, or math or science process to another. At a certain point in the telling, ring a bell and inject an unexpected element that requires the performance of some multiple intelligence capacity (for example, the three little pigs are deaf, so the wolf can only communicate with them by drawing pictures). The other student must perform it, then tell what happens next.

➤ **Illustrating a Lecture with MI "Stuff."** Put an outline of a lecture or a concept that is central to the day's lesson on the overhead or board. Start working through it, pausing at certain points where you ask students to do multiple intelligences tasks related to what you've been presenting; for example, a piece of music they would play, a physical movement they would perform, a visual image they would draw, a natural phenomenon they would inject, and so on.

➤ **Intelligence "Workout" Routines.** For certain rote learning or memorization tasks in a given subject area, help students devise eight ways of using *mnemonic devices* to learn the information. Then have them create a routine for themselves to practice the information (for example, "rap" times tables, visual symbols for the parts of speech, or body gestures for science concepts).

Commentary: Multiple Intelligences and the Learning Process

The Exploring Multiple Intelligence Capacities with a Partner strategy helps students use more complex cognitive abilities. By consciously incorporating the different ways of knowing, students learn to move their thinking beyond the basic facts to an understanding of process, dynamics, and complex relationships in the material; and further, to the ability to apply, transfer, integrate, and synthesize their learning.

EXPLORING INTELLIGENCE CAPACITIES WITH A PARTNER

Beyond-the-Classroom Exploration and Discovery

The ultimate goal of this exercise is to enrich students' experience of working with others beyond the formal academic situation. Therefore, the activities here should be focused more on self-development; that is, helping students discover ways that the various intelligences can become a regular part of their relating to and with others.

Beyond-the-Classroom Exploration and Discovery Applications

➤ **Potential MI-Coach Survey.** Ask students to list people they know beyond the school environment who exemplify strength and comfort in intelligence areas in which the students need some help. Have students then interview these people and discuss how they might coach them.

➤ **Mentoring the Young.** Have students find someone younger than themselves who is part of their life beyond school. They are to create a plan to work with this person to help them develop some of the multiple intelligence skills and capacities that are strong in the students' lives.

➤ **Video Partners.** Have students list multiple intelligence capacities they want to develop more in their personal lives beyond the classroom. Then help them research videos they might rent and/or things they might tape on TV where people are demonstrating the how-tos of those capacities. Brainstorm with students how these videos can help them improve their MI capacities.

Commentary: Multiple Intelligences and Everyday Life
Students should be encouraged to find a partner or "intelligence buddy" they can work with outside of school; someone who is also interested in expanding his or her own intelligence capacities. They should be encouraged to help each other think of ways that more of the capacities of all the intelligences can become a regular part of their daily lives. In doing so they are both directly and indirectly preparing themselves for a more holistic experience of living.

Exploring Intelligence Capacities with a Partner
(Elementary)

Tell the story of the "Three Little Pigs" in a song.	**Spell your name with your body.**
Listen to a story and tell it to someone else.	**Make numbers into people and animals.**
Have a conversation with a rock, a plant, or an animal.	**Tell a partner some of the questions you have about life.**
Look at a picture and tell a story about it.	**Make up a number pattern to stump a friend.**

Exploring Intelligence Capacities with a Partner
(Middle School)

Tell a story you've read recently through song, rap, and music.	**Read something, making different sounds for the punctuation marks.**
Draw pictures to show what goes on in adding, subtracting, multiplying, and dividing.	**Concentrate on an object from nature and record your feelings and thoughts about it.**
Tell a story about a picture. What do you think is happening?	**Draw a picture of an experience while a partner tells you about it.**
Make up body movements or gestures to match a piece of music.	**Create a secret code for the alphabet; then write a message using the code.**
Tell a partner how to do something; then watch her or him do it!	**Make up a drama about something you've studied in science.**

Exploring Intelligence Capacities with a Partner
(Secondary)

Create a "Shakespeare Rap" to tell the story of a play.	Make up an outline for a television soap opera based on a scientific process.
Write a story in which the characters are mathematical operations, symbols, or processes.	Listen to a piece of music and draw any shapes, designs, images, and pictures it evokes in you.
Pretend you can have a conversation with an object, process, animal, or plant from the natural world. What advice would you seek? How would it answer your questions?	Draw a picture or diagram (with color!) of how to find the hypotenuse of a right triangle, the "x" factor in an equation, or a square root.
"Illustrate" a piece of poetry with appropriate background sounds, rhythms, tones, and other noises.	Make a logical outline that explains the emotional flow and impact of a piece of music.
Make up a series of gestures or physical movements to embody key concepts or ideas you have been studying.	Create a skit to show a scientific process, a math formula, or the classical structure of a persuasive speech.
Write a description of your opinion of a piece of art—what you like, don't like, what it "says" to you, and so on.	Listen to a partner tell you how she or he solved a problem; then explain the process to others.
Make a list of "life questions" raised by a piece of poetry or other literature.	Imagine the digestive system, the respiratory system, the circulatory system, and the brain having a conversation about a current events topic. Record what each might say.

Pathways of Learning © 2000 Zephyr Press, Tucson, Arizona • 800-232-2187 • http://zephyrpress.com

Teacher's Personal Reflection Log

EXPLORING INTELLIGENCE CAPACITIES WITH A PARTNER

I have the following thoughts/insights about the Exploring Intelligence Capacities with a Partner strategy:

I feel that the Exploring Intelligence Capacities with a Partner strategy can help me in my teaching in the following ways:

As a learning process, the Exploring Intelligence Capacities with a Partner strategy includes the following benefits for my students:

I have the following specific ideas for using the Exploring Intelligence Capacities with a Partner strategy in my classroom in the near future:

I think the Exploring Intelligence Capacities with a Partner strategy can be used beyond the classroom and school in the following ways:

Intelligence Triggers

INTRODUCTION

This exercise gives students an opportunity to state what helps them turn on the different intelligences. While we all have all eight ways of knowing, certain gimmicks or techniques may give us access to certain intelligences more quickly and effectively than other techniques.

OBJECTIVE

The goal of the exercise is to make students aware of the methods, tools, and techniques students use to gain quick access to each intelligence, and to allow them to name their favorite methods.

DISCUSSION

One of the key research findings related to the theory of multiple intelligences is that, given the intelligences' basis in the neurological system, they are easily triggered or awakened through certain external and internal stimuli. The key to using this information effectively to enhance one's use of multiple intelligences in everyday life is knowing what these awakening triggers are. In my first book, *Eight Ways of Knowing* (revised 1998), I present numerous exercises, games, puzzles, and practices for achieving this awakening. This exercise is designed to create a strategic awareness of what is involved in accessing the various intelligence modalities. It is also important to recognize, however, that every awakening exercise or technique does not work equally well for each person, given the diversity of our sociocultural backgrounds.

EXPLORATION AND DISCOVERY BASE EXERCISE: INTELLIGENCE TRIGGERS

Exercise Procedures

1. Pass out a marking pen and eight 3"-by-5" self-stick notes, one for each intelligence, to each student.

2. Project the eight intelligences Toolbox (pp. 175–176) on the overhead or post the chart on the board. Say, *"In this exercise we are going to create a Multiple Intelligence Toolbox to help us use all of our intelligences in our classroom. We will start by brainstorming a list of favorite tools and activities for each intelligence."*

   Note: Refer to Multiple Intelligence Toolbox to help students think of additional tools.

3. Go through the intelligences one by one, asking students to write their favorite tool for accessing each intelligence, one tool for one intelligence per self-stick note.

4. Divide the board or a wall in the classroom into eight sections, one for each intelligence. Give students a couple of minutes to stick their self-stick notes in the appropriate sections.

5. As a whole class, look at the tools listed, clustering any that are the same. After organizing the tools, make a couple of summary statements regarding what the organization tells you: "It looks like a lot of us really like to draw," or "There doesn't seem to be a favorite for this one—look at the variety of tools we like."

6. Have students form groups of two or three with their neighbors. The groups' first task is to understand the tools suggested for triggering each intelligence and add any other tools they think of as a team. Be on hand to answer questions as they arise.

7. When students have completed their discussion of the tools, pass out the work sheet on page 177 to each student. Have students individually choose two tools for each intelligence that they like and that work best for them, and write

them on the work sheet by the pluses under the appropriate intelligence. Then have them list by the minuses on the work sheet one tool for each intelligence that may work for someone else but does nothing for them.

8. Have students concentrate on one intelligence at a time and share with their groups the tools they listed on the work sheets. Make sure each student explains why she or he marked certain tools.

   Note: The information on the work sheets can help you plan future exercises, so you may want to have students sign the toolboxes and to collect the signed toolboxes. You can then include in your lessons multiple intelligence teaching strategies that take into account the things your students like, and you can determine those tools your students need help to use effectively.

9. Lead the class in the following implications reflection:

   • *What did you find interesting about creating the toolbox? What was exciting? Surprising? Confusing? Helpful?*
   • *If you were going to explain our toolbox to someone who wasn't here today, such as one of your parents, a younger brother or sister, or one of your grandparents, what would you tell that person the toolbox is?*
   • *In what ways do you think the toolbox can help you with your daily classroom work? How can it help you with your homework?*

   Note: You may want to leave the list of the brainstormed tools up as a permanent reference.

Parallel Curriculum Interface

INTELLIGENCE TRIGGERS

Personal Exploration and Discovery

We all have at least eight ways of knowing; they are part of our biology and neurology as human beings. Intelligence Triggers work with this reality by helping students learn how to access and/or activate the various intelligences within their own brain, mind, body systems. This knowledge enables them to rapidly "turn on" various regions of the brain—those regions which are responsible for certain of our multiple intelligence abilities.

Personal Exploration and Discovery Exercises

➤ **What Got Triggered for You?** Show students a video that is full of action, glorious visual effects, and so on. During the movie, ask students to be aware of which of their intelligences are being stimulated. Afterwards, discuss what happened and the triggering techniques the film maker used. Also ask how students knew a particular intelligence had been triggered.

➤ **Triggering Your Own Intelligence.** Introduce students to a lesson by telling them your objective for the lesson and the particular intelligence that you will be emphasizing as the teaching and learning mode. Allow students to take a few minutes to prepare themselves to use the target intelligence by using whatever trigger works best for them.

➤ **Triggering Others' Intelligences.** Play a game where an intelligence is named and students, working in teams, are given a specified time to brainstorm all of the ways that the named intelligence could be triggered in other people. The team to come up with most gets to try out their triggers on the rest of the class and to name the next intelligence.

Commentary: Personal MI Exploration and Discovery

The notion of being able to trigger the intelligences at will is a fascinating self-discovery for most students. When introducing this concept to students you may need to have a series of triggering (or awakening) exercises followed by reflection on what got turned on in the process of the exercise. This will help students to recognize when an intelligence has in fact been triggered, as well as what works and doesn't work for them.

INTELLIGENCE TRIGGERS

Academic Exploration and Discovery

The Intelligence Triggers strategies will help students become more active, involved, and responsible learners. When students understand that you are focusing the teaching and learning process in one of the intelligence areas, it makes learning the material more interesting and fun for them.

Academic Exploration and Discovery Strategies

➤ **Awakening Intelligence in Others.** Divide students into groups of three or four. Give them an outline of lessons you have planned for a week and the particular intelligence emphasis you have decided for each lesson. The groups are to create the "awakening the intelligence stage" (see *Eight Ways of Knowing*) for their assigned lesson. For each lesson during the week, the respective group leads the class in triggering the intelligence that will be emphasized.

➤ **Intelligent Report Options.** Assign students a research report about specific content you want them to investigate as part of a particular unit of study. They are to use at least two intelligences in their research and reporting, beyond verbal/linguistic intelligence. Ask them to turn to a partner to discuss various options, getting ideas from each other. Have each student submit a written report plan.

➤ **Test Options and Alternatives.** Have students work with each other to prepare for an upcoming examination. Encourage them to use any of the intelligences (or combinations of them) to make sure they are getting the required information. Also ask them for input on their ideas for creating an intelligence-fair test that would let them use different intelligences to demonstrate mastery of academic material.

Commentary: Multiple Intelligences and the Learning Process
The more students understand the intelligences, the more they can become advocates for themselves and their own learning needs. This becomes the case as students progress from early childhood education through the secondary years and beyond. Students quickly see that we all have the full learning potentials represented by each of the intelligences within our bio-neurological makeup. Work with all of the ways of knowing to access both the intelligence you're using in a given lesson, or, when appropriate, an intelligence that might help students more. The stretch into less-developed intelligence areas is good—it's called growth, and is often a catalyst for human transformation.

INTELLIGENCE TRIGGERS

Beyond-the-Classroom Exploration and Discovery

The Intelligence Triggers exercises are probably among the easiest to transfer beyond the classroom into everyday life. In daily living, we all need a wide variety of ways to deal with the challenges, issues, problems, and concerns we face. The triggers approach suggests making a strategic decision about which intelligence would be most useful in finding a solution, and then accessing that intelligence. These exercises (and others you create) challenge students to do this for themselves beyond the confines of the classroom.

Beyond-the-Classroom Exploration and Discovery Applications

> ➤ **Intelligence Triggers in Everyday Life.** On the overhead projector or blackboard, display a timeline of a day, starting with getting up, getting ready, breakfast, traveling to school, and so on. In small groups, ask students to make a list of the "given" intelligence triggers that are part of each section of the timeline; for example, sounds, images, conversation with others, physical movement, and so on. Have students list ideas for helping themselves be more aware of these triggers.

> ➤ **Special Situation MI Access.** Have students list a variety of challenging situations they face on a regular basis. Then have them brainstorm which of the eight intelligences could help them deal with these situations. Finally, have students list things they could do when that situation arises to rapidly access the intelligences they think could help.

> ➤ **Triggers in a Group.** Ask students to think about groups and/or clubs of which they are a part (including their families) and try to recall times when they needed to access other intelligences to help them with an issue or concern they were facing. Have students brainstorm intelligence-triggering strategies that could help a group move into using the different intelligences in these situations in the future.

Commentary: Multiple Intelligences and Everyday Life

Once you are inside a strategically chosen intelligence, you can explore all the possibilities it has to offer. You must convince students that they can trust the information they receive from the different intelligences. Get students to "step inside" the intelligences to explore all of its possibilities. Begin with small experiments, always providing opportunities for students to share their experiences and what they are discovering about triggering their eight intelligence beyond the classroom. Then, move to more involved and complex processes. Underscore the importance of first triggering the intelligence in the brain, then moving forward from there.

Teacher's Reference
Multiple Intelligence Toolbox[4]
(Elementary)

TOOLS TO HELP YOU BE SMART!

Verbal/Linguistic
Telling jokes
Writing words
Reading
Speaking

Logical/Mathematical
Solving problems
Finding patterns
Counting
Thinking

Visual/Spatial
Molding clay
Drawing
Painting
Pretending

Intrapersonal
Being alone
Telling about feelings
Asking questions
Telling about thinking

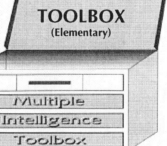

TOOLBOX
(Elementary)

Multiple
Intelligence
Toolbox

Musical/Rhythmic
Singing
Listening to music
Creating music
Making rhythm

Interpersonal
Talking to others
Listening
Being on a team
Cooperating

Naturalist
Growing things
Collecting natural stuff
Raising animals
Classifying nature
Using things found in nature

Bodily/Kinesthetic
Playing sports
  and games
Acting
Dancing
Exercising

4. Adaped from Lazear, David. *Eight Ways of Knowing*. Palatine, Ill.: Skylight, 1998.
Pathways of Learning © 2000 Zephyr Press, Tucson, Arizona • 800-232-2187 • http://zephyrpress.com

Teacher's Reference
Multiple Intelligence Toolbox[5]
(Middle School & Secondary)

Verbal/Linguistic
- Reading
- Vocabulary
- Formal speech
- Journal or diary keeping
- Creative writing
- Poetry
- Oral debate
- Impromptu speaking
- Humor or telling jokes
- Storytelling

Logical/Mathematical
- Abstract symbols and formulas
- Outlining
- Graphic organizers
- Number sequences
- Calculation
- Deciphering codes
- Forcing relationships
- Syllogisms
- Problem solving
- Pattern games

Bodily/Kinesthetic
- Folk or creative dance
- Role-playing
- Physical gestures
- Drama
- Martial arts
- Body language
- Physical exercise
- Mime
- Inventing
- Sports

Visual/Spatial
- Guided imagery
- Active imagination
- Color schemes
- Patterns and designs
- Painting
- Drawing
- Mind mapping
- Pretending
- Sculpture
- Pictures

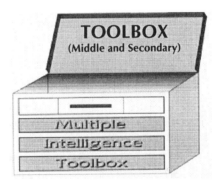

TOOLBOX
(Middle and Secondary)

Multiple
Intelligence
Toolbox

Interpersonal
- Giving feedback
- Intuiting others' feelings
- Cooperative learning strategies
- Person-to-person communication
- Empathy practices
- Division of labor
- Collaboration skills
- Receiving feedback
- Sensing others' motives
- Group projects

Musical/Rhythmic
- Rhythmic patterns
- Vocal sounds and tones
- Music composition and creation
- Percussion vibrations
- Humming
- Environmental sounds
- Instrumental sounds
- Singing
- Tonal patterns
- Music performance

Intrapersonal
- Silent reflection methods
- Metacognition techniques
- Thinking strategies
- Emotional processing
- "Know thyself" practices
- Mindfulness practices
- Focusing and concentration skills
- Higher-order reasoning
- Complex guided imagery
- "Centering" practices

Naturalist
- Archetypal pattern recognition
- Caring for plants/animals
- Conservation practices
- Environmental feedback
- Hands-on labs
- Nature encounters/field trips
- Nature observation
- Natural world simulations
- Species classification (organic/inorganic)
- Sensory stimulation exercises

5. Adapted from Lazear, David. *Eight Ways of Knowing.* Palatine, Ill.: Skylight, 1998.
Pathways of Learning © 2000 Zephyr Press, Tucson, Arizona • 800-232-2187 • http://zephyrpress.com

Intelligence Triggers
(All Grades)

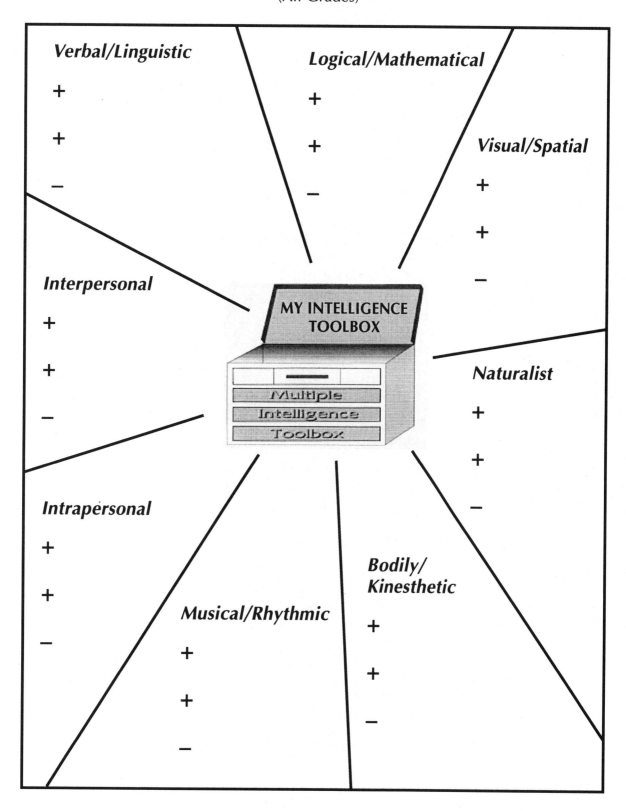

Teacher's Personal Reflection Log
INTELLIGENCE TRIGGERS

I have the following thoughts/insights about the Intelligence Triggers strategy:

I feel that the Intelligence Triggers strategy can help me in my teaching in the following ways:

As a learning process, the Intelligence Triggers strategy includes the following benefits for my students:

I have the following specific ideas for using the Intelligence Triggers strategy in my classroom in the near future:

I think the Intelligence Triggers strategy can be used beyond the classroom and school in the following ways:

EXPLORATION AND DISCOVERY BASE EXERCISE: INTELLIGENCE COACHING

Exercise Procedures

1. Assign the class to work with partners. Try to pair each student with a partner who has different intelligence strengths and weaknesses from her or his own.

2. Tell students their task is to coach each other on how to use the eight ways of knowing to improve their performance in school. On the overhead or board, show students the coaching model or process that is appropriate for their grade level (see pp. 184–186).

3. Explain the coaching process as follows:

> *For the next month (or longer, if students seem ready and willing), we are going to experiment with being intelligence coaches for each other. At the end of each week you will meet with your coach and review the week. You will share with your partner homework you have done and tests you have taken, and you will talk generally about how the week has gone. As you share, you are to discover the areas in which your partner had difficulty and discuss how your partner might have employed different intelligences to help. In light of this conversation, you will help your partner think of ways she or he can use the intelligences in the coming week. When your coaching session is over, each of you will have an intelligence action plan for improving your performance during the next week.*

You may need to point out that it is okay for students to get together to coach each other at times other than those you set aside, but that once a week they will have time in class to coach each other.

4. Discuss any issues you feel will clarify the process and its intent and answer any questions students have.

Intelligence Coaching

INTRODUCTION

This exercise teaches students how they can help and encourage each other to use the full spectrum of their intellectual capacities, both in school and beyond the classroom.

OBJECTIVE

The goal of the exercise is to teach students the basic steps of the coaching model and to have students practice using the model to be more successful in school.

DISCUSSION

Learning to coach others in the intelligences is probably the most advanced process presented in this book. Coaching requires not only a great deal of sensitivity to other people, but also an in-depth knowledge of the intelligences. Nonetheless, students are fully capable of coaching each other in the manner described in the exercise if they are taught how to do it, are given time to practice, and are given time at least once a week to work on their coaching relationships.

5. Give students a chance to practice the coaching process using a relatively simple situation. Your goal in this step is to allow students to learn the process so they feel comfortable with the process and with relating to each other in this way. Later, they will transfer the coaching process to academic situations. See the examples for possible practice scenarios.

6. Give the pairs time to try the coaching model and to get to know each other in this new way.

7. At the end of the allotted time, have the partners thank each other for the help each has given. Ask students to talk about what happened, sharing the positive and negative aspects of being each other's coaches:

- *What was the best part of being a coach for your partner? What was the worst part?*
- *Did you like coaching? Why or why not?*
- *Are you willing to try coaching for a month and see how you feel then?*
- *What questions did this exercise raise for you? What parts of the process don't you understand?*
- *In what ways do you think this kind of coaching might help you?*

Note: These questions might also be used after the weekly coaching session to get students' feedback on how it is going.

Parallel Curriculum Interface

INTELLIGENCE COACHING

Personal Exploration and Discovery

As students get to know the intelligences in themselves and each other, one thing they learn is that we all need help. Fostering this attitude is key to the Intelligence Coaching process. As you create coaching exercises (or use the ones suggested here), remind students that this need for help is not a deficiency, it's a gift. We need to be able to draw on each other's strengths.

Personal Exploration and Discovery Exercises

➤ **Planning for "Peak Performance."** Ask students individually to list two to three upcoming situations in which they feel they will need to perform at their absolute best; for example, an oral report, sporting event, music recital, final exam, and so on. Then, have them get together with their coaching partner to help each other create winning plans; for example, mental rehearsal, verbal affirmations, practice trial runs, visual diagrams of steps involved, and so on.

➤ **Evaluating Problem-Solving Strategies.** Have students write down the steps they usually go through when trying to solve a problem. As coaching partners, compare their problem-solving steps, then discuss pluses and minuses. Then create a new approach incorporating the best steps from both of their approaches.

➤ **MI Coaching Vocabulary.** For each intelligence have students brainstorm some of the language that is appropriate for the different intelligences they can use to help someone they are coaching in the different areas; for example, visualize, make a picture in your mind for visual/spatial intelligence, or move with it or act it out for bodily/kinesthetic. Then have students try the words and phrases when they are coaching each other.

Commentary: Personal MI Exploration and Discovery

Intelligence Coaching exercises assume students have a working knowledge of the intelligences and the creative possibilities inherent within each of the eight ways of knowing. It also assumes that students trust their coach. Help students refine their coaching skills and give genuinely helpful advice to each other. As students learn more about how the various intelligences can be used, the more they can be a regular part of their repertoire for daily living.

INTELLIGENCE COACHING

Academic Exploration and Discovery

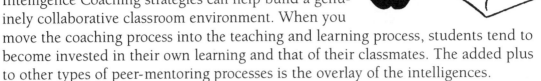

Intelligence Coaching strategies can help build a genuinely collaborative classroom environment. When you move the coaching process into the teaching and learning process, students tend to become invested in their own learning and that of their classmates. The added plus to other types of peer-mentoring processes is the overlay of the intelligences.

Academic Exploration and Discovery Strategies

➤ **Intelligent Test Preparation.** Have students work with their coaches to prepare for an upcoming test. Each member of the coaching team is to tell the other how he or she will prepare for the test using the eight ways of knowing. Partners are then to work with each other on the review, helping each other use the intelligence strategies discussed earlier. Be on hand as a resource person to assist.

➤ **Unit Reviews.** At the conclusion of a unit of study, have students gather in their coaching teams to discuss, review, and pull the unit together. The coaching teams are to choose an intelligence as the medium for the review, and then produce their summary. Be prepared for anything here, from murals, to songs, mind maps, outlines, and creative dances.

➤ **What Went Wrong?** After you have corrected a test or a homework assignment, have students work with their coaches to understand and correct mistakes. Encourage them to discuss how they used the different ways of knowing with the assignment or test and to think of intelligent things they could do next time to improve their performance. Allow students to retake the test or redo the homework.

Commentary: Multiple Intelligences and the Learning Process

Students already have some knowledge about each others' intelligence capacities, even if all they know is who's really good at such things as drawing, music, acting, and so on. The coaching process brings to bear the full spectrum of intelligence possibilities in the classroom. Be present to facilitate the coaching process if students get stuck, off task, or if peer-relationships issues arise. Generally, however, it is best to stay out of the way and allow the process to carry itself. You may be pleasantly surprised by the results.

INTELLIGENCE COACHING

Beyond-the-Classroom Exploration and Discovery

At the heart of the Intelligence Coaching process is the ability to give and receive feedback (including constructive criticism) from others. This ability is a key to success in terms of the people skills needed in almost every conceivable job beyond school.

Beyond-the-Classroom Exploration and Discovery Applications

➤ **Coaching Diary or Reflective Journal.** Students should keep a record of the feedback and advice they receive in the course of their normal daily life. They are to classify each entry under the different intelligences and notice the gaps; that is, where they are not getting balanced advice from the perspectives of all of the intelligences. They should create a plan in their journal for getting advice from others that includes all the intelligences.

➤ **Intelligence Specific Coaches.** Students should find someone whom they trust to be their mentor or guide in the different intelligences. Whenever they find themselves needing advice on using one of the intelligences, they should call upon this coach to help them "break loose." Students are to ask this person to also use them in the same way. Remember, these outside coaches may not know the terminology of multiple intelligences, but they may still have a great deal to share related to the intelligences.

➤ **Being a Coach to Others.** Have students think of several people they know beyond the school setting who are facing some challenge or issue in their lives. The students should think about which of the eight intelligences could really help deal with this issue or challenge. Then, students should plan how they could coach these people in using these multiple intelligences.

Commentary: Multiple Intelligences and Everyday Life

We are often hesitant to admit the need for help. We fear we are infringing on other people's time to ask them to consult with us on our projects, issues, or challenges. This coaching process beyond the classroom asks students to find relationships where the coaching is a mutually beneficial process. Coaches could be fellow students, a family member, or some other person they know who manifests strength in one of the intelligence areas.

Intelligence Coaching
(Elementary)

HELPING EACH OTHER

Coaching Steps

1. **SHARE your work**
2. **TELL about hard times**
3. **SHARE ideas to help**
4. **PLAN next steps**

Find Eight Ways to . . .

Meet new friends	**Tell a good story**
Make a hard decision	**Learn to use good manners**
Learn spelling words	**Teach counting to 25**

Intelligence Coaching
(Middle)

COACHING YOUR PARTNER

Coaching Steps

1. SHARE basic information
2. DISCUSS your feelings
3. Track PAST intelligence strategies used
4. Think of new INTELLIGENCE strategies to help
5. PLAN for next week

Practice Scenarios

1. Talk about a difficult decision you made in the last year. *How could the eight ways of knowing have helped you?*

2. Pretend you can replay a past family problem. *Think of ways the eight intelligences could have been used.*

3. Share some homework or a test that you "bombed." *What new intelligence strategies would you use if you could redo the homework or retake the test?*

4. Talk about an argument with a friend. *How can you use the eight intelligences to work things out?*

5. Discuss some things you really want to buy. *Think of at least eight money-raising ideas—one for each of the intelligences.*

6. Discuss saying "NO!" to drugs. *How could you use the language of each intelligence to say "NO!"*

Intelligence Coaching
(Secondary)

COACHING MODEL

Coaching Steps

1. **Share basic information**
2. **Intelligence analysis/processing (Feelings)**
3. **Intelligence strategy plotting (Past)**
4. **Intelligence strategy plotting (Future)**
5. **Intelligence action planning (Performance)**

Practice Scenarios

1. **Discuss a family situation with which you feel you could use some help. Help each other understand the situation and think of alternatives.**

2. **Think through a problem your school is facing. With your partner, explore all the options you can think of for solving it.**

3. **Coach each other on a recent school assignment that was difficult or on which you received a low grade. What could you have done to do better on the assignment?**

4. **Discuss multiple approaches to a peer relations issue you are facing. *Note:* Stay focused on your own, not another's, problem.**

5. **Give each other advice and think of ideas about using the eight intelligences to resist the temptation to do drugs, including alcohol.**

6. **Think together about dealing creatively with challenges you'll face when you finish high school (for example, career directions, college, a job, marriage, and so on).**

Pathways of Learning © 2000 Zephyr Press, Tucson, Arizona • 800-232-2187 • http://zephyrpress.com

Teacher's Personal Reflection Log

INTELLIGENCE COACHING

I have the following thoughts/insights about the Intelligence Coaching strategy:

I feel that the Intelligence Coaching strategy can help me in my teaching in the following ways:

As a learning process, the Intelligence Coaching strategy includes the following benefits for my students:

I have the following specific ideas for using the Intelligence Coaching strategy in my classroom in the near future:

I think the Intelligence Coaching strategy can be used beyond the classroom and school in the following ways:

Exercises for Reflective Use of the Intelligences

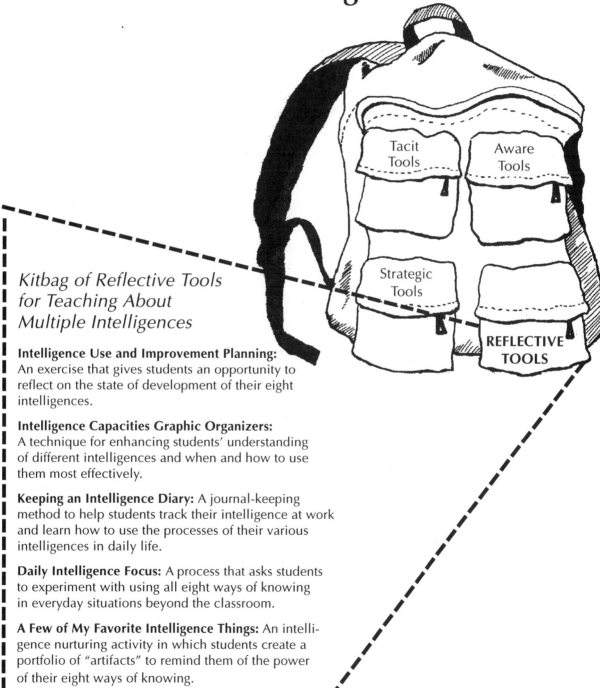

Kitbag of Reflective Tools for Teaching About Multiple Intelligences

Intelligence Use and Improvement Planning:
An exercise that gives students an opportunity to reflect on the state of development of their eight intelligences.

Intelligence Capacities Graphic Organizers:
A technique for enhancing students' understanding of different intelligences and when and how to use them most effectively.

Keeping an Intelligence Diary: A journal-keeping method to help students track their intelligence at work and learn how to use the processes of their various intelligences in daily life.

Daily Intelligence Focus: A process that asks students to experiment with using all eight ways of knowing in everyday situations beyond the classroom.

A Few of My Favorite Intelligence Things: An intelligence nurturing activity in which students create a portfolio of "artifacts" to remind them of the power of their eight ways of knowing.

Veronica was a sixth-grade student who, for the past two years, had teachers who used multiple intelligences as a regular part of their teaching. These teachers also worked with students regularly to help students understand as much as possible about the intelligences: how the different intelligences work (that is, the neurobiological processes involved) and how to improve or strengthen all of the intelligences. The teachers also encouraged students to use all eight ways of knowing in homework assignments, on tests, in processing lessons, in reports, and so on.

During a parent-teacher conference, Mrs. Rodriguez, Veronica's sixth-grade teacher, had a conversation with Veronica's father.

Veronica's father asked, "What is this stuff you are teaching about different intelligences? I thought your job was to teach the three Rs."

Mrs. Rodriguez responded by asking, "What has Veronica told you?"

Veronica's father related a situation that occurred in their home one evening in the last few weeks: "We were having a family discussion about how to deal with a certain problem we were facing. A fairly heated argument broke out because everyone had a different idea about what should be done. Suddenly, Veronica took over the conversation and said we needed to be thinking about the problem in more ways than just one! She said that she has learned some things in school that she thought could help us. Then she suggested that we needed not only to talk about the problem, but we should also draw pictures of it, act it out, create a song about it, and take some individual quiet time to reflect on it. We all thought she was nuts, but we were clearly not getting anywhere with the argument approach. So we tried some of the things she suggested. And you know what? It got us beyond arguing. We started listening to each other's opinions and ideas in a new way. It was really quite amazing!"

Mrs. Rodriguez responded, "Well, this is exciting to me. One of the ways I know I am teaching well is if students take what they are learning in the classroom into their everyday lives. Yes, you are right, my job is to teach the three Rs, but we have discovered that not all students learn and know in the same way. Teaching students about different ways of learning and knowing is helping them understand the three Rs much better. I'm sure you have noticed that Veronica is doing much better in school."

The father said, "Oh, don't get me wrong—I'm not complaining. I'm just very interested; her suggestions made a big difference in our discussion. And they helped us move toward a solution to the problem. I'm glad you're teaching her these things. Is there a way parents could learn about these different ways of learning too?"

Mrs. Rodriguez was able to invite Veronica's father and mother to join a school-sponsored parents' workshop dealing with multiple intelligences.

☆   ☆   ☆

EXPLORATION AND DISCOVERY BASE EXERCISE: INTELLIGENCE USE AND IMPROVEMENT PLANNING

Exercise Procedures

1. Give each student a copy of the appropriate planning work sheet (pp. 197–199). Each student works with a partner brainstorming a list of several story characters (elementary) or historical or literary figures (middle or secondary), each of which embodies one of the intelligences. If you teach middle or secondary students, also have them brainstorm contemporary occupations that require strength in the capacities related to each intelligence. Give students ten to fifteen minutes to brainstorm with their partners.

2. Get a quick cross-section of the responses students wrote on their charts.

3. Give students ten to fifteen minutes without their partners to think of examples of situations in which the students like to use each intelligence most. They will come up with eight situations, one for each intelligence.

   Note: For the elementary level, you may need to lead students through the questions one by one, depending on verbal and writing skills. Let students draw their answers if they need to.

4. After the allotted time, have students share their responses their partners. Make sure that they discuss each situation and ask each other questions about it. As they get ideas from their partners, students may want to add to or change their responses in some or all parts of the chart; they may do so as long as the situations are still those in which the students enjoy using the intelligence. You are after honest reflection here, not conformity.

5. Have students exchange charts with their partners. Each person considers what his or her partner has said about each situation and then writes practical intelligence advice, suggesting

Intelligence Use and Improvement Planning

INTRODUCTION

In this lesson students have the opportunity to reflect on the state of their eight intelligences. The students look into the past, consider the present, and think about the future.

OBJECTIVE

The goal of the exercise is to help students create plans for working consciously to improve their eight ways of knowing, and for integrating the ways more fully into their everyday lives.

DISCUSSION

The ability to be self-reflective is unique to the human species, as far as we know. In this book we see the possibilities of this dynamic gift operating on almost every page. In some ways this exercise puts a capstone on all of the work I have been suggesting regarding the eight intelligences: how students use them and how students can strengthen them.

ways the partner might use the other seven intelligences to expand her or his approaches to each situation. It may help students to give them a formula such as, "Have you considered trying . . ." or "In this situation you might think about using . . ." After they complete their writing have the partners decide which one of them will be person A and which will be person B. Person A will be the listener and person B the speaker. Have them go through the following process:

- Person B gives person A advice regarding possible other intelligent approaches to each situation person A listed.
- As person B speaks, person A listens carefully to the suggestions. Person A is not to argue or disagree, but may ask questions for clarification.
- When Person B is finished giving advice, person A thanks person B for the wise counsel.

7. Have students repeat the process with the roles reversed; person B is the listener and person A is the speaker and advice giver.

8. When the students have finished giving each other advice, have them work individually again. They will rank the suggestions they received from their partners, beginning with "things I think I may want to try next time . . ." and ending with "thank you very much, but I don't want to try that idea." For elementary levels, have each student draw the picture suggested on the work sheet.

9. Lead the whole class in the following reflection on the lesson:

- *What are some things you heard from your partner when you were the listener?*
- *What are some things you said as the speaker or advice giver?*
- *What were your feelings when your partner was giving his or her advice?*
- *What were your feelings when you were giving advice?*
- *How did this activity help you?*
- *What did you learn about yourself and your intelligences as you did this activity?*

Parallel Curriculum Interface

INTELLIGENCE USE AND IMPROVEMENT PLANNING

Personal Exploration and Discovery

Just like any skill we have developed in our lives, the capacities of the various intelligences can be enhanced, developed, and strengthened. These exercises provide students with a variety of opportunities to become actively and consciously involved in growing their own intelligence.

Personal Exploration and Discovery Exercises

➤ **The Possible Human.** Ask students to imagine themselves as a person whose intelligence potential is fully activated. Have them make a list of all those things they think might be different in their life from the way things are now. Tell them to close their eyes and get a picture of themselves as that person. Have them open their eyes and draw a symbol that will remind them of this possibility. Suggest they post this symbol someplace where they will see it every day.

➤ **Setting Intelligence Improvement Goals.** Ask students to make two columns on a piece of paper and to label the first column "Now" and the second "6 Months." For each intelligence, have them write a few notes to themselves regarding where they are now (relative strengths and weaknesses) and where they'd like to be in six months (skills to develop). Then ask them to get with a partner to create a plan to help them reach their six-month goals.

➤ **Setting Intelligence-Use Goals.** Have students individually list the sections of a normal day in their lives. For each section of their day, list how they use the intelligences. Now have them assign each intelligence a number that estimates the percentage of a normal day they use each intelligence. Finally, have students create a plan for intentionally incorporating the lower-percentage intelligences into their day more frequently.

Commentary: Personal MI Exploration and Discovery

The exercises presented here assume that students are at the reflective level of learning about and understanding their own multiple ways of knowing; that is, they see the value of multiple intelligences and want to make them a greater part of their daily living. As you work with students on these exercises, your role should be that of helping them set realistic goals that are compatible with the developmental research on the intelligences (see *Eight Ways of Knowing*).

INTELLIGENCE USE AND IMPROVEMENT PLANNING

Academic Exploration and Discovery

Intelligence Use and Improvement Planning exercises ask students to take all they know about multiple intelligences, in general, and their own intelligence profile, specifically, to enhance their learning of the required material and/or concepts. In other words, this will help them approach their studies with more intelligence.

Academic Exploration and Discovery Strategies

➤ **Intelligent Schoolwork.** Have students make a list of the different subjects or content areas that are part of a normal day/week in school. They then are to list the intelligence(s) that they use the most when doing work related to each subject or content area. Then, with a partner, brainstorm ideas for extending the use of all eight ways of knowing in each of these curriculum areas.

➤ **Unit Analysis and Enhancement.** Lay out a particular unit for students, explaining its goals and the learning tasks involved. Ask them to expand the scope of the unit by making sure that all the intelligences are involved as much as possible. This should include not only an analysis of the actual content to be learned, but also the teaching/learning process for mastering the material.

➤ **Special Report/Project Planning.** Have students lay out a plan for incorporating all the intelligences into a report or project. Ask them to share their plan with a partner, to receive his or her feedback, suggestions, and help on incorporating intelligences they find difficult to use. Ask them to hand in their plans for your approval once the partners feel they have solid direction for the report/project.

Commentary: Multiple Intelligences and the Learning Process
This strategy takes one instantly to the higher-order thinking areas. Students must not only deeply understand the cognitive processes of the different intelligences, but also know how to transfer this knowledge so they are using the intelligences to enhance and deepen their learning of certain concepts and/or curricular material.

INTELLIGENCE USE AND IMPROVEMENT PLANNING

Beyond-the-Classroom Exploration and Discovery

By the time you get to these exercises, students will already have begun to think about applying multiple intelligences outside of school. As you design similar exercises, your goal is to help students find even more ways the multiple intelligences can be incorporated into their lives beyond the classroom.

Beyond-the-Classroom Exploration and Discovery Applications

➤ **Intelligence in the Past.** Ask students to think about their lives in the past and to make a list or five to ten situations, events, and experiences where they wish they had known about the eight intelligences. After completing their lists, have them share these with a neighbor. For discussion have students ask: "How might the eight ways of knowing have made a difference in the outcomes?"

➤ **Intelligence in the Future.** Have students consider their lives over the next year. Ask them to list five to ten events they are anticipating, both exciting and difficult ones. Then, have them share their lists with a partner. For discussion have students ask: "How can your knowledge about the eight ways of knowing help you in these situations you are anticipating? What do you need to do to remind yourself to use all eight?"

➤ **Balancing MI in My Week.** Ask students to analyze the past week of their lives, noting when, where, and how they used the eight intelligences. Which intelligences were dominant? Which were underutilized? Then ask them to make a plan for next week, that represents more of a balance between all the intelligences.

Commentary: Multiple Intelligences and Everyday Life

These application exercises will help students include the intelligences as a given part of their daily experience of living—almost without thinking about it. In order for this to happen, however, students must have a fairly clear grasp of the various cognitive strategies of the different intelligences as well as when and how to use them. Gaining this understanding is the goal of the strategic level. Once students understand the range of strategic possibilities, the reflective level will often follow on its own. These exercises are intended to "jump start" this process.

Intelligence Use and Improvement Planning
(Elementary)

Think of story characters who . . .	**Think of when you . . .**
Like to talk, read, or write	Like to talk, read, or write
Like to be really active or exercise	Like to be really active or exercise
Like to solve problems	Like to solve problems
Like music, singing, or making sounds	Like music, singing, or making sounds
Like to pretend, dream, or draw	Like to pretend, dream, or draw
Like working with others	Like working with others
Like to be alone and think about stuff	Like to be alone and think about stuff
Like to be outside, or with plants and animals	Like to be outside, or with plants and animals

Draw someone who likes to do all of these things!

Intelligence Use and Improvement Planning
(Middle School & Secondary)

	Historical/Literary Figures	Present-Day Occupations	When I Like to Use Each Intelligence
Verbal/Linguistic			
Logical/Mathematical			
Visual/Spatial			
Bodily/Kinesthetic			
Musical/Rhythmic			
Interpersonal			
Intrapersonal			
Naturalist			

Notes on my partner's advice:

Teacher's Personal Reflection Log

INTELLIGENCE USE AND IMPROVEMENT PLANNING

I have the following thoughts/insights about the Intelligence Use and Improvement Planning strategy:

I feel that the Intelligence Use and Improvement Planning strategy can help me in my teaching in the following ways:

As a learning process, the Intelligence Use and Improvement Planning strategy includes the following benefits for my students:

I have the following specific ideas for using the Intelligence Use and Improvement Planning strategy in my classroom in the near future:

I think the Intelligence Use and Improvement Planning strategy can be used beyond the classroom and school in the following ways:

Pathways of Learning © 2000 Zephyr Press, Tucson, Arizona • 800-232-2187 • http://zephyrpress.com

EXPLORATION AND DISCOVERY BASE EXERCISE: INTELLIGENCE CAPACITIES GRAPHIC ORGANIZERS

Exercise Procedures

This exercise is really four separate mini-exercises, each one using a different graphic organizer to analyze the capacities of the different intelligences. Each section outlined below constitutes one such graphic organizer exercise. See the grade-appropriate examples on pp. 205–207.

Mini-Exercise 1: Intelligence Analysis Using a Web

1. Introduce students to webbing by leading them in a practice exercise using things within the classroom: defining the characteristics of clothes, attributes of the overhead projector, and so on.
2. Have students get into eight groups. Students will be in the same group throughout the four lessons in this activity. Assign each group one of the eight intelligences.
3. Students are to draw a web on a piece of newsprint and list on the rays of the web as many of the defining attributes of their assigned intelligence as they can think of.

Intelligence Capacities Graphic Organizers

INTRODUCTION

This exercise is designed to help students understand the various capacities or skills of the eight intelligences more fully, so that students can decide when to use which intelligence to achieve certain goals in everyday life.

OBJECTIVE

The goal of this exercise is to help students clearly define the capacities and skills that are related to each intelligence using cognitive or graphic organizers.

DISCUSSION

Cognitive research indicates very clearly the powers of using graphic or cognitive organizers to teach students thinking skills. These organizers are so effective because they are in synch with how the brain organizes and processes information in a functional manner, moving from general concepts to specific parts and pieces. A graphic organizer simply helps to make this process visible so that we can work with the process, enhance it, and use it with greater consciousness and intention. My adaptation of graphic organizers to the intelligences focuses first on creating an awareness of the different capacities we all have as human beings, and second, on ways to integrate this awareness into daily living. The more we learn about our different ways of knowing (be their eight or eighty), the more we can bring our full intellectual potential to bear on solving the problems and dealing with the challenges facing our planet today.

4. When students have completed this task, have them put a star by the critical attributes of their assigned intelligence, the attributes that are most important and unique to that intelligence.

5. Post and discuss the webs (see discussion suggestions at the end of these procedures).

Mini-Exercise 2: Intelligence Analysis Using a Triangle Chart

1. Introduce students to the triangle chart by leading them in a practice exercise: do something, such as taking a bite out of an apple, and have the class brainstorm what it looks like, sounds like, and feels like.

2. Have students get in their groups. Assign each group one of the eight intelligences, making sure that each group is working on a different intelligence from the one they worked on in the first mini-exercise.

3. Have each group make a triangle chart on a piece of newsprint and have them brainstorm as much information as they can on what it looks like (what they see when this intelligence is in operation), what it sounds like (the sounds they hear when this intelligence is being used), and what it feels like (the emotional responses they associate with this intelligence).

4. Post and discuss the triangle charts (see discussion suggestions at the end of these procedures).

Mini-Exercise 3: Intelligence Analysis Using a Matrix

1. Introduce students to the use of a matrix by leading them in a practice exercise: show the class several items or pictures and have the students classify the items based on certain criteria (color, size, shape, material, use, and so on).

2. Have students get into their groups. Assign each group to work on one of the eight intelligences, making sure that each group is working on a different intelligence from the two they worked on in the previous mini-exercises.

3. Each group is to make an intelligence matrix on a piece of newsprint using categories such as those in the examples. The groups fill in the various boxes of the matrix with as much information as they can, related to the operation and uses of the assigned intelligences.

4. Post and discuss the matrices (see discussion suggestions at the end of these procedures).

Mini-Exercise 4: Intelligence Analysis Using a Venn Diagram

1. Introduce students to the Venn diagram by having them practice comparing and contrasting various things in the classroom: the people sitting on one side of the room to the people on the other, for example.
2. Have students get into their groups. Each group will focus on one of the eight intelligences. Make sure they are working on a different intelligence from the three they worked on in the previous mini-exercises.
3. Have each group make six Venn diagrams on a piece of newsprint. Next have the students label each Venn with their assigned intelligence in the left circle and each of the other intelligences in each right circle and proceed to compare and contrast their assigned intelligence with each of the other seven intelligences. Similarities will go in the overlapping sections of the diagram; differences will go in the separate parts of the circles. If the group was assigned musical/rhythmic intelligence, for example, the first Venn would compare and contrast musical/rhythmic intelligence and bodily/kinesthetic, the next would be musical/rhythmic and visual/spatial, and so on.
4. Post and discuss the Venn diagrams when they are completed (see discussion suggestions at the end of these procedures).

General Discussion to Follow Each Mini-Exercise

Ask the class to make general observations as they look at the different graphic organizers: similarities (things that show up on two or more charts), uniqueness (things that are on only one of the charts), and so on. Ask the following questions:

- *What do you find especially interesting about the charts? What is exciting about them? What confuses you?*
- *What new insights into the eight ways of knowing do these charts give you?*

Give students a few minutes to write in their journals a response to the question, "What new ideas do I have about how to use the intelligences in my everyday life beyond school?"

Parallel Curriculum Interface

INTELLIGENCE CAPACITIES GRAPHIC ORGANIZERS

Personal Exploration and Discovery

Working with graphic organizers will help students develop effective patterns for thinking. When graphic organizers are applied to multiple intelligences, they assist students in developing a deeper understanding of the various cognitive processes involved when working with each intelligence.

Personal Exploration and Discovery Exercises
(See page 207 for organizers.)

> ➤ **Ranking Ladder.** Begin by having students rank-order the intelligences several ways; for example, from favorite to least favorite, strongest to weakest, needs work the most to the least, and so on. Have them talk with three other students and notice similarities and differences.

> ➤ **KWL.** Have students list items on a chart with three columns: (1) "Know" (things I know about the intelligences), (2) "Want to Know" (things I want to know), and (3) "Learned" (things I have learned about the eight ways of knowing). Ask students to share items from the first two columns, then create a class KWL chart and leave it posted. Add to the "L" column as appropriate.

> ➤ **Thought Tree.** Have students put the name of one of the intelligences in the top box of a tree organizer. In the next row of boxes, students will start making associations with the intelligence. Then in the next row, they will make associations with the associations. Tell students to make one thought tree for each intelligence, then compare the associations on the different thought trees.

> ➤ **PMI.** Give students time to evaluate each of the eight ways of knowing by writing about the "Pluses" of each intelligence for them, the "Minuses," and what they find "Interesting" about each. Have several volunteers share their thoughts with the rest of the class. See if there are common feelings and thoughts in the class.

Commentary: Personal MI Exploration and Discovery

Students often assume that there is little connection between what they do in school and their lives beyond school. Having them work with Intelligence Capacities Graphic Organizers can help them bridge their use of the intelligences in the classroom to nonschool situations. As much as possible, build these nonschool reflections into their work with the organizers.

INTELLIGENCE CAPACITIES GRAPHIC ORGANIZERS

Academic Exploration and Discovery

The Intelligence Capacities Graphic Organizers strategy can force students to think about, and hopefully understand, the material you are teaching on many more levels. This strategy indirectly permits them to consider the use of the intelligences as a regular part of their own repertoire for learning. It allows them to learn from others' use of the intelligences, whether this is in a piece of literature, a historical period, and so on.

Academic Exploration and Discovery Strategies
(See pages 205–206 for organizers.)

> ➤ **MI Character Webs.** In literature or when studying certain historical figures, have students web these figures' uses of the different intelligences. Discuss the effect the intelligences had on the story or historical events, as well as how things might have been different had other intelligences been used.

> ➤ **Content Classification Matrices.** Have students create a chart with column heads that represent the key concepts involved in a unit of study. In the left-hand column, list the eight intelligences. Have students review the unit by remembering and classifying both the content studied and the learning activities used to cover the concepts listed in each column.

> ➤ **Analyzing Social Studies and History.** Have students create a matrix, web, or other graphic organizer as appropriate, for analyzing how the various intelligences shaped a culture or a historical era. Ask students to think about how these cultures and/or historical periods might have been different had other intelligences been dominant.

Commentary: Multiple Intelligences and the Learning Process
Multiple intelligences have always been a part of people's lives, whether or not they were labeled as such. By introducing the Graphic Organizers strategy, you are indirectly promoting the regular incorporation of all eight intelligences into students' personal lives, both in and outside of the formal classroom.

INTELLIGENCE CAPACITIES GRAPHIC ORGANIZERS

Beyond-the-Classroom Exploration and Discovery

These exercises help students begin and/or expand the conscious use of all eight intelligences as part of their regular daily life. As students analyze what they are studying via the graphic organizer strategies, using the intelligences becomes embedded in how they look at life. They may be informally webbing someone else's behavior in a social situation, creating a matrix as they watch a TV show or movie, or doing intelligence-based Venns when analyzing various situations in the news.

Beyond-the-Classroom Exploration and Discovery Applications
(See pages 205–207 for organizers.)

► **Bridging Snapshots.** For each intelligence, have students create a set of ideas for using the intelligence beyond the classroom. Try to come up with very practical ideas, something that one could take a snapshot of. When students have completed one set of "snapshots," have them share their ideas with each other.

► **Life Challenges Matrix.** Have students create a chart which lists certain issues, problems, or challenges they are facing beyond the classroom across the top. Down the side of the chart list the eight intelligences. Ask students to brainstorm things they can do to use the various intelligences to help them deal with the issue, problem, or challenge listed in each column.

► **Graphic Organizers and Peer/Family Relationships.** Have students devise different multiple intelligence-based graphic organizers to help them more fully analyze and understand some of their personal relationships beyond the classroom. For example, do multiple intelligences character webs of members of their family, use a Venn to compare and contrast the different intelligence strengths of their circle of friends, and so on.

Commentary: Multiple Intelligences and Everyday Life

Initially, the suggestion that multiple intelligence should be a given part of how we approach the challenges, issues, and problems of daily living may see like a stretch. But as we find ways to use the intelligences more, we will, without even having to think about it, use all the intelligences as a matter of course. This is quite natural; it is simply a matter of recovering the full range of intellectual potentials we all have as human creatures.

Intelligence Capacities Graphic Organizers
(Elementary)

WEB

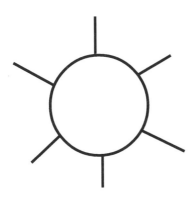

What do you do when you're using this way of knowing?

TRIANGLE

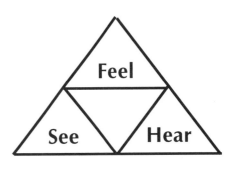

- **Tell what you see**
- **Tell what you hear**
- **Tell what you feel**

CHART

Seeing	Reading	Drawing
Speaking	Action	Writing
Listening	Touching	Thinking

Make an "X" in each box that is true for your way of knowing

VENN

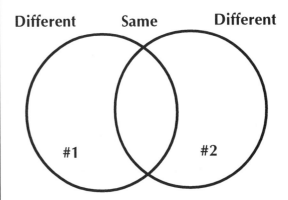

How are two ways of knowing the same and different?

Intelligence Capacities Graphic Organizers
(Middle School & Secondary)

ATTRIBUTE WEB

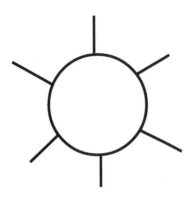

1. List the attributes of your assigned intelligence on the rays of the web.
2. Put an asterisk (*) by the attributes that are unique to this intelligence.

TRIANGLE CHART

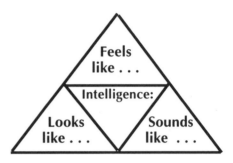

For your assigned intelligence list
- the "looks like" (what you see)
- the "sounds like" (what you hear)
- the "feels like" (what you feel, your emotions)

CLASSIFICATION MATRIX

Intelligence:

	In School	In the Community	In the World
In Myself			
In Friends			
In Others			

1. Study and discuss the top and side categories on the matrix.
2. Fill in the center boxes with examples of the intelligences that honor the top and side intersections.

VENN DIAGRAM

Assigned Intelligence: Comparing Intelligence:

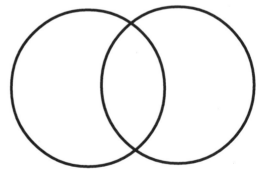

1. On the left and right, list ways your assigned intelligence and another intelligence are different from each other.
2. In the middle, list ways in which they are similar.

Pathways of Learning © 2000 Zephyr Press, Tucson, Arizona • 800-232-2187 • http://zephyrpress.com

More Graphic Organizers
(All Grades)

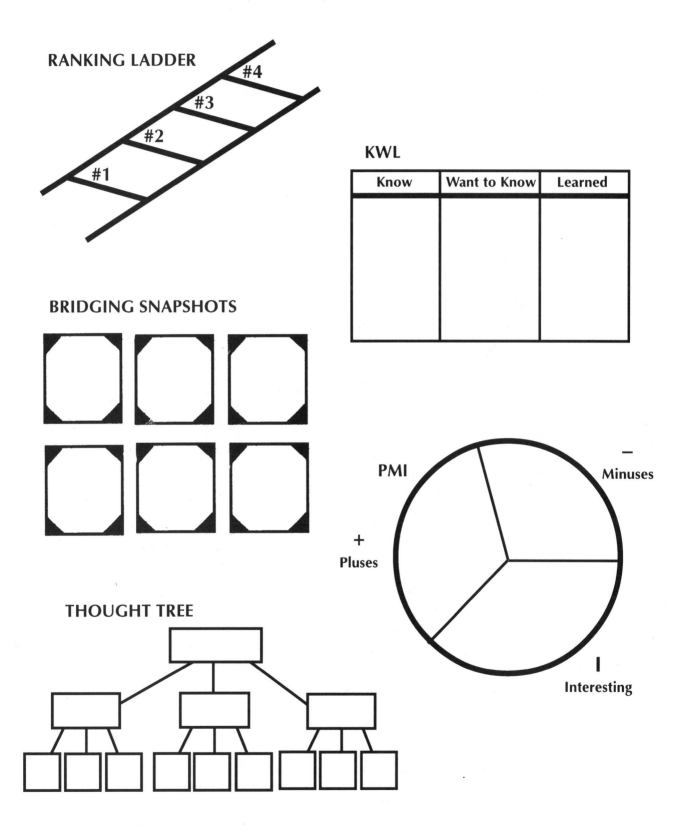

RANKING LADDER

#4

#3

#2

#1

KWL

Know	Want to Know	Learned

BRIDGING SNAPSHOTS

PMI

− Minuses

+ Pluses

I Interesting

THOUGHT TREE

Teacher's Personal Reflection Log
INTELLIGENCE CAPACITIES GRAPHIC ORGANIZERS

I have the following thoughts/insights about the Graphic Organizers strategy:

I feel that the Graphic Organizers strategy can help me in my teaching in the following ways:

As a learning process, the Graphic Organizers strategy includes the following benefits for my students:

I have the following specific ideas for using the Graphic Organizers strategy in my classroom in the near future:

I think the Graphic Organizers strategy can be used beyond the classroom and school in the following ways:

Pathways of Learning © 2000 Zephyr Press, Tucson, Arizona • 800-232-2187 • http://zephyrpress.com

EXPLORATION AND DISCOVERY BASE EXERCISE: KEEPING AN INTELLIGENCE DIARY

Exercise Procedures

1. Give each student a special notebook or folder that is to be an Intelligence Diary. Tell students they are to reflect on their intelligences each day and to make an entry about their reflections in their diaries. They will make entries for one month.

2. Introduce students to the appropriate reflection models in the examples (pp. 214–215) or other models you create. Suggest that your students try a variety of reflective approaches during the course of the month. Following are instructions for using each model shown.

   • **Model 1:** Provide a series of "finish this phrase" writing stems or lead-ins to help students get started. Students are to write their responses to one or more of the phrases in their Intelligence Diaries.

   • **Model 2:** Create a set of doing stems for students to use to reflect on the day or on a particular lesson. These stems are lead-ins, like those above, but they ask students to do more than just write about the day. Make sure that the stems require students to use all eight intelligences to respond.

   • **Model 3:** This model suggests that students pretend their intelligences are animals (elementary) or people (middle or secondary). The students also pretend they can converse with the animals or people. To prepare for the process, students should create some questions they would like to ask their intelligences. During the pretending part of the exercise, students should record the answers they get from the different intelligences.

Keeping an Intelligence Diary

INTRODUCTION

This exercise helps students foster a metacognitive awareness of their own intelligence processes. Students will learn a variety of journaling techniques by which they can become more skilled at tracking their intelligences.

OBJECTIVE

The goal of this exercise is to introduce students to the discipline of keeping a journal or log and to catalyze in them an interest to do so.

DISCUSSION

Keeping a journal or log is a powerful tool of transformation. By their very nature, journals cause one to be introspective, and that very introspection has the potential to open new realms of thought and experience. As we become aware of ourselves, and, in a sense, take a step back and watch ourselves, we gain new power over our lives. We are much less likely to abdicate responsibility for our actions. We are less apt to fall into the feeling that we are victims of someone else's decisions. And we are less likely to get stuck in various kinds of habitual, robotlike behavior patterns. Following are some keys to keeping journals, logs, or diaries successfully: (1) write entries on a regular basis (daily or every other day); (2) make the exercise fun, creative, and relaxing so that you will look forward to it; (3) get a special notebook and special recording media (colored pens, markers, paints, clay, tape recorder, construction paper, and so on); and (4) do your writing in a special place (where you will not be disturbed for five to ten minutes) and at a special time of the day (generally at its end).

- **Model 4:** Encourage students to invent new models and approaches to reflect on the day or on a particular lesson. The manner in which students reflect is not important; that they reflect is extremely important. Just make sure that the students document what they did and what they learned.

3. Once a week, ask students to share what is happening and what they are learning as they keep their Intelligence Diaries. Following are some examples of questions you may use:

    - *Will some of you volunteer to share one entry from your diaries? Let's try to get a variety of types of entries, such as something you've written, drawn, sung, and so on.*

    - *What are your feelings about this exercise? Did you like it? Why or why not?*

    - *What are you learning about yourself as you reflect in this way each day?*

    - *What tips can you give to others about how to make journaling go easier? How to make it more fun? Other approaches to the task you have invented?*

Parallel Curriculum Interface

KEEPING AN INTELLIGENCE DIARY

Personal Exploration and Discovery

The Intelligence Diary exercises listed here just barely scratch the surface of the creative journaling possibilities related to the various intelligences. These exercises can include such things as intelligence-use logs, personal intelligence growth and development reflective journals, daily-weekly-monthly multiple intelligences experience diaries, or even a portfolio which documents the role of the intelligences in one's life.

Personal Exploration and Discovery Exercises

➤ **Sculpting/Painting/Drawing Your Reflections.** Give students clay, paints, or colored markers and instruct them to create a visual expression of their thoughts and feelings. The expression can be a literal picture or simply a series of designs, shapes, and colors. Tell students to trust their intuitions and their first impulse of what they want to make.

➤ **The Sounds and Music of the Day.** Have students create a chart that shows the different parts of their days. For each segment, have them decide on the appropriate sound and/or music that they would play as an accompaniment. Once students have orchestrated their day, have them get with a partner and share the sounds and music of the day.

➤ **Naming the Patterns of the Day.** Have students create a time line of one day, from waking up until bedtime. Have them list key events that happened and plot them at the appropriate place on the time line. Then, have students look back over the day for patterns (that is, groupings of events) or divisions in the day. Have them create titles for these groupings or for the different segments of the day.

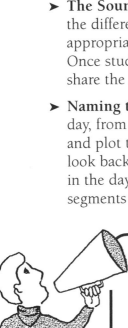

Commentary: Personal MI Exploration and Discovery

The key to any kind of Intelligence Diary or journal, regardless of the form, is to ask students to step back and reflect directly on their journey using the eight ways of knowing. This very act of stepping outside of and observing one's self tends to catalyze a more conscious use of the intelligences. Once students are conscious about anything in their lives, they suddenly have control over it and can assume more responsibility for it. At this meta-intelligence reflective level, this responsibility is directly related to grasping MI as an integral part of effective daily living.

KEEPING AN INTELLIGENCE DIARY

Academic Exploration and Discovery

The Intelligence Diary strategy helps students find links between what they are studying in the classroom and real life. The key is to create diary-writing or journaling tasks which ask students to express their feelings about the material using all eight intelligences, as well as to explore meaningful connections between what they are studying and their own lives.

Academic Exploration and Discovery Strategies

➤ **The Montage Journal.** Give students a sheet of heavy paper, magazines with lots of pictures, scissors, and glue. Instruct them to create an all-pictures reflection on a particular lesson of the day. Tell them to remember that the colors they choose also can communicate their feelings and thoughts.

➤ **The Audio-Cassette Log.** Allow students to speak their thoughts into a tape recorder. Maybe try something like an Oprah Winfrey–style question-and-answer show, where you (or other students) interview each other about reflections on a lesson or the day.

➤ **The Kinesthetic Journal.** Ask each student to make up a short pantomime or charade which says, through body language, what they think or feel about a lesson. Then have each perform his or her drama for the class, with the rest of the class trying to guess what he or she is saying.

➤ **Reflections through Poetry.** Teach students the structure of a limerick and then have them create limericks that share their thoughts and feelings about a lesson. You could also work with other poetry forms such as haiku, free verse, iambic pentameter, and so on.

Commentary: Multiple Intelligences and the Learning Process
Students, consciously or unconsciously, tend to assume a "Show me how this is important!" attitude. As teachers, we can provide students with occasions that allow them to create these connections for themselves. When you are working at the reflective level of teaching students about the multiple intelligences, your role is helping students discover meaningful connections between their everyday lives and their learning in the classroom.

KEEPING AN INTELLIGENCE DIARY

Beyond-the-Classroom Exploration and Discovery

The very act of asking students to brainstorm beyond-the-classroom ideas for diaries and journals may be the key to getting them committed to this kind of reflection.

Beyond-the-Classroom Exploration and Discovery Applications

➤ **A Multimodal Diary/Journal.** Students are to create a diary or journal process to reflect on a day, week, or month using all of the intelligences (see example on pp. 214–215). Make sure that the process involves using the unique cognitive mode for each of the intelligences respectively.

➤ **Intelligence-Focused Reflections.** Have students imagine that each intelligence has its own independent existence. Reflect on the day, week, or month from this perspective. For example, what are the primary shapes, images, colors, textures of today, this week, this month? What association patterns of nature, animals, weather conditions, physical formations, and so on, do you make?

➤ **Daily or Weekly MI-Media Processing.** For the next eight weeks, have students target one intelligence for each week. Throughout the week they are to use the target intelligence as much as possible in their reflections on the week; for example, one week's process may be through painting, another's through poetry-writing, and still another's through encounters with the natural world.

Commentary: Multiple Intelligences and Everyday Life

The Intelligence Diary exercises that you create and use at this level ask students to incorporate some kind of formal reflective process as part of their normal, daily routine, such as thinking about and/or planning the next day's activities or evaluating the past day. The more you can get the students involved in planning suggestions for these reflective activities, the more follow-through you will find.

Keeping an Intelligence Diary
(Elementary)

MODEL 1
Stems (writing)

I wanted to sing when . . .

Today I used my body to . . .

It was fun today when . . .

I want to go outside today when . . .

It was hard today when . . .

Something I made today was . . .

I talked with a friend about . . .

An animal/plant I thought about today was . . .

I felt really smart today when . . .

It really made me think when . . .

I wanted to be alone today when . . .

Something I read today was . . .

I used numbers today for . . .

MODEL 2
More stems (doing)

Draw something from the day.

Make up a song about today.

Do an action from the day.

Talk to a partner about the day.

Make a rhyme about the day.

Paint the colors of your day.

Beat out the rhythms of your day.

Be silent and remember the day.

Act out how you feel about today.

Make sounds you heard today.

MODEL 3

What is your favorite way of knowing?

What kind of animal would it be?

Pretend you can talk to your "knowing animal." What would it say?

What would your "knowing animal" say or ask you?

MODEL 4

Make something to remind you of what you learned today.

Keeping an Intelligence Diary
(Middle School & Secondary)

MODEL 1
Journal Writing Starters

- *I used my _____ intelligence most today in the following situations:*

- *I had the most trouble using _____ intelligence today because . . .*

- *The time today when I used the most intelligences at the same time was . . .*

- *Something I learned today about how I think and learn was . . .*

- *I had the most fun today when I was using my _____ intelligence because . . .*

- *A new idea I had about how all eight ways of knowing can help me in my life is . . .*

- *The biggest difficulty I'm having using my eight ways of knowing is . . .*

MODEL 2
Journal Doing Starters

- *An image or picture I have of this day is . . .* (Draw it.)

- *If today were a song, it would be . . .* (Sing it.)

- *My inner feelings about today are . . .* (Meditate on it.)

- *A body movement or gesture for today is . . .* (Do it.)

- *A thought I've had today is . . .* (Write it.)

- *I want to talk with someone about . . .* (Discuss it.)

- *A thought pattern I find interesting is . . .* (Think about it.)

- *If today was a plant, animal or weather condition, it would be . . .* (Go outside to experience it.)

MODEL 3
A Chat with My Intelligence

1. Pretend your eight intelligences are eight people you can talk to. Close your eyes and imagine what they look like.

2. Now pretend that you are having a chat with them. Spend a minute with each of these "intelligence persons" and ask them each a question.

3. Imagine you hear them answering your questions. What is their message for you? (Remember that their answers may not be in words!)

4. In your journal, write what happened. What did your intelligences communicate to you that you want to remember?

5. Turn to a person sitting near you and share what happened.

MODEL 3
Inventing New Journaling Ideas

Make up eight new ideas for reflecting on the day—one idea for each intelligence.

Teacher's Personal Reflection Log

KEEPING AN INTELLIGENCE DIARY

I have the following thoughts/insights about the Intelligence Diary strategy:

I feel that the Intelligence Diary strategy can help me in my teaching in the following ways:

As a learning process, the Intelligence Diary strategy includes the following benefits for my students:

I have the following specific ideas for using the Intelligence Diary strategy in my classroom in the near future:

I think the Intelligence Diary strategy can be used beyond the classroom and school in the following ways:

Pathways of Learning © 2000 Zephyr Press, Tucson, Arizona • 800-232-2187 • http://zephyrpress.com

EXPLORATION AND DISCOVERY BASE EXERCISE: DAILY INTELLIGENCE FOCUS

Exercise Procedures

1. Pass out a copy of the appropriate 8-day intelligence planner (pp. 222–223) to each student. Say, "The exercise we are about to start will take eight days to complete. You will choose an intelligence to focus on for each day. You'll then have some time to create a plan in which you will include every way you can think of to incorporate the day's intelligence into all that you do."

2. Explain how to use the 8-day planner:

   - Before beginning, students will work on their own and draw a picture or image (elementary) or write the name of an intelligence (middle and secondary) in the space provided for each day. Each day is to have a different intelligence focus. As the days come up, students will focus on the intelligence they have listed.

   - After students have finished listing the focuses, ask the students how they decided which intelligence to assign to which day. Was their choice random, or did they have a rationale?

   - Now have students list at least eight ideas of what they will do to implement the assigned focus, one for each day.

   - After students have come up with one idea for each day, have them share ideas with a partner. Both partners then will come up with one more idea for each day.

   - Have students thank their partners and find other partners. With the new partners they are to repeat the process, coming up with one more idea for each day. At the end of these two rounds of working with a partner, each student will have at least three ideas for each day.

   Note: Stress to your students that *it's okay to steal ideas from each other!*

Daily Intelligence Focus

INTRODUCTION

In this exercise, students are assigned to focus on different intelligence skills and capacities for eight days. The students are asked to experiment with using the intelligences consciously in new situations.

OBJECTIVE

The goal of the exercise is to help students transfer their knowledge about the intelligences into the task of daily living beyond the classroom.

DISCUSSION

In some ways the intelligences are like any skills or capacities we have—the more we use them, the better they become. We often let ourselves fall into various kinds of routine patterns of behavior and thinking. As a matter of course, we generally do not venture into areas that require risk and with which we are uncomfortable. We often prefer the so-called tried and true over the new and uncertain. The Daily Intelligence Focus exercise is a way to interrupt this propensity, thus giving students (and teachers) a way to step beyond the predictable boredom of "every day is the same as the day before." Not only can this exercise make each day more interesting, it can strengthen all of our intelligence capacities, many of which will not get exercised if we are simply left to our regular routines.

- Have students thank each other for the ideas and then pull the class back together as a whole group.

3. Lead students in the following sharing discussion:

- *Who would like to share some of the great ideas he or she got from a partner?*
- *Look at your own planning work sheet and pick the day you think is the most interesting. What are you going to try that day?*
- *Pick the day that looks most boring or predictable. Share your ideas for that day. Ask the whole class for other ideas that could "juice up" that day so it isn't so boring and predictable.*
- *Which day are you looking forward to the most? Why?*

4. Say, "*A part of your homework assignment each day is to spend five minutes reflecting on the day and reviewing the ideas you tried. The most important part of the lesson is this debriefing at the end of the day. Write what happened, how you felt, and what you learned as you focused on and experimented with the intelligence of the day.*"

5. At the end of the eight days, schedule a time for students to share what happened and what they learned about their intelligences. Ask students if they would like to continue the exercise for another eight days.

Parallel Curriculum Interface

DAILY INTELLIGENCE FOCUS

Personal Exploration and Discovery

The Daily Intelligence Focus exercises are based on the research finding that intelligence can be taught, enhanced, developed, and strengthened. These exercises, and others you create, ask students to focus their understanding of the eight intelligences in a variety of situations, including with other people, their own use of the intelligences, products people have created using the different intelligences, and so on.

Personal Exploration and Discovery Exercises

➤ **Fine-Tuning Intelligence Capacities.** Assign students an eight-day experiment where they pretend that their various intelligence capacities are on a rheostat and can be turned up higher (that is, emphasized) and turned down lower at will. Each day of the experiment, they are to focus on one intelligence and experiment with turning it up and down. At the end of the experiment, ask students to share their experiences.

➤ **People Watching with an Intelligent Eye.** Assign students to experiment with watching people involved in various group situations. Ask them to keep a log of what they learned about different intelligences' strengths and weaknesses by listening and watching people.

➤ **Focus to Foci.** Provide an opportunity for students to experience typical art forms created by various intelligences; for example, a painting, a symphony, a dance, reading poetry, and so on. Ask students to focus their full attention on the art form and, secondarily, to be aware of what else is catalyzed by these art forms, such as other times and places in their lives, other people, pets, feelings, images, food, and so on.

Commentary: Personal MI Exploration and Discovery

These exercises directly or indirectly ask students to use their eight intelligences as an analytic screen for looking at others or themselves. The ultimate goal of these exercises is to help students understand that the intelligences are tools that can give them new levels of understanding and appreciation for almost any situation in which they find themselves. For even more reflection practice, have students brainstorm their own application scenarios where they would like to use the intelligences as an analytic screen.

DAILY INTELLIGENCE FOCUS

Academic Exploration and Discovery

The use of the Daily Intelligence Focus strategy with your academic content requires students to finely hone their understanding and use of the eight intelligences. This strategy asks students to look at the curriculum from a wide variety of angles—at least eight! In doing so, they will rapidly move beyond a simple regurgitation of facts and figures. Require them to use the various ways of knowing to demonstrate their knowledge. This will give you new glimpses of their understanding of the material you are trying to teach.

Academic Exploration and Discovery Strategies

➤ **Multimodal Listening and Note-Taking.** When listening to a lecture, ask students to take notes using all of their intelligences; that is, record what the person is saying but add to this images or pictures, song titles or sounds that come to mind, notes about physical gestures that could embody the ideas being communicated, humorous comments you would like to make, and questions you would like to ask.

➤ **MI Academic Goals.** Ask students to target their learning of different academic concepts using specific intelligences. During the specified time frame, they are to focus on using the distinct capacities of the target intelligence to enhance, deepen, and expand their learning of the academic material at hand.

➤ **Intelligent Homework Assignments.** When you give students a homework assignment, ask them to choose (or you assign) at least three intelligences they must use to present their completed work. Over time, make sure to balance assignments so they are using all the intelligences in the completion of various homework assignments.

Commentary: Multiple Intelligences and the Learning Process
The more levels on which students process any experience in their lives (including learning) the more they truly understand. The benefits of using this strategy are at least twofold: it helps students integrate specific curricular material into their lives and, secondly, it deepens their understanding of the various intelligences and how they can be employed as a part of learning in almost any situation.

DAILY INTELLIGENCE FOCUS

Beyond-the-Classroom Exploration and Discovery

As you create these beyond-school applications of the Intelligence Focus exercise, think about all those situations in which everyone is required to process information. Create the exercises around using all the intelligences to process this data on more levels.

Beyond-the-Classroom Exploration and Discovery Applications

➤ **TV Watching with a Focus.** Assign students to experiment with watching TV shows or videos with part of their attention tracking the occurrences of the eight intelligences; for example, music, sounds, colors, settings and props, relationships, and so on. The students are then to write a short report about how the producers used the intelligences and to what ends.

➤ **Sorting the News.** Assign students to read a newspaper or news magazine and sort each story into the eight intelligences areas. You could also have them look for the eight intelligences within a single article. Students should "read between the lines" for the "intelligence news," which may not be the same as the news being overtly reported in the article.

➤ **MI Socializing.** When students are in any situation where they are relating to and interacting with other people, have them turn on their eight multiple intelligence receptors to help them more fully experience the situation. For example, tune their attention to the colors and textures of the situation: the body language being used, the sounds, tones, rhythms, and beats of the situation, and so on.

Commentary: Multiple Intelligences and Everyday Life

Students are bombarded with more information than they can handle. However, as they learn to process information on more levels of their brain, mind, body system, they can learn to take in and understand a lot more. As students are encouraged to use all their intelligences to process everything that happens in their lives, new levels of their experience of and appreciation for the complexity of daily living may emerge.

Daily Intelligence Focus
(Elementary)

How will you be smart each day?

MONDAY	TUESDAY	WEDNESDAY	THURSDAY	FRIDAY
Make a picture of Monday's way:	Make a picture of Tuesday's way:	Make a picture of Wednesday's way:	Make a picture of Thursday's way:	Make a picture of Friday's way:
IDEAS: What will I do or try?	IDEAS: What will I do or try?	IDEAS: What will I do or try?	IDEAS: What will I do or try?	IDEAS: What will I do or try?

Eight Ways of Being Smart

Words, language, and speech	Counting and finding patterns	Drawing, sculpting, and painting	Body movement and action	Singing, sounds, and drumming	Talking and listening to others	Being alone and thinking	Nurtures plants and animals

Daily Intelligence Focus
(Middle School & Secondary)

My plan for being intelligent this week

MONDAY	TUESDAY	WEDNESDAY	THURSDAY	FRIDAY
Intelligence focus:	Intelligence focus:	Intelligence focus:	Intelligence focus:	Intelligence focus:
IDEAS: What will I do or try? 1. 2. 3. 4. 5.	IDEAS: What will I do or try? 1. 2. 3. 4. 5.	IDEAS: What will I do or try? 1. 2. 3. 4. 5.	IDEAS: What will I do or try? 1. 2. 3. 4. 5.	IDEAS: What will I do or try? 1. 2. 3. 4. 5.

Eight Ways of Being Smart

Verbal/ Linguistic	Logical/ Mathematical	Visual/ Spatial	Bodily/ Kinesthetic	Musical/ Rhythmic	Inter-personal	Intra-personal	Naturalist

Teacher's Personal Reflection Log
DAILY INTELLIGENCE FOCUS

I have the following thoughts/insights about the Daily Intelligence Focus strategy:

I feel that the Daily Intelligence Focus strategy can help me in my teaching in the following ways:

As a learning process, the Daily Intelligence Focus strategy includes the following benefits for my students:

I have the following specific ideas for using the Daily Intelligence Focus strategy in my classroom in the near future:

I think the Daily Intelligence Focus strategy can be used beyond the classroom and school in the following ways:

Pathways of Learning © 2000 Zephyr Press, Tucson, Arizona • 800-232-2187 • http://zephyrpress.com

EXPLORATION AND DISCOVERY BASE EXERCISE: A FEW OF MY FAVORITE INTELLIGENCE THINGS

Exercise Procedures

1. Ask students to bring a medium-sized box to class. On the day you begin this lesson, introduce the idea of an "intelligence kitbag" to the class by saying,

   Over the next three weeks you will be putting various things into the box. You will choose things that help you be aware of and use all eight ways of knowing, both in your studies and in your life beyond the classroom. This box will become your multiple intelligences kitbag. The kitbag is like a doctor's bag, which contains the basic tools he or she needs to be a good doctor. The intelligence kitbag contains tools, techniques, methods, and so on that you need to be the most intelligent person you can be! It may also contain examples of things you and others have produced using the different intelligences. It should contain items that are reminders of your multiple intelligence capabilities as well as items that are somehow inspiring to you.

2. Begin by giving students time to cover and decorate their boxes. You want students to invest some time and energy in creating their kitbags so that the boxes will have the students' personal touches and will remind the students' of their eight ways of knowing as soon as they see the boxes. Make sure that you have all the materials on hand for students to decorate their kitbags: paints, colored markers, colored paper, and so on.

   Note: In the next step of the lesson, you will be asked to show students your kitbag as an example. So if you haven't created one yet, now is an excellent time to do so!

A Few of My Favorite Intelligence Things

INTRODUCTION

This exercise asks students to create a kitbag that contains their favorite tools and techniques for each of the eight intelligences, the ones they enjoy using most. The exercise is most appropriate after students have a fair degree of familiarity with the intelligences and have been working with them for some time.

OBJECTIVE

The goal of this exercise is to help students create tangible evidence of the power and benefit of the eight ways of knowing, and to catalyze a deep resolve to integrate the intelligences into their everyday living.

DISCUSSION

Many of our cultural traditions have taught us the importance of symbols in our lives. Human beings are symbol-making creatures. We live by our symbols. They tell us who we are, what we are doing with our lives, and why. They communicate the meaning and purpose of our existence. In this exercise, students are asked to create a kitbag that contains items that symbolize for them the eight ways of knowing. The very act of collecting the items will be profoundly important to many students, for they are not only putting things in their kitbags that remind them of the eight intelligences, but at some deep, unconscious level, they are symbolizing their full potential as human beings. The objects they choose will likely be things that evoke many latent potentials that can provide a deeper, fuller, and richer experience of living.

3. Show students your intelligence kitbag, displaying the items and explaining why the kitbag is important to you and how it helps remind you of the eight intelligences.

4. Ask students to brainstorm a list of items that represent the different intelligences and that they might want to include in their kitbags (see suggestions in the examples on pp. 231-232 to "prime the pump" as needed). Ask students to think about the following questions to get started:

   • *What are the tools, techniques, strategies, and methods for each intelligence that work best for you?* (Responses should be things that get the students into the modality of each intelligence quickly: a favorite audiotape, a set of colored marking pens, a Rubik's cube, a book of poetry, and so on.)

   • *What things could you put into the kitbag that would symbolize for you the different ways of knowing?* (Responses should symbolize and call to mind the essence of each of the intelligences: how it operates, its unique language, its core capacities, how to trigger it in the brain, and so on.)

   • *What things could you include, which you have produced or created, as examples of your different intelligences at work?* (Students should include artifacts that, when the students see them, will remind the students of their multiple intelligence capacities.)

5. After students have some ideas of what they might include in their kitbags, tell them that they have three weeks to work on creating their kitbags. They are to have at least one item for each intelligence. At the end of the three weeks they will have an opportunity to share what is in their kitbags with other students.

6. Kitbag sharing:

   • Place students into groups of three or four.
   • Have the students in each group proceed in round-robin fashion, with students sharing in turn what items they put in their kitbags and how they plan to use those items. Have each student explain why she or he chose particular items and tell how she or he plans to use those items. It is best to deal with one intelligence at a time, with each student in the group sharing the items she or he has collected for one intelligence before moving on to the next intelligence. Sharing in this way keeps the conversation more lively and interesting because students will go around the group eight times.

7. Consider setting up individual student-teacher conferences to go through students' kitbags with them.

- Compare your and your students' notes on what you have observed the students doing as they were involved in various learning activities, and comment on the items they have included in their kitbags.
- Make additional suggestions of things students may want to consider including in the kitbag.

Note: This conference is a great opportunity to reflect with students on the development of their own intelligence capacities. Offer any advice you may have on exercises and practices that could help the students capitalize on their strengths and strengthen their weaker intelligences.

- Make suggestions for extending the intelligences into situations beyond the formal academic world: relationships with peers, family, resolving conflicts, and so on.
- Share your own struggles and breakthroughs in working with the intelligences.
- Let students know of your concern and support to help them develop their full intellectual potential.

Parallel Curriculum Interface

A FEW OF MY FAVORITE INTELLIGENCE THINGS

Personal Explorations and Discovery

Philosophers have frequently observed that humans are symbol-makers; once we have created symbols, they, in turn, tend to create us. This set of exercises involves students in creating a variety of ways to symbolize. Include artifacts from each of the different ways of knowing to symbolize the importance of using all eight intelligences.

Personal Exploration and Discovery Exercises

➤ **"Once Upon an Intelligence . . ."** Have students make up an adventure story in which the hero or heroine is a fully actualized multiple intelligence being. You might begin with the whole class brainstorming ideas. Give them time to write and share their stories.

➤ **Personal Art Gallery.** Give students an opportunity to find or create things to put on the wall of their bedroom to remind them of the eight intelligences; for example, a picture for each intelligence, an object for each intelligence, and so on.

➤ **Personal Orchestra.** Have students brainstorm pieces of music that are appropriate for each of the intelligences. The music should remind them of the eight ways of knowing; that is, communicate what each intelligence is like.

➤ **Intelligence Gestures.** Have students create a hand signal or gesture for each of the intelligences (like sign language). Suggest to students that they use these gestures during the day to remind them of their full intellectual potential.

Commentary: Personal MI Exploration and Discovery
Much of what goes on as students work with this process will be highly intuitive, and thus may be beyond realms of logical analysis and rational explanation. Your main goal is to have students create a variety of personal daily reminders to be "all that they can be" intellectually. In some ways, the very process of creating these Favorite Intelligence Things can become a symbol of the possibility of living one's daily life on multiple levels.

A FEW OF MY FAVORITE INTELLIGENCE THINGS

Academic Exploration and Discovery

While it is an error to equate the intelligences with certain academic disciplines or content, it is interesting to look occasionally at the curriculum in this way. The content of some curricular areas seems to favor certain intelligences (for example, language arts has obvious connections to verbal/linguistic intelligence). When students understand this, they are then free to strategize how they can best master various academic material.

Academic Exploration and Discovery Strategies

➤ **Intelligence Curricular Connections.** Ask students to analyze the content of various academic areas using the screen of MI. Which intelligences seem to dominate or be the favorites of given subject areas? Then ask students to see if they find the other intelligences more subtly present within the specific curricular content.

➤ **My Favorite Intelligences for "X" Content.** Ask students to analyze the various subject areas of the curriculum and to say which intelligences help them the most when trying to learn the related content. Ask them to be as specific as possible about how they use the intelligences to help.

➤ **Others' Favorite Intelligence Things.** In different content areas, have students note which intelligences various people tend to favor; for example, characters in literature; famous historical figures; the aspects of a story problem in math; scientists or inventors and their experimental and discovery process; and so on.

Commentary: Multiple Intelligences and the Learning Process
These strategies helps students realize that any content can be learned in a variety of ways. That is, the seeming intelligence relationship of the content does not dictate how it must be taught and/or learned. The academic use of the Favorite Intelligence Things strategy recognizes some of the content biases and allows students to move beyond these in the teaching and learning process.

A FEW OF MY FAVORITE INTELLIGENCE THINGS

Beyond-the-Classroom Exploration and Discovery

As you create additional Favorite Intelligence Things exercises, remember that your goal is to help students create powerful reminders for themselves to use all their intelligences every day. You want them to create a series of artifacts which they can display and encounter every day. These artifacts should be symbolic reminders of the importance of multiple intelligences.

Beyond-the-Classroom Exploration and Discovery Applications

➤ **Intelligence Hero/Heroine Biographies.** Assign students to create a booklet which contains at least one biographical sketch of a person (famous or otherwise, historical or fictional) who is an exemplar of strength in each of the intelligence areas. Students also should try to get a photo of the person(s), an example of something they produced or created, and a brief outline of their life (things that influenced them, family situation, special experiences, and so on).

➤ **Multiple Intelligences Daily Ritual.** Help student create a quick, ritualistic rehearsal of the eight ways of knowing that they could use each day to remind themselves to use all of their intelligences during the day. The ritual should involve things that are typical of the modality for each intelligence; for example, drawing something, making sounds or singing, physical movement or gesture, and so on.

➤ **A Dialogue with My Intelligences.** Ask students to pretend their eight intelligences are an inner advisory council upon which they can call when they need advice on solving a problem or meeting a challenge. Have students notice which are the "favored" members of the council. Also have them think of situations beyond school when they feel it would be helpful to "convene the council."

Commentary: Multiple Intelligences and Everyday Life
From biological, neurological, and psychological perspectives, these kinds of exercises deal with intelligence archetypes. In psychology, archetypes are exemplars of the human journey. They communicate what is possible in our own development. These exercises give students opportunities to create and find symbols that tell them "I am a multiple-intelligent being whose full potential is in a state of becoming."

A Few of My Favorite Things
(All Grades)
SUGGESTIONS FOR PERSONAL INTELLIGENCE KITBAGS

Verbal/Linguistic

Tools/Techniques/Strategies/Methods
* new, strange, or fun vocabulary words
* humor: puns, jokes
* oral or written expression of ideas
* academic debate
* storytelling or hearing stories

Symbols of Verbal/Linguistic Knowing
* a favorite piece or book of poetry
* a famous speech that "changed things"
* examples of glorious metaphors or similies
* a clever story with a surprise ending
* a complex verbal puzzle

Creative Examples (personal)
* an essay you wrote that you still like
* an important poem you wrote
* an award for public speaking
* a really good story you can tell
* a debate you won

Logical/Mathematical

Tools/Techniques/Strategies/Methods
* mind-stretching puzzles or activities
* finding interesting patterns in the ordinary
* creating number patterns to stump others
* work to solve a problem
* learn new thinking patterns

Symbols of Logical/Mathematical Knowing
* a catalogue of cognitive organizers
* pictures of famous problem solvers
* the most exciting pattern you know
* formulas that have changed the world
* a montage of math symbols

Creative Examples (personal)
* the most difficult problem you have solved
* a list of times when you need math in your life
* steps of your problem-solving method
* successful attempts at doing math
* some clever thinking you've done

Visual/Spatial

Tools/Techniques/Strategies/Methods
* a box of paints or colored marking pens
* a box of modeling clay
* an example of the mind-mapping process
* gestalt-shift images or puzzles
* an effective active imagination process

Symbols of Visual/Spatial Knowing
* a favorite picture or piece of sculpture
* a montage of favorite colors
* a three-dimensional image or a hologram
* an object that is meaningful to you
* an unusual or interesting map or diagram

Creative Examples (personal)
* something you've drawn
* a painting you have done
* something you made from clay
* an intriguing pattern or design you created
* a collage of different textures or touches

Bodily/Kinesthetic

Tools/Techniques/Strategies/Methods
* physical exercise (dancing, jogging)
* different kinds of walking
* role-playing or acting out
* sports and physical activities
* inventing or making something

Symbols of Bodily/Kinesthetic Knowing
* action pictures or posters
* video of a fine physical performance
* picture of a bodily/kinesthetic hero
* list of favorite body language gestures
* list of favorite action-packed movies

Creative Examples (personal)
* an award for physical accomplishment
* a picture of you doing something great
* your personal exercise routine
* a video of a dance you created
* a program from a play you were in

CHAPTER 5

A Few of My Favorite Things
(All Grades)
SUGGESTIONS FOR PERSONAL INTELLIGENCE KITBAGS

Musical/Rhythmic

Tools/Techniques/Strategies/Methods
★ various kinds or styles of music tapes
★ a tape of interesting sounds
★ a tape of various kinds of beats or rhythms
★ a chart of when you like what music
★ a tape of sounds from the environment

Symbols of Musical/Rhythmic Knowing
★ examples of the use of music in society
★ sounds you make in order to communicate
★ things you have learned by putting them to music
★ a list of music that alters your moods
★ a list of favorite music and why you like it

Creative Examples (personal)
★ a song or tune you wrote
★ your use of music to express yourself
★ a song you can play, sing, or hum
★ your part of a musical creation
★ a program from a musical performance you were in

Interpersonal

Tools/Techniques/Strategies/Methods
★ good person-to-person communication
★ positive group interdependence
★ genuine empathy with others
★ effective cooperative behavior
★ team spirit or identity "gimmicks"

Symbols of Interpersonal Knowing
★ a product of a team effort
★ example of team support or encouragement
★ consensus-building procedures
★ checklist of an "effective team"
★ pictures of exemplary teams

Creative Examples (personal)
★ your contribution to a team effort
★ a list of successful teams you have been on
★ a personal success that was due to team effort
★ a time when you transcended yourself while part of a team
★ an experience when you used reflective listening

Intrapersonal

Tools/Techniques/Strategies/Methods
★ self-reflection experiences
★ awareness of feelings and emotions
★ "who am I" questioning investigations
★ transpersonal sense of the self methods
★ higher-order thinking or reasoning skills

Symbols of Intrapersonal Knowing
★ personal identity symbols
★ personal goals, objectives, or directions
★ a list of personal heroes
★ a list of key personal values or beliefs
★ your technique for inner renewal

Creative Examples (personal)
★ personal goals or objectives you have attained
★ times you have trusted your intuition
★ your most creative accomplishments
★ moments when you had acute mindfulness
★ moments of deep concentration

Naturalist

Tools/Techniques/Strategies/Methods
★ picture of nature
★ list of nature places you like to go to
★ list of sounds from nature you enjoy
★ list of things you learned from nature
★ symbols of your connection to nature

Symbols of Naturalist Knowing
★ picture of a scene in nature
★ picture of a favorite animal
★ tape-CD of environmental sounds
★ special objects from the natural world
★ a dried flower, leaf, and so on

Creative Examples (personal)
★ a nature-based collage
★ photo of "my nature spot"
★ reflective writing about an experience in nature
★ an object with some special meaning
★ a statement on "my conservation efforts/goals"

Teacher's Personal Reflection Log

A FEW OF MY FAVORITE INTELLIGENCE THINGS

I have the following thoughts/insights about the A Few of My Favorite Intelligence Things strategy:

I feel that the A Few of My Favorite Intelligence Things strategy can help me in my teaching in the following ways:

As a learning process, the A Few of My Favorite Intelligence Things strategy includes the following benefits for my students:

I have the following specific ideas for using the A Few of My Favorite Intelligence Things strategy in my classroom in the near future:

I think the A Few of My Favorite Intelligence Things strategy can be used beyond the classroom and school in the following ways:

6

The Multiple Intelligence School

A FUTURE SCENARIO

For a moment pretend that you have mysteriously shown up in a culture that has no education system and that you have been assigned to invent, from scratch, such a system. What would you create? What would the curriculum be? Whom would you select as teachers? Where would the teaching or learning take place?

In Howard Gardner's book *The Unschooled Mind: How Children Think and How Schools Should Teach,* he presents a compelling and intriguing new image of the educational process. I suggest you read the following quotation from this book, and after each section, close your eyes and try to visualize the scene the words suggest. You might even have some paper and markers nearby so you can sketch what you see with your mind's eye.[6]

6. The quotation is from Gardner 1991; the format and suggestions for visualization and drawing exercises are mine.

Imagine an education environment in which youngsters at the age of 7 or 8, in addition to or perhaps instead of attending a formal school, have the opportunity to enroll in a children's museum, a science museum, or some kind of discovery center or exploratorium. As part of this educational scene, adults are present who actually practice the disciplines or crafts represented by the various exhibitions.

Pause, visualize, and draw.

During the course of their school, youngsters enter into separate apprenticeships with a number of these adults. Each apprentice group consists of students of different ages and varying degrees of expertise in the domain or discipline. As part of the apprenticeship, the child is drawn into the use of various disciplines. . . . The student's apprenticeships deliberately encompass a range of pursuits, including artistic activities, activities requiring exercise and dexterity, and activities of a more scholarly bent.

Pause, visualize, and draw.

Most of the learning and most of the assessment are done cooperatively; that is; students work together on projects that typically require a team of people having different degrees of and complementary kinds of skills. Thus, the team assembling the bicycle might consist of half a dozen youngsters, whose tasks range from locating and fitting together parts to inspecting the newly assembled systems to revising a manual or preparing advertising copy.

Pause, visualize, and draw.

The assessment of learning also assumes a variety of forms, ranging from the student's monitoring her own learning by keeping a journal to "the test of the street"—does the bicycle actually operate satisfactorily, and does it find any buyers?

Pause, visualize, and draw.

Because the older people on the team, or "coaches," are skilled professionals who see themselves as training future members of their trade, the reasons for activities are clear, the standards are high, and satisfaction flows from a job well done.

Pause, visualize, and draw.

And because the students are enrolled from the first in a meaningful and challenging activity, they come to feel a genuine stake in the outcome of their (and their peers') efforts.

Pause, visualize, and draw.

In another publication, Gardner (1990) suggests that in a multiple intelligence school students might spend half of each day studying the traditional subjects but in very nontraditional ways. Students would master the content of particular subject areas by creating a variety of projects, experiments, and exhibitions. For example, they might be given problems to solve that people in the real world face, such as designing a new playground, investigating conflicting reports about an event in the community, or creating advertisements for a school function. They would spend the second half of the day out in the community exploring their classroom learning in context: by visiting museums and discovery centers, and by getting involved in apprenticeships or by bringing the community into the classroom.

If we are talking about implementing the theory of multiple intelligences fully in our schools, we are talking about an educational system that is radically different from what we currently have. In this final chapter, I will explore some implications of using the theory and practice behind multiple intelligences for restructuring schools. I believe that something similar to what I am suggesting is a vital part of the reinvention of the educational paradigm for the new millennium. In fact I would even suggest there may be no greater tool for transforming education today than restructuring our schools so they are places that teach students how to be more intelligent beings!

From the perspective of multiple intelligence theory, *the paramount restructuring goal is to promote the fullest possible intellectual development of our students*. I believe that there are four restructuring areas with which we need to be concerned, each of which promotes our students' full intellectual development.

OVERVIEW

Restructuring the Curriculum
(Teaching FOR Multiple Intelligences)

We promote the full intellectual development of our students when we explicitly teach them the core skills of each of the eight intelligences. This area involve restructuring the curriculum. We must evaluate the curricula of our various educational institutions to ensure that within them students are learning the specific sets of core skills necessary to be able to utilize the full spectrum of these students' intellectual capabilities. This analysis must take us far beyond but include verbal/linguistic and logical/mathematical skills, which are the current biases of our Western educational systems.

Restructuring Instruction
(Teaching WITH Multiple Intelligences)

We promote the full intellectual development of our students when we present every lesson using multiple teaching and learning strategies and encourage students to process information using all eight intelligences. This area involves restructuring instructional technologies and practices. We must reconsider our own teaching methodologies and techniques to ensure that we teach everything in multiple ways; not all students know, understand, perceive, and learn in the same way. Instruction must be more individualized and tailored to students' varying intelligence strengths and weaknesses.

Restructuring the Learning Process
(Teaching ABOUT Multiple Intelligences)

We promote the full intellectual development of our students when we help them learn about their intelligences and how those intelligences function, and when we work with parents to help them understand the eight ways of knowing. This area involves reinventing the learning process itself. We must find the time to provide students with opportunities to learn about their own multiple intelligence capacities. Students need occasions to explore and develop their various ways of knowing, both within the traditional school setting and in their lives beyond the classroom.

Restructuring Assessment
(Multimodal Testing through the Multiple Intelligences)

We promote the full intellectual development of our students when we provide intelligence-fair testing to determine relative strengths and weakness in all intelligence areas and when we use a wide variety of testing modes to evaluate students' academic progress. This area involves restructuring the way we assess students at all levels. We must create appropriate and authentic means for examining students' various intelligence capabilities as well as students' learning in specific subjects and content areas. We need to be teaching students to transfer intelligence across the curriculum and into their lives beyond the school situation.

RESTRUCTURING THE CURRICULUM

Please do the survey on page 240 before reading this section.

Multiple Intelligence Capacities or Skills

In some ways we can view our intelligence capacities as the building blocks necessary to utilize the various ways of knowing fully and effectively. Without these building blocks, the full potential of a particular intelligence is not available to us. Think for a moment what it would be like to try to teach mathematical problem solving if your students didn't have the skills of number sequencing, basic calculation, and recognition of patterns. What would happen if you tried to teach English to students who did not possess the skills of reading, writing, verbal communication, and humor? The logical/mathematical and the verbal/linguistic ways of knowing would simply not be fully available to those students.

As educators, we may be more familiar with the background capacities students must master in order to be skillful in the language arts and math, but we may not realize that the same kind of careful skill instruction is needed to help students develop capacities in each of the intelligence areas. That is, if we want students to be able to use the full spectrum of their intellectual capabilities, they must be taught explicitly the skills of each intelligence, in the same manner as we currently teach students the ABCs, counting, vocabulary, arithmetic operations, and so on. If we want them to develop their visual/spatial capacities, for example, we must explicitly teach them such things as how to use their active imaginations, how to make graphic representations, how to manipulate images, and how to find their way around a given location. If we want them to develop their musical/rhythmic intelligence, we must teach them how to recognize the meaning of various sounds and tones, how to produce meaningful tones themselves, and how to carry a tune.

The Multiple Intelligence Capacities Inventory Wheels (see pp. 262–263) suggests a categorization of different capacities, potentials, and skills that are necessary if one is to use the eight intelligences effectively. Howard Gardner sometimes refers to these as "sub-intelligences." They represent various sets of core capacities inherent in human beings' central nervous system. We can consciously develop these core capacities and improve them through various kinds of exercises and practices. (See *Eight Ways of Knowing* if you are not familiar with these.)

It is crucial that we teach all of these capacities to all students, and the capacities must be integrated or embedded in the curriculum itself. We must not consider development of multiple intelligence capacities an "add on." I suggest that we need to restructure our curriculum guides so that, as we present the curriculum, we are developing our students' multiple intelligences. In doing so we will be helping students actualize their full intellectual potential.

Restructuring the Curriculum
What skills and capacities should we be teaching?

Teaching FOR Multiple Intelligences Survey

Place an "X" in the box by any item that you feel is true of your regular teaching approaches.

☐ My classroom provides students with a sensory-rich learning environment (i.e., opportunities to see, touch, smell, taste, hear, and think about each lesson).

☐ My students are aware of the eight ways of knowing.

☐ I teach my students how to access or trigger the eight intelligences within their own brain/mind/body systems.

☐ I am aware of the capacities my students need beyond the traditional three Rs and I am teaching them these skills.

☐ I provide opportunities for students to practice using different ways of knowing and learning that go beyond the traditional verbal/linguistic and logical/mathematical modes.

☐ I am aware of and use various practices for helping my students amplify the full spectrum of their intellectual capabilities.

What I am suggesting has nothing whatsoever to do with what our culture usually calls "talent," whether it be musical, artistic, mathematical, dramatic, literary, or what have you. We all possess all eight ways of knowing, and likely many more than eight. We can use these ways to acquire knowledge, understand our world, improve our ability to solve problems, create, and meet the challenges we face in our daily lives whether or not the larger culture would call us talented.

Developmental Pathways of the Intelligences

How do the intelligences develop? When do the different capacities and skills normally appear in human development? What can we do to assist and catalyze the development of the full spectrum of intellectual capabilities?

We are most likely familiar with Jean Piaget's (1972) brilliant picture of the journey of children's cognitive development. We must remember, however, that Piaget's work dealt mostly with the development of logical/mathematical intelligence. One of the keys for launching a true transformation of the curriculum is to flesh out Piaget-type models to include pictures of how each of the intelligences evolves and matures, including the necessary inputs and catalysts along the way.

In the second edition of *Eight Ways of Knowing* (1998) I outline four stages that represent the general evolution of an intelligence:

1. The first and earliest stage is the *acquisition of the basic capacities and skills* for each intelligence. This could also be called the "novice stage." This stage is more or less guaranteed for the general population both by our biological makeup and by the various socialization processes of our cultures. These capacities are generally learned almost by osmosis, from family, environment, and other factors that are part of our early childhood experiences.

2. The second broad stage of development involves an *expanded and more complex development of all intelligence skills*. This stage begins most often when children start their formal education. They learn to expand their basic skills and to use them in various problem-solving tasks. They also learn the "language" and "symbol systems" for each of the intelligences.

3. The third stage involves *the development of higher-order intelligence capacities* and generally begins with a person's secondary schooling. During this period of intellectual development students learn to integrate the eight intelligences into their normal daily functioning, to employ different ways of knowing to help attain personal goals, and to use many modes to solve problems and meet challenges.

4. The final developmental stage is often directly related to one's *vocational or avocational pursuits*. This level usually represents mastery as

well as the conscious use of one's intelligences to be of service to the larger social order.

In public education we have often relied on our so-called fine arts programs and "extracurricular" activities to teach the skills and develop the intelligence capacities that go beyond the so-called academic subjects, which tend to emphasize the development of verbal/linguistic and logical/mathematical skills. I believe we must hang onto and expand our fine arts programs, for it is often these so-called extra parts of the curriculum that teach students the basic capacities and skills they need to use the different ways of knowing. Unfortunately, these curricular offerings are the first to be cut when school districts face necessary budget cuts. In light of this, I strongly advocate that every classroom teacher must find and teach the "fine arts" components that are part of every subject area. Or even better, let us thoroughly integrate the fine arts and academic curricula; it's time to take the "extra" out of "extracurricular" and make it all curricular!

Curriculum Analysis Exercise*

How Intelligent Is Your Curriculum?

In this exercise you will have an opportunity to take a new look at the curriculum you are teaching and to analyze it in terms of the multiple intelligences. You will be using the Multiple Intelligence Capacities Wheels (pp. 262–263).

1. Make a copy of the Curriculum Analysis work sheet on page 243.
2. Review the capacities related to the intelligences on the Capacities Inventory Wheels (pp. 262–263). After reviewing each, make notes of the impressions you have of your curriculum on the Curriculum Analysis Work Sheet:

   - In the first column, note specific areas (for example, academic subjects, after-school activities, special classes, and so on) in which students are explicitly taught the capacities or skills of the various intelligences.
   - In the second column, rank the intelligences from strongest to weakest in terms of the numbers of skills that are part of what is taught in your school.

3. Now spend some time creating a new curricular vision—a vision in which the fine arts are integrated completely into the so-called academic subjects and one in which the extracurricular is curricular:

   - In the third column, list three to five areas in which you see fresh, new opportunities to teach students the skills of the eight intelligences.

*Permission to reprint Curriculum Analysis Exercise granted by Phi Delta Kappa.

Pathways of Learning © 2000 Zephyr Press, Tucson, Arizona • 800-232-2187 • http://zephyrpress.com

Curriculum Analysis Work Sheet

	WHERE CURRENTLY TAUGHT	RANK	NEW OPPORTUNITIES TO TEACH	RANK	TOTAL
Verbal/Linguistic intelligence					
Logical/Mathematical intelligence					
Visual/Spatial intelligence					
Bodily/Kinesthetic intelligence					
Musical/Rhythmic intelligence					
Intrapersonal intelligence					
Interpersonal intelligence					
Naturalist intelligence					

- In the fourth column, rank the intelligences based on these new ideas. Compare this new ranking with your previous one. What differences do you notice?

4. Now total the two rankings, the skills that are currently being taught and the new opportunities for teaching the skills, in the fifth column.

   - Write three to five statements about what these lists reveal about the directions curriculum reform needs to take in your school or district.
   - Brainstorm a list of strategic steps you can take *in your current position* to begin the process of restructuring curriculum. Include both immediate and long-range strategies.

RESTRUCTURING INSTRUCTION

Please do the survey on page 245 before reading this section.

Staging Multiple Intelligence Lessons

Generally speaking, there are four stages to teaching with multiple intelligences. These stages make teaching compatible with how the brain actually works. When we teach in brain-compatible ways, we get better thinking and information processing, higher levels of creativity, greater transfer of learning, raised self-esteem, and higher degrees of motivation from our students. Dr. Jean Houston (1980) at the Foundation for Mind Research has researched the idea of multiperceptual learning and states the following:

> We are as different from each other as snowflakes; and each of us has, especially in childhood, a special penchant for different ways of exploring our world. In order to preserve the genius and developmental potential of childhood, one must quite simply give the universe back to the child, in as rich and dramatic a form as possible.
>
> *Multiperceptual learning,* we have found, is a key to this gifting. In school curricula and programs . . . the child is taught to think in images as well as in words, to learn spelling or even arithmetic in rhythmic patterns, to think with his whole body— in short, to *learn school subjects, and more, from a much larger spectrum of sensory and cognitive possibilities.* (emphasis mine)

Art Costa (1991) supports this multimodal concept. He notes that there are fourteen characteristics of intelligent behavior. "Using all the senses" is one of these ways of knowing and being intelligent:

> Language, culture, and physical learning are all derived from our senses. To know a wine it must be drunk; to know a role it must be acted; to know a game it must be played; to know a dance it must be moved; to know a goal it must be

Restructuring Instruction
How can we help more kids succeed more of the time?

Teaching WITH Multiple Intelligences Survey

Place an "X" in the box by any item that you feel is true of your regular teaching approaches.

☐ **My daily classroom teaching integrates multiple intelligence strategies and tools into lessons that deal with the different subject areas.**

☐ **I encourage and require my students to process information from a lesson using all eight ways of knowing.**

☐ **In my lesson planning, I think through how to teach every lesson using all eight intelligences even if I don't use all eight in each lesson.**

☐ **I have a system that tracks my teaching to make sure that I use all eight intelligences every week and that I am teaching in an intelligence-balanced manner.**

☐ **I am experimenting with new forms of authentic academic assessment that take into account the eight intelligences.**

☐ **I know how to stage lessons so that they are compatible with the neurobiological functioning of the different intelligences.**

envisioned. Those whose sensory pathways are open and alert absorb more information from the environment than those whose pathways are oblivious to sensory stimuli.

We can observe students using their senses when they touch objects in their environment, when they request that a story or rhyme be read again and again, or when they act out roles. Often, what they say tells us that their senses are engaged: "Let me see, let me see . . . " "I want to feel it . . ." "Let me try it . . . " "Let me hold it . . . "

As children mature, we can observe that they conceive and express many ways of solving problems by the use of the senses. . . . Their expressions use a range and variety of sensory words: "I feel like . . . " "It touches me," "I hear your ideas," "It leaves a bad taste in my mouth," "Get the picture?"

The diagram on page 247 is from *Eight Ways of Teaching* and is a model for staging intelligence-compatible lessons.

Stage 1: Awakening the Intelligences[7]

Since each intelligence has a neurological and biological base, we can consciously activate the intelligences by performing certain brain/mind exercises, such as those suggested in the second chapter. The goal of the awakening stage in a lesson is to stimulate specific areas of the brain/mind/body system to wake up certain intelligence capacities that may be dormant.

For example, if you want to activate visual/spatial capacities, the mere act of passing out colored markers, paints, crayons, or clay will often do the job. If you want to trigger bodily/kinesthetic capacities in a lesson, any kind of physical movement, including dance, role-playing, and body gestures, will suffice. In many ways the specific media of an intelligence are in and of themselves a message to latent intelligence capacities in the brain to "wake up and get ready for action!"

In this awakening stage we are concerned first with becoming aware that we do in fact possess multiple ways of knowing and learning, and second with learning techniques for stimulating the different intelligences within the brain/mind/body system.

Stage 2: Amplifying the Intelligences

We can enhance, strengthen, and improve each of the intelligences. In some ways intelligence capacities are like any skill we possess: the more we practice the better we become. The goal of the amplifying stage is to focus on developing or strengthening intelligence areas in which one is uncomfortable or weak.

To improve students' interpersonal intelligence capacities, for example, you must teach them certain relational skills, such as listening,

7. The following description is adapted with permission from the PDK Fastback series. Pathways of Learning © 2000 Zephyr Press, Tucson, Arizona • 800-232-2187 • http://zephyrpress.com

What Does It Take to Teach Intelligence?[8]

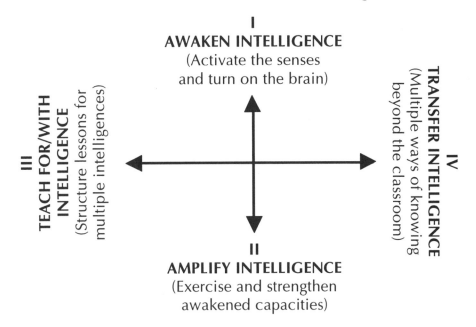

I
AWAKEN INTELLIGENCE
(Activate the senses
and turn on the brain)

III
TEACH FOR/WITH INTELLIGENCE
(Structure lessons for multiple intelligences)

IV
TRANSFER INTELLIGENCE
(Multiple ways of knowing beyond the classroom)

II
AMPLIFY INTELLIGENCE
(Exercise and strengthen
awakened capacities)

Stage I
AWAKEN INTELLIGENCE

Since each intelligence is related to the five senses, we can activate or trigger the intelligences. This stage involves exercises and activities that use the following bases: sight, sound, taste, touch, smell, and speech; communication with others; and the inner senses, such as intuition, metacognition, and spiritual insight.

Stage II
AMPLIFY INTELLIGENCE

This stage involves practices for expanding, deepening, and nurturing an awakened or activated intelligence. As with any skill, not only can we awaken our intelligence skills but we can improve and strengthen them if we use them regularly. And, like any skill, they will go back to sleep or atrophy if we do not use them.

Stage III
TEACH FOR/WITH INTELLIGENCE

This stage involves learning how to use, to trust, and to interpret a given intelligence through knowing, learning, and understanding tasks. I use classroom lessons that emphasize and use different intelligences to teach with intelligence.

Stage IV
TRANSFER INTELLIGENCE

This stage integrates an intelligence into daily living, and we learn to apply it appropriately to solving problems and meeting the challenges we face in the "real world." The goal of this stage is for the intelligence to become a regular part of our cognitive, affective, and sensory lives.

8. Adapted from Lazear, David. *Eight Ways of Teaching*. Palatine, Ill.: Skylight, 1998.

encouraging others, reaching consensus, and so on, and then give them opportunities to practice the skills. If you want to amplify musical/rhythmic capacities, work to help students develop recognition of different sounds, practice matching a rhythmic pattern or tune produced by another, or learn to express emotions through sound alone.

In this stage, we are concerned with learning how particular intelligences function and how to work to improve them. We must understand the different capacities and skills of the intelligences, how to access them, and how to use these capacities or skills effectively.

Stage 3: Teaching with the Intelligences

Once an intelligence has been awakened and we have learned to strengthen our skills in using it, we can employ the intelligence to gain specific information or acquire knowledge. The goal of the teaching stage is to present content-based lessons that apply different ways of knowing to the teaching and learning process required to master academic material.

One can learn vocabulary words with the body, for example, physically "embodying" the words' meanings (bodily/kinesthetic). You can teach the parts of a tree by having students make clay models of trees that illustrate the different parts (visual/spatial). Students can learn the states and capitals by creating a rap or song with the information (musical/rhythmic).

We must remember that about 95 percent of the material we have to teach as educators comes prepackaged in a verbal/linguistic or a logical/mathematical form. In planning lessons, however, we must not be bound by this packaging. We can and should design lessons that emphasize all eight ways of knowing.

Stage 4: Transferring the Intelligence

The final stage is to integrate the intelligences into one's daily living. This integration includes learning how to apply the intelligences to solve problems and to meet challenges faced in the world beyond the classroom. The goal of the transfer stage is to make the intelligences a regular part of one's cognitive, affective, and sensory repertoire for living.

Once students have learned how to succeed in a cooperative learning situation, for example, they can transfer the same skills to their family to improve the relating and cooperation among family members (interpersonal). Or they can use reflective logs beyond the classroom by keeping daily or weekly journals to reflect on their lives (intrapersonal).

We must teach our students how to use all of the intelligences to improve their effectiveness in dealing with the issues and challenges they encounter in the task of daily living. This task is primarily one of learning strategies for approaching all aspects of living on multiple levels, with a variety of problem-solving methods that engage the full spectrum of the intelligences.

You may be asking, "What about time? I've got so much to cover and only a limited time in which to do it!" Art Costa (1991) has observed that one of the effects contemporary cognitive research has had on today's educational systems is that taking precious classroom time to teach students how to think and learn is gaining wider acceptance:

> As a result of this wider acceptance, thinking skills are not being viewed as mere additions to an already overcrowded, time-squeezed, cemeterial compendium of scopes and sequences. Rather teachers are finding comfort, agreement, and rededication in some common goals—that process is as important as product; that thoughtful and reflective thinking (rather than coverage) is acceptable once again; and that students' production of knowledge is as important as their reproduction of knowledge.

In the staff development workshops I conduct, the question, "How can we teach the way you're suggesting when we have so much we have to cover in a normal school day?" is often raised. In one such training, a high school history teacher asked the group if they knew Webster's definition of the verb "to cover." He informed us that its primary meaning is "to hide from view." He then posed the provocative question, "Is this in fact what we're doing when we are so preoccupied with covering the curriculum? Maybe," he suggested, "we should be uncovering the curriculum for our students. Maybe this is a far greater service to them!"

His statements apply beautifully to teaching with multiple intelligences. The good news about teaching with multiple intelligences is that doing so is not an additional task to what we have to teach anyway. I am not suggesting that we should be teaching more "stuff" in an already over-stuffed curriculum. But I am suggesting that we teach the old stuff in a radically new way!

When we work with the intelligences in daily lessons, the key is first to trigger the eight ways of knowing within the class, which gives students an opportunity to practice using the full spectrum of their intelligences, and then to move into the lesson at hand utilizing the intelligence(s) that have been awakened and the skills that students have practiced. The Multiple Intelligences Toolbox in chapter 3 is a quick lesson planning device to help you easily move anything you have to teach to multiple levels of knowing, learning, and understanding. One very effective use of the Multiple Intelligences Toolbox is as a brainstorm aid for exploring the multiple intelligence possibilities for a given lesson. Simply select one tool from each intelligence and then plan the lesson around those tools. (If you are unfamiliar with the "MI toolbox" and how to use it in detailed lesson planning, see *Eight Ways of Teaching,* 1998.)

RESTRUCTURING THE LEARNING PROCESS

Please do the survey on page 251 before reading this section.

Reinventing the Learning Process: Meta-Intelligence as Transformational Process

In some ways, the restructuring or reinventing of the learning process integrates all that I have suggested in the previous parts of this chapter. I have called this area "meta-intelligence. As you have seen in this book, it is the most complex and probably the most holistic aspect of working with the multiple intelligences. Teaching about multiple intelligences assumes and encompasses teaching for and with the intelligences! The chart on page 252 illustrates this idea.

Brain-Based Teaching and Learning

The tacit level involves learning how to access or trigger the different intelligences in the brain/mind/body system. Generally this awakening can be achieved through exercises, games, puzzles, and the like that are designed to stimulate different areas of the brain.

The aware level involves an understanding of the modalities by which each intelligence processes information. Each intelligence has its own language and method of processing. For example, the language and processing modality of visual/spatial intelligence is colors, textures, shapes, images, patterns, designs, and pictures. Visual/spatial intelligence simply does not understand such things as alphabets, words, sentences, paragraphs, and the like.

The strategic level involves the ability to call upon the eight ways of knowing to assist you in a variety of situations. For example, putting something you're having a hard time remembering to music, expressing or changing feelings through physical exercise or movement, or drawing diagrams to help someone understand an idea.

The reflective level involves knowing how to bring a number of intelligences to bear on a single issue or topic. This level requires knowledge of how each intelligence works and what it takes to access its wisdom and input quickly.

Intelligence Enhancement and Expansion

The tacit level involves knowledge of practices for strengthening and improving the intelligences. Through the disciplined exercising of different intelligence skills, one can strengthen those skills by using all eight ways of knowing. Remember, "practice makes perfect."

Restructuring the Learning Process
How can we help kids reach their full learning potential in school?

Teaching ABOUT Multiple Intelligences Survey

Place an "X" in the box by any item that you feel is true of your regular teaching approaches.

☐ **My students are aware of and know how to use different tools to access their own multiple ways of knowing, understanding, and learning in a lesson.**

☐ **I am working to create intelligence profiles for each of my students so that I am aware of their strengths and weaknesses in each of the intelligences.**

☐ **In my weekly lesson planning, I include time for students to be "meta-intelligent" (i.e., to think about, evaluate, understand, and work on improving all eight ways of knowing).**

☐ **I am providing information and training that teaches parents how to deal with multiple intelligences and how to use and nurture the intelligences at home.**

☐ **I have a plan for moving my students through the different meta-intelligence levels, from the tacit to the reflective.**

☐ **My students keep an intelligence portfolio in which they reflect on what they are learning about themselves and their own intelligence potentials and keep ideas they have for applying the eight ways of knowing to life beyond the school.**

Dynamics of Meta-Intelligence

Brain-Based Teaching and Learning (teaching FOR multiple intelligences)	Intelligence Enhancement and Expansion (teaching WITH multiple intelligences)	Appropriate Transfer and Application (teaching ABOUT multiple intelligences)
• **knowledge of the various intelligence triggers** (tacit level) • **understanding the language of each intelligence** (aware level) • **ability to access the intelligences in varying situations** (strategic level) • **knowing how to switch between the intelligences** (reflective level)	• **knowledge of intelligence-amplifying practices** (tacit level) • **understanding the symbol systems of the intelligences** (aware level) • **ability to interpret or process intelligence data accurately** (strategic level) • **knowing one's own intelligence strengths or weaknesses** (reflective level)	• **knowledge of different meta-intelligence levels** (tacit level) • **understanding intelligence translation processes** (aware level) • **ability to utilize the intelligences to solve problems** (strategic level) • **knowing when to use which of the eight intelligences** (reflective level)

Pathways of Learning © 2000 Zephyr Press, Tucson, Arizona • 800-232-2187 • http://zephyrpress.com

The aware level involves understanding what Gardner calls "notational systems." Each intelligence has its own symbol system for communication. For example, the symbol system for musical/rhythmic intelligence is notes arranged on a staff that represent a tune to be played at a specified rhythm and pitch. This symbolic or notational dimension of the intelligences is what allows their wisdom and knowledge to be transmitted.

The strategic level involves the accurate interpretation of various kinds of information generated by the intelligences. Developing the ability to read and understand that information is a matter of learning to recognize certain patterns of communication, to interpret and appreciate the meaning of nonverbal data, and to process traditional information in multiple, nontraditional ways.

The reflective level involves the skills of accurately evaluating one's own intelligence strengths and weakness. It also involves knowledge of such things as exercises or practices for improving weaker intelligences and knowing how to use a stronger way of knowing to train a weaker one.

Appropriate Transfer and Application

The tacit level involves knowledge of the various stages of meta-intelligence (or teaching about the intelligences) and skill in helping others learn about, explore, and come to understand something of their own multiple ways of knowing, understanding, perceiving, and learning.

The aware level involves an understanding of the "translation process" involved in working seriously with multiple intelligences; namely, translating verbal/linguistic information into other modalities. For example, you can translate geometric formulas into a dance, vocabulary words into clay sculptures, or the parts of a cell into a rap.

The strategic level involves the ability to use all eight intelligences to solve problems and to deal with challenges faced in the task of living. This ability involves skill in problem analysis and an understanding of the creative process, as well as how to tap into higher levels of creativity and thinking through the intelligences.

The reflective level involves knowing when to use which intelligence to deal with what situation. At this level, the eight ways of knowing are no longer something external to one's being; they have become fully integrated and are a part of the "equipment" one uses in the task of effective living.

RESTRUCTURING ASSESSMENT

Please do the survey on page 255 before reading this section.

The Assessment Conundrum:
"To Test or Not to Test? That Is the Question!"

A major concern in teaching about multiple intelligences is how to assess students' intelligence capacities so we can help them be better learners, and how to evaluate their academic progress. To address the first concern, we must devise ways to help us recognize and understand students' relative strengths and weaknesses in the eight intelligence areas. This assessment is obviously important, as current research indicates that intelligence is not fixed or static as we once thought. In fact, intelligence appears to be a dynamic, continually evolving process.

This information is important from at least three perspectives:

1. We can help students develop a fuller spectrum of intellectual abilities to use in the classroom, and in their lives beyond the classroom.
2. We can find new strategies for helping students use their stronger intelligences to succeed in school.
3. We can use a student's strength in one intelligence to strengthen a weakness in another.

Howard Gardner suggests that when we try to assess the intelligences of students, we need a profile of their intelligences, not decontextualized scores. The process of intelligence assessment is somewhat akin to putting together a jigsaw puzzle: no single piece of the puzzle gives you the whole picture; only when all the pieces are together do you see the whole. The job is to figure out what makes each student tick intellectually, that is, to figure out how students best know, understand, perceive, and learn. Gardner believes that with about ten hours of careful observation of students involved in various activities and learning tasks, we can get a fairly accurate intelligence profile of our students. We can use this information to help them master their studies and deal with everyday problems and challenges, and to give them vocational guidance counseling later in their educational journey.

The second area of authentic assessment involves employing multiple intelligence ways to evaluate students' academic progress. My concern here again is to gain a holistic picture of what students know—beyond what can be demonstrated on the typical paper-and-pencil test. We can rest assured that even the best students know more than they can adequately show on most of the tests we give. I am not suggesting that there is something wrong with paper-and-pencil tests, as long as we keep them in their proper place and don't try to make them the sole indicator of what a student knows or has learned in a given lesson or unit.

Pathways of Learning © 2000 Zephyr Press, Tucson, Arizona • 800-232-2187 • http://zephyrpress.com

Restructuring Assessment
How can we use assessment to give us an
authentic picture of the whole child?

Authentic Assessment Survey

Place an "X" in the box by any item that you feel is true
of your regular teaching approaches.

☐ **I allow and encourage my students to demonstrate what they
have learned using a wide variety of methods, including, but
not limited to, paper-and-pencil methods.**

☐ **I know how to help students transfer their unique ways of
knowing and learning to perform successfully on required,
standardized tests.**

☐ **I continually watch my students as they are involved in various
learning tasks or activities to gain a fuller picture of their
intelligence profiles.**

☐ **I am experimenting with the creation and testing of
intelligence-fair ways to assess students' academic progress.**

☐ **I am experimenting with a new kind of whole child report
card that not only evaluates academic skills, but also provides
feedback on the different intelligence skills and capacities the
student has mastered.**

☐ **I provide administrators and my fellow teachers with the most
up-to-date information about multiple intelligence research,
including inviting them to observe applications I am using in
my classroom.**

Project Spectrum

Project Spectrum is an innovative research effort focused on assessment in early childhood. It is based on Gardner's work. In the February 1991 edition of *Educational Leadership* Mara Krechevsky summarizes five key factors of Spectrum's assessment system. I believe that these hold clues for all levels and may help us solve the assessment conundrum:

1. **Blurring the lines between curriculum and assessment.** This means that teachers gather information from their careful observation of students who are involved in a wide variety of learning tasks and activities. No single paper-and-pencil test (nor any other single test) should be used to determine what a student knows or has learned in a particular unit. We should be assessing how our students are doing all of the time, not just on traditional exams, and we should be doing so by using a wide variety of forms such as student-created portfolios, reflective logs and journals, videos of students demonstrating something they have learned, and so on.

2. **Embedding assessment in meaningful, real-world activities.** Rather than focusing on skills that are meaningful in the school context only, Project Spectrum suggests that assessment be focused on abilities and skills relevant to achieving rewarding roles later in life. In other words, what we teach and how we test should be grounded in the real world outside of the school setting. Nowhere in real life does anyone ever encounter the typical standardized test that calls for the simple regurgitation of memorized facts and information (except perhaps when applying for a driver's license). Life is about application—it is about doing something with what we know! Instead of having students spend hours memorizing the rules of grammar, why not have them create a class newspaper and try to instill in them the love of communicating their ideas to others? Or have them create something that requires the meaningful use of math facts, processes, and operations?

3. **Using measures that are "intelligence fair."** Most standardized tests view students' learning only through the glasses of verbal/linguistic and logical/mathematical abilities. Why not allow students to use a wide range of media to demonstrate what they know and have learned? Experiment with allowing students to use nontraditional ways that go beyond the verbal/linguistic and logical/mathematical to demonstrate their knowledge of a topic. For example, on a math test, you might involve bodily/kinesthetic knowing by couching it in terms of body movement itself, including gestures, physical action, role-play, dance, or inventing, while a science test using visual/spatial knowing would involve drawing, painting, active imagination, and sculpting as the primary means by which students demonstrate what they have learned.

4. **Emphasizing children's strengths.** This assessment factor emphasizes giving students the experience of success in school by creating learning activities and lessons that encourage the students to know and learn using their stronger intelligences. Krechevsky suggests that this approach not only increases students' sense of self-esteem, but can spark in them awareness of ways to use their strengths to improve other intelligence areas that are not as strong. I know of few adults who could stand or would tolerate a continual deficit-based assessment of their performance (that is, "let me tell you all the areas where you are failing!"). Yet we often expect our students to survive twelve years (or more) of these assessments. Why not, instead, ask children who are strong in sports to create a new game about the Bill of Rights? Or have students who love music and rhythm illustrate a story with music and sound? As I mentioned earlier, I believe that we must always remember that anything we have to teach can be taught and learned in a wide variety of ways. We must not be bound by the verbal/linguistic and logical/mathematical prepackaging that controls more than 95 percent of our curriculum materials!

5. **Attending to the stylistic dimensions of performance.** This factor involves carefully tracking how students approach different learning tasks and activities. How do they interact with the material? How do they relate to each other in the midst of a lesson? Project Spectrum is as concerned about students' working styles as with their cognitive skills. In *Eight Ways of Knowing,* I suggest allowing students an opportunity to play a variety of intelligence skill-related games, such as Pictionary™, crossword puzzles, Twister™, Name that Tune™, and so on. You can learn a great deal about your students' working styles by carefully observing how they approach the game, regardless of the game they have chosen. In the Project Spectrum experiment many students exhibit a great deal of focus, reflection, and skill when they are working in an area in which they feel strong and comfortable.

Conclusion

TRANSFORMING AND RESTRUCTURING
THE PLACE CALLED SCHOOL

In *Control Theory in the Classroom*, William Glasser suggests that the most important issue confronting us in American education is that well over 50 percent of the students who inhabit our classrooms day in and day out have absolutely no desire to learn what we are trying to teach them. He suggests further that their lack of interest is not their problem; it is the educators' problem. Until we find a way to make getting an education worth their while, all of our efforts at restructuring curriculum and re-forming school policy may be only an interesting diversion.

How do we approach the task of making education worth students' while? How do we increase the payoff now? Glasser notes that there are five basic needs with which every student comes into our classrooms and which all students will find a way to meet in any way they can:

> **Love:** Students want to feel that others love and value them. They need to feel accepted.
>
> **Independence:** Students want to experience a sense of freedom and independence. They need to feel that they can make decisions on their own.
>
> **Fun:** Students want and need to enjoy the situation in which they find themselves and will very often go to extreme lengths to create fun if they don't think there is enough fun.

Security: Students need to feel a basic sense that things are right with the world. This need is more difficult to meet, given the lack of stability in many homes today.

Power: Students want to feel in control of what happens to them. They want to have a say in those things that are shaping their lives, even if it is only during a forty-five minute period.

What if we could find ways to meet these five basic needs every day within our classrooms? What if the payoff of education was that these needs were regularly met and fulfilled? Glasser suggests that the percentage of students "on board with their education" would likely be far higher.

One of the main reasons that I am so excited about multiple intelligences is that I believe, and have witnessed in hundreds of schools and districts across North America, that this approach to teaching and learning addresses these basic needs. I have seen students who have experienced failure in their studies for years suddenly experience success. I have seen countless teachers experience a renewed excitement for their chosen profession. I have experienced dramatic shifts in both students' and teachers' levels of self-esteem as they discover ways to affirm their unique ways of knowing and discover that they are not "weird" or "strange" just because they do not excel in verbal/linguistic or logical/mathematical intelligence capacities. I invite you to join this journey of self-discovery and to likewise invite your students to begin to know themselves intellectually.

Appendix

MULTIPLE INTELLIGENCE CAPACITIES INVENTORY WHEELS

The following diagrams include a summary of the capacities and skills related to each of the intelligences. These skills must be taught explicitly to students if the students are to learn how to use all eight ways of knowing. Just as students must be taught the alphabet, how to make words, and how to read and write if they are to be strong in verbal/linguistic intelligence, they must be taught such things as how to use the active imagination, how to do graphic representation, and how to see relationships between different objects in space if they are to be strong in visual/spatial intelligence. I suggest that you use these wheels as a checklist to evaluate your child's relative strengths and weaknesses in each intelligence area. Then use some of the activities listed in chapter 1 to give your child opportunities to exercise and practice using all of his or her intelligences at home.

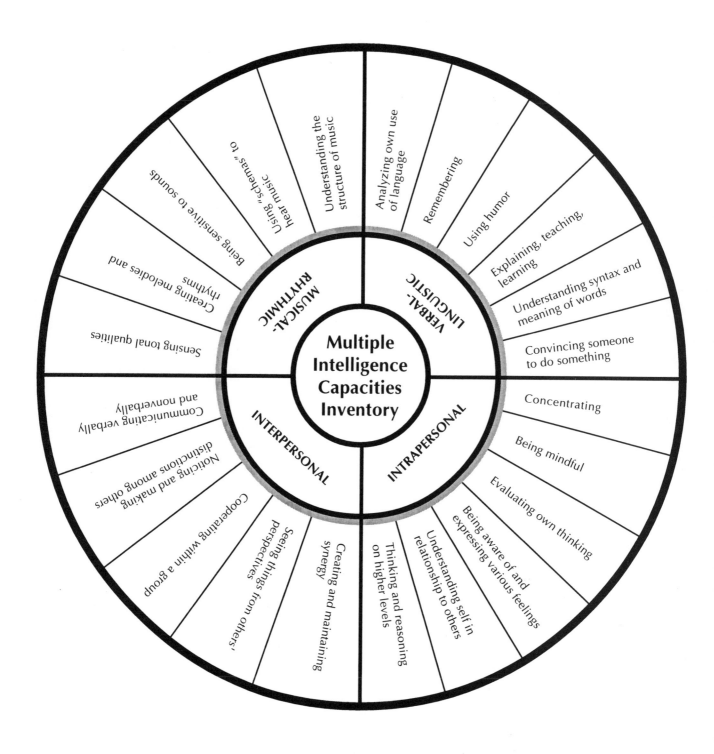

The wheel diagram "Multiple Intelligence Capacities Inventory" contains the following labels:

MUSICAL-RHYTHMIC
- Understanding the structure of music
- Using "schemas," to hear music
- Being sensitive to sounds
- Creating melodies and rhythms
- Sensing tonal qualities

VERBAL-LINGUISTIC
- Analyzing own use of language
- Remembering
- Using humor
- Explaining, teaching, learning
- Understanding syntax and meaning of words
- Convincing someone to do something

INTRAPERSONAL
- Concentrating
- Being mindful
- Evaluating own thinking
- Being aware of and expressing various feelings
- Understanding self in relationship to others
- Thinking and reasoning on higher levels

INTERPERSONAL
- Communicating verbally and nonverbally
- Noticing and making distinctions among others
- Cooperating within a group
- Seeing things from others' perspectives
- Creating and maintaining synergy

*Adapted from David Lazear's *Eight Ways of Knowing: Understanding Multiple Intelligences* (Palatine, Ill.: Skylight, 1998).

Pathways of Learning © 2000 Zephyr Press, Tucson, Arizona • 800-232-2187 • http://zephyrpress.com

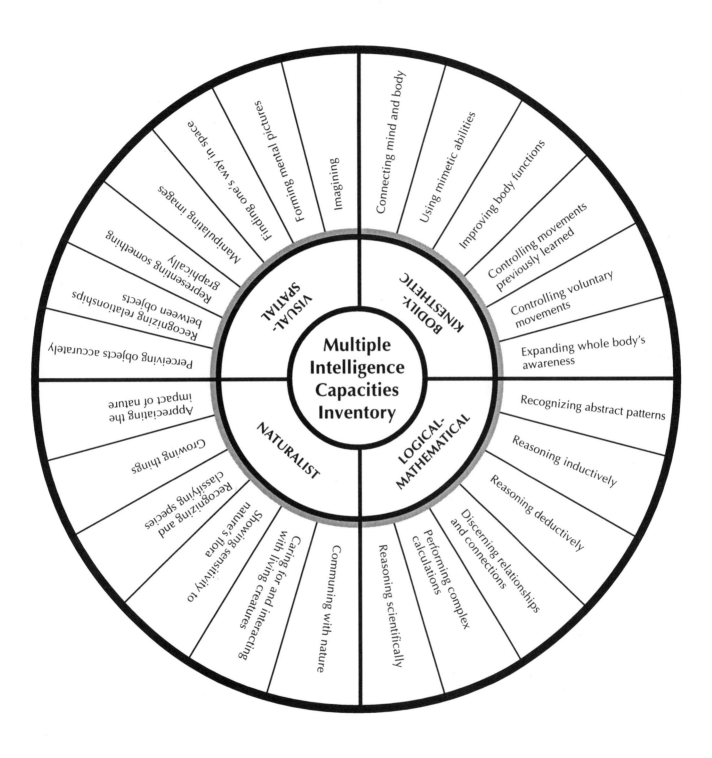

The wheel diagram "Multiple Intelligence Capacities Inventory" contains the following:

VISUAL-SPATIAL
- Imagining
- Forming mental pictures
- Finding one's way in space
- Manipulating images
- Representing something graphically
- Recognizing relationships between objects
- Perceiving objects accurately

BODILY-KINESTHETIC
- Connecting mind and body
- Using mimetic abilities
- Improving body functions
- Controlling movements previously learned
- Controlling voluntary movements
- Expanding whole body's awareness

LOGICAL-MATHEMATICAL
- Recognizing abstract patterns
- Reasoning inductively
- Reasoning deductively
- Discerning relationships and connections
- Performing complex calculations
- Reasoning scientifically

NATURALIST
- Appreciating the impact of nature
- Growing things
- Recognizing and classifying species
- Showing sensitivity to nature's flora
- Caring for and interacting with living creatures
- Communing with nature

*Adapted from David Lazear's *Eight Ways of Knowing: Understanding Multiple Intelligences* (Palatine, Ill.: Skylight, 1998).

Pathways of Learning © 2000 Zephyr Press, Tucson, Arizona • 800-232-2187 • http://zephyrpress.com

Bibliography

Alexander, F. *The Use of the Self: Its Conscious Direction in Relation to Diagnosis, Functioning, and the Control of Reaction.* Downey, Calif.: Centerline Press, 1984.

Ambruster, B., and T. Anderson. *The Effect of Mapping on the Free Recall of Expository Tests.* Tech. Rep. No. 160. Urbana-Champaign, Ill.: University of Illinois, Center for the Study of Reading, 1980.

Anderson, R., and W. Biddle. "On Asking People Questions about What They Are Reading." In G. Brower (ed.), *The Psychology of Learning and Motivation.* New York: Academic Press, 1975.

Arlin, P. "Teaching as Conversation." *Educational Leadership* 48 (2), 1990.

Armstrong, T. *In Their Own Way: Discovering and Encouraging Your Child's Personal Learning Style.* Los Angeles: J. P. Tarcher, 1987.

———. *Seven Kinds of Smart: Identifying and Developing Your Many Intelligences.* New York: Penguin Books, 1993.

Assagioli, R. *The Act of Will.* New York: Viking Press, 1973.

Ausubel, D. *Educational Psychology: A Cognitive View.* New York: Holt, Rinehart, Winston, 1968.

Bacon, F. "Of Studies." In W. Louis (ed.), *Century Readings in the English Essay.* New York: Appleton-Century-Crofts, 1939.

Bartlett, F. *Thinking.* New York: Basic Books, 1958.

Bellanca, J., and R. Fogarty. *Blueprints for Thinking in the Cooperative Classroom.* Rev. ed. Palatine, Ill.: Skylight Publishing, 1986.

———. *Catch Them Thinking.* Palatine, Ill.: Skylight Publishing, 1991.

Benson, H. *The Relaxation Response.* New York: Morrow, 1975.

Beyer, B. *Practical Strategies for the Teaching of Thinking.* Boston: Allyn & Bacon, 1987.

Bloom, B. *Taxonomy of Educational Objectives.* New York: David McKay, 1956.

Bogen, J. *Some Education Aspects of Hemispheric Socialization.* Pomona, N.Y.: Dromenon, 1979.

Boulding, K. *The Image.* Ann Arbor: University of Michigan Press, 1966.

Bruner, J., J. Goodnow, and G. Austin. *A Study of Thinking*. New York: Wiley, 1956.

Buzan, T. *Use Both Sides of Your Brain*. New York: Dutton, 1991.

Caine, R., and G. Caine. "Understanding a Brain-Based Approach to Learning and Teaching." *Educational Leadership* 48 (2): 66–70, 1990.

Campbell, D. *Introduction to the Musical Brain*. Richardson, Tex.: Magnamusic-Baton, 1983.

Campbell, J. *The Improbable Machine: What the Upheavals in Artificial Intelligence Research Reveal about How the Mind Really Works*. New York: Simon and Schuster, 1989.

Campbell, L. *Tomorrow's Education Today*. Seattle: The Pegasus School, 1985.

Campbell, L., B. Campbell, and D. Dickenson. *Teaching and Learning through Multiple Intelligences*. Seattle: New Horizons for Learning, 1992.

Chomsky, N. *Language and Mind*. New York: Harcourt Brace Jovanovich, 1968.

Churchill, Winston. *My Early Life: A Roving Commission*. New York: Scribner, 1987.

Costa, A. "Mediating the Metacognitive." *Educational Leadership* 42 (3): 57–62, 1984.

———. "The School as a Home for the Mind." In Costa, *Developing Minds*.

———. "Teaching for Intelligent Behavior." *Educational Leadership* 39 (1): 29–31, 1981.

———. "Thinking Skills: Neither an Add-on nor a Quick Fix." In *Developing Minds*.

Costa, A., ed. *Developing Minds*. Rev. ed. Alexandria, Va.: Association for Supervision and Curriculum Development, 1991.

Culicover, P., and Wexler, P. *Formal Principles of Language Acquisition*. Cambridge, Mass.: MIT Press, 1980.

Curry, L. "A Critique of the Research on Learning Styles." *Educational Leadership* 48 (2): 50–52, 1990.

Dansereai, D., et al. "Development and Evaluation of a Learning Strategy Training Program." *Journal of Educational Psychology* 71 (1): 1979.

Davidson, J. "The Group Mapping Activity for Instruction in Reading and Thinking." *Journal of Reading* 26 (1): 52–56, 1982.

de Bono, E. *Lateral Thinking: Creativity Step by Step*. New York: Harper and Row, 1973.

Dickinson, D. *New Developments in Cognitive Research*. Seattle: New Horizons for Learning, 1987.

Dunne, J. *The Way of All the Earth: Experiments in Truth and Religion*. New York: Macmillan, 1972.

Feldenkrais, M. *Awareness through Movement: Health Exercises for Personal Growth*. New York: Harper and Row, 1977.

Ferguson, M. *The Aquarian Conspiracy: Personal and Social Transformation in the 1980's*. Los Angeles: J. P. Tarcher, 1980.

Feuerstein, R. *Instrumental Enrichment*. Baltimore, Md.: University Park Press, 1980.

Fogarty, R., and J. Bellanca. *Patterns for Thinking, Patterns for Transfer*. Palatine, Ill.: Skylight Publishing, 1989.

———. *Teach Them Thinking*. Palatine, Ill.: Skylight Publishing, 1986.

Gardner, H. "Developing the Spectrum of Human Intelligences: Teaching in the Eighties, a Need to Change." *Harvard Educational Review,* 1987.

————. *Developmental Psychology: An Introduction.* Boston: Little Brown, 1982.

————. "Do Babies Sing a Universal Song?" *Psychology Today,* December 1981.

————. *Frames of Mind: The Theory of Multiple Intelligences.* New York: Harper and Row, 1983.

————. *Multiple Intelligences: The Theory in Practice.* New York: Basic Books, 1993.

————. *The Unschooled Mind: How Children Think and How Schools Should Teach.* New York: Basic Books, 1991.

Gawain, S. *Creative Visualization.* New York: Bantam Books, 1978.

Gazzaniga, M. *Mind Matters: How Mind and Brain Interact to Create Our Conscious Lives.* Boston: Houghton Mifflin, 1988.

Gendlin, E. *Focusing.* New York: Everest House, 1978.

Glasser, W. *Control Theory in the Classroom.* New York: Perennial Library, 1986.

Graham, I. "Mindmapping: An Aid to Memory." In B. Steinfield (ed.), *Planetary Edges.* Toronto: The Institute of Cultural Affairs, 1988.

Guilford, J. *Way Beyond IQ.* Buffalo, N.Y.: Creative Education Foundation, 1979.

Harman, W. *The Global Mind Change.* Indianapolis: Knowledge Systems, 1988.

Harman, W., and H. Rheingold. *Higher Creativity.* Los Angeles: J. P. Tarcher, 1985.

Hart, Leslie. *Human Brain and Human Learning.* Village of Oak Creek, Ariz.: Books for Educators, 1983.

Houston, J. *Lifeforce: The Psycho-historical Recovery of the Self.* New York: Delacorte Press, 1980.

————. *The Possible Human: A Course in Extending Your Physical, Mental, and Creative Abilities.* Los Angeles: J. P. Tarcher, 1982.

————. *The Search for the Beloved: Journeys in Sacred Psychology.* Los Angeles: J. P. Tarcher, 1987.

Hubbard, B. *Manual for Co-Creators of the Quantum Leap.* Irvine, Calif.: Barbara Marx Hubbard, 1985.

Institute of Cultural Affairs. *5th City Pre-School Education Manual.* Chicago: Institute of Cultural Affairs, 1968.

————. "Imaginal Training Methods." *Image: A Journal on the Human Factor.* April–June, 1981

Johnson, D., R. Johnson, and E. J. Holubec. *Circles of Learning.* Edina Minn.: Interaction Book Company, 1986.

————. *Cooperation in the Classroom.* Edina, Minn.: Interaction Book Company, 1988.

Kagan, S. *Cooperative Learning Resources for Teachers.* San Juan Capistrano, Calif.: Resources for Teachers, 1990.

Kazantzakis, N. *The Saviours of God.* New York: Simon and Schuster, 1960.

Laird, C. *The Miracle of Language.* New York: Fawcett Publications, 1957.

Langer, S. *Reflections on Art.* New York: Arno Press, 1979.

Lawrence, D. "Search for Love." In V. de Sola Pinto and F. Roberts (eds). *The Complete Poems of D. H. Lawrence.* New York: Viking Press, 1959.

Lazear, D. *Multiple Intelligence Approach to Assessment: Solving the Assessment Conundrum.* Tucson, Ariz.: Zephyr Press, 1998a.

————. *Eight Ways of Knowing: Teaching for Multiple Intelligences.* Palatine, Ill.: Skylight Publishing, 1998b.

————. *Eight Ways of Teaching: The Artistry of Teaching with Multiple Intelligences.* Palatine, Ill.: Skylight Publishing, 1998c.

————. *Teaching for Multiple Intelligences.* Bloomington, Ind.: Phi Delta Kappa, 1992.

Leonard, George. *The Silent Pulse: The Search for the Perfect Rhythm that Exists in Each of Us.* New York: Dutton, 1986.

Loye, D. *The Sphinx and the Rainbow: Brain, Mind, and Future Vision.* Boulder, Colo.: New Science Library, 1983.

Lozonov, G. *Suggestology and Outline of Suggestology.* New York: Gordon & Breach, 1978.

Machado, L. *The Right to Be Intelligent.* New York: Pergamon Press, 1980.

MacLean, P. "On the Evolution of Three Mentalities." In S. Arieti and G. Chryanowski (eds.), *New Dimensions in Psychiatry: A World View.* Vol. 2. New York: Wiley, 1977.

Markley, O. "Using Depth Intuition in Creative Problem Solving and Strategic Innovation." *Journal of Creative Behavior* 22 (2): 85–100, 1988.

Masters, R., and J. Houston. *Listening to the Body: The Psychophysical Way to Health and Awareness.* New York: Delacorte Press, 1978.

————. *Mindgames.* New York: Delacorte Press, 1972.

McTighe, J. "Teaching for Thinking, of Thinking, and about Thinking." In M. Heiman and J. Slomianko (eds.), *Thinking Skills Instruction: Concepts and Techniques.* Washington, D.C.: National Education Association, 1987.

McTighe, J., and F. Lyman. "Cueing Thinking in the Classroom: The Promise of Theory-Embedded Tools." *Educational Leadership* 45 (7): 18–24, 1988.

Monroe, R. *Far Journeys.* Garden City, N.Y.: Doubleday, 1985.

Nat Hahn, T. *The Miracle of Mindfulness.* New York: Beacon Press, 1988.

O'Conner, J., and J. Seymour. *Introduction to Neurolinguistic Programming.* London: Mandala, 1990.

Orff, C. *The Schulwerk.* M. Murray, trans. New York: Schott Music Corporation, 1978.

Perkins, D. *Knowledge as Design.* Hillsdale, N.J.: Lawrence Erlbaum Associates, 1986.

Piaget, J. *The Psychology of Intelligence.* Totowa, N.J.: Littlefield Adams, 1972.

Pribram, K. *Holonomy and Structure in the Organization of Perception.* Stanford, Calif.: Stanford University Press, 1974.

————. *Languages of the Brain: Experimental Paradoxes and Principles in Neuro-psychology.* Englewood Cliffs, N.J.: Prentice-Hall, 1971.

Progoff, I. *At a Journal Workshop: The Basic Text and Guide for Using the Intensive Journal.* New York: Dialogue House Library, 1975.

Rico, G. *Writing the Natural Way: Using Right-Brain Techniques to Release Your Expressive Powers.* Los Angeles: J. P. Tarcher, 1983.

Rosenfield, I. *The Invention of Memory: A New View of the Brain.* New York: Basic Books, 1988.

Russell, P. *The Brain Book.* New York: E. P. Dutton, 1976.

———. *The Global Brain: Speculations on the Evolutionary Leap to Planetary Consciousness.* Los Angeles: J. P. Tarcher, 1983.

Samuels, M., and N. Samuels. *Seeing with the Mind's Eye: The History, Techniques, and Uses of Visualization.* New York: Random House, 1975.

Schmeck, R., ed. *Learning Strategies and Learning Styles.* New York: Plenum Press, 1988.

Shone, R. *Creative Visualization.* New York: Thorson's Publishers, 1984.

Slavin, R. *Cooperative Learning.* New York: Longman, 1983.

Snowman, J. "Learning Tactics and Strategies." In G. Phy and T. Andre (eds.), *Cognitive Instructional Psychology: Components of Classroom Learning.* New York: Academic Press, 1989.

Springer, S., and G. Deutsch. *Left Brain, Right Brain.* New York: W. H. Freeman, 1985.

Steiner, R. *Music in Light of Anthroposophy.* London: Anthroposophical, 1925.

Sternberg, R. *Beyond I.Q.: A Triarchic Theory of Human Intelligence.* New York: Cambridge University Press, 1984.

———. *Intelligence Applied: Understanding and Increasing Your Intellectual Skills.* San Diego: Harcourt Brace Jovanovich, 1986.

Sternberg, R., L. Okagaki, and A. Jackson. "Practical Intelligence for Success in School." *Educational Leadership* 48 (1): 35–39, 1990.

Vaughn, F. *The Inward Arc.* Boulder, Colo.: The New Science Library, 1986.

von Oech, R. *A Kick in the Seat of the Pants: Using Your Explorer, Artist, Judge, and Warrior to Be More Creative.* New York: Perennial Library, 1986.

———. *A Whack on the Side of the Head: How to Unlock Your Mind for Innovation.* New York: Warner Books, 1983.

Vygotsky, L. *Thought and Language.* Cambridge, Mass.: MIT Press, 1986.

Walsh, R., and F. Vaughn, eds. *Beyond Ego: Transpersonal Dimensions in Psychology.* Los Angeles: J. P. Tarcher, 1980.

Walters, J., and H. Gardner. "The Development and Education of the Intelligences." Position paper. Chicago: Spencer Foundation; New York: Carnegie Corporation, 1984.

Weinstein, M., and J. Goodman. *Playfair.* San Luis Obispo, Calif.: Impact, 1980.

Wilber, K. *The Atman Project.* Wheaton, Ill.: Quest Books, 1980.

———. *Eye to Eye: The Quest for the New Paradigm.* Garden City, N.Y.: Anchor Books, 1983.

Index